AN ATTEMPT TO ROB OUR TWO BANKS HERE WAS MADE BY
THE DALTONS. THE CITIZENS ARE FIGHTING THEM IN THE
STREETS. THREE OF THE ROBBERS HAVE BEEN KILLED
AND ONE CAPTURED SO BADLY WOUNDED THAT HE WILL
DIE BEFORE NIGHT. ONE ESCAPED AND WENT TOWARDS
THE OKLAHOMA LINE RIDING A FAST HORSE. PLEASE TRY
TO CAPTURE HIM IF HE REACHES OKLAHOMA.

—*Telegram from the Mayor of Coffeyville, Kansas,
to U.S. Marshal Chris Madsen, October 5, 1892*

A legend was born the day the Dalton Gang died on the
quiet streets of Coffeyville, Kansas. Now the truth behind that legend is revealed by one of the West's most
able historians.

Harold Preece has based his story on extensive research.
He interviewed relatives, friends, and foes of the Daltons, and he consulted the hitherto closed files of the
Pinkerton Agency, the Railway Express Agency, and the
archives of the Historical societies of Missouri and
Fresno, California. The result is <u>The Dalton Gang</u>—
the first complete, documented account of the rise and
fall of the bandit brothers whose ruthless crimes
terrorized the West.

"Harold Preece does an excellent job on his factual
presentation of the Daltons and their times . . . a well-
documented, fast-moving saga."

—*Saint Louis Post-Dispatch*

"*The Dalton Gang* seems to just about tie up the subject
for all time, and can be classified as either exciting reading or authentic history of the post-Civil War days."

—*Fort Worth Star Telegram*

SIGNET Books You'll Want to Read

THE DALTON GANG

END OF AN OUTLAW ERA

Harold Preece

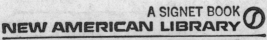

A SIGNET BOOK
NEW AMERICAN LIBRARY
TIMES MIRROR

FOR BENJI ATER
whose spirit kept a writer going

Published as a SIGNET BOOK
by arrangement with Hastings House, Publishers, Inc.,
who have authorized this softcover edition.
A hardcover edition is available from Hastings House,
Publishers, Inc.

 SIGNET TRADEMARK REG. U.S. PAT. OFF. AND FOREIGN COUNTRIES
REGISTERED TRADEMARK—MARCA REGISTRADA
HECHO EN CHICAGO, U.S.A.

SIGNET, SIGNET CLASSICS, MENTOR, PLUME AND MERIDIAN BOOKS
are published by The New American Library, Inc.,
1301 Avenue of the Americas, New York, New York 10019

FIRST PRINTING, MAY, 1964

3 4 5 6 7 8 9 10 11

PRINTED IN THE UNITED STATES OF AMERICA

CONTENTS

LIST OF ILLUSTRATIONS

ACKNOWLEDGMENTS

MY TASK of doing this first book of complete scope on the Dalton Gang could not have been realized without much help, practical and spiritual, from friends and colleagues who contributed generously of their time and attention.

The Pinkerton Archive files on the Daltons, in New York City, were opened to me; I am most grateful to Bernard F. Boyce, assistant secretary-treasurer of the Pinkerton National Detective Agency, and to George O'Neill, assistant to the Agency's director of public relations. Homer Croy's help was indispensable; he generously made available his own large store of unpublished material on Oklahoma's most notorious outlaw gang. Bouquets are also due to Harry Sinclair Drago, who knew Emmett Dalton personally; to Edwin V. Burkholder, native Kansas author and my close friend; and to Keene and Roscoe D. Wallis, kinsmen of Florence Quick, Bob Dalton's inamorata.

I am grateful to Evelyn Cunningham for preliminary publicity; to William Nevins, for much fine talk about our native West during the book's progress; to Horace Montague and his late wife, Ella, for their constant encouragement; to my sister and brother-in-law, Katherine and Sam Luparello, for much concrete assistance; to Angela Hawley, for more goodness than I can define in words; and to Lavinia Dobler, for much hospitality.

For valued aid in research, on both this and former works, I am indebted to three good friends of the American-history section of the New York Public Library—Mrs. Shirley L. Spranger, Leon Weidman, and Frederick Willerford. Nyle H. Miller of the Kansas Historical Society contributed much valuable editorial material on the Dalton book. Similar help came from the Kentucky Historical Society, the Historical Society of Missouri and the Fresno, California, Historical Society; from Mrs. Thelma Mires, great-granddaughter of Bill Dalton; and from Fred Hedges, mayor of Coffeyville, Kansas. Enlightening material was provided by the REA Express organization (formerly the Railway Express Company), the Santa Fe Railway and the Missouri, Kansas and Texas Railway (the Katy).

I want to express my appreciation to several fellow Southwesterners who have been of endless cumulative help in my interpretations of a great and colorful land. They are Orin L. Crain, newsman and fraternity brother; Bill Burchardt, editor of *Oklahoma Today;* John Ben Shepperd, who loves the old boys and the old tales; Edmunds Travis, who broke me in as a writer for the Austin *Statesman;* Glenn Shirley, who knows every old outlaw hideout in Oklahoma; Ziggie Hunter, who published some of my first writing on the West; and J. Frank Dobie, who urged me to start writing about it.

A deep and loving tribute in memoriam is rendered to my wife, Ruth Kruskal Preece, whose charity would have extended even to road agents. Upon the book itself lies the impact of that long and creative association with my friend and editor, Don Ward; he made me work like a cowhand on a long drive, and this is what emerged at trail's end.

For other friends whose names I must regretfully omit for lack of space—*muchas gracias!*

H. P.

BUCKSHOT BELT

THIS was a wild land in a wild age of the American empire, a natural arena that was a proper setting for a thunderous rehearsal of the Civil War. Split-up and shot-up country. A region of stark terrain and a mood of murder. A 25,000-square-mile section, bisected by sullen rivers, with broad pastures where dead men turned up as often as dead horses, and thorny brakes bristled like the daggers of its rival gangs of guerrillas. A land where, said wry jokesters, the settlers made soup from gunpowder and the fancy women of the tough frontier towns wore spikes on their nipples.

It was the area of the Kansas-Missouri border where the abolitionist counties of eastern Kansas bucked in endless showdowns the pro-slavery counties of western Missouri. The rest of America knew it for its merciless gun sprees between transplanted New Englanders bearing efficient new weapons called "Beecher's Bibles" and émigré Southerners sometimes carrying inherited Kentucky long rifles. Men of guts, all of them, on both sides willing to share their last crust with a friend or spend their last bullet on a foe.

Here they fought: Kansas Jayhawkers and Missouri Border Ruffians, torch finishing what gun began. Nobody ever gave this fierce segment of the Louisiana Purchase territory a name suited to its way of life—and death. The Buckshot Belt, it might have been called, with mutually warring chieftains like Jim Lane of Kansas and William Clarke Quantrill of Missouri standing as godfathers for its baptism of gore.

It was bad country for peaceful people. Often they plowed their fields with short arms tied to plow handles for ready defense against raiders from one or another side of the border. Of all this element, wanting just to live, none hated the gun more than a man and a woman who were destined to produce a whole brotherhood of gunslingers.

The man was Lewis Dalton, a roaming, shiftless six-foot ex-Kentuckian whose "one passion was for fast horses" and who had slept in livery stables all over the Belt while swapping them. The woman was tiny, waspish Adeline Dalton, born in Cass County, Missouri, but of Kentucky ancestry derived through Virginia.

Each had highly personal reasons for detesting trigger play. Jovial Lewis Dalton always maintained that he'd had enough of killing while serving under General Zachary Taylor during the Mexican War. Actually, he had piped men to battle as a fifer rather than standing musket to musket with them.[1] It had been a strange sort of enlistment for a character who boasted so much and so often about being "Irish." For Scotch-Irish earlier troopers like him had whaled the tar out of the British under their racial kinsman, Andy Jackson, at New Orleans.[2]

Adeline Dalton had seen her father, Colonel Charles Younger, buried from the unhappy circumstance of being a Southern abolitionist who had freed his slaves, only to be bushwhacked by Kansas Unionists believing that the Colonel was pulling a smart Dixie trick. After the slaying the family had moved to Jackson County, where a town called Kansas City was beginning to be built as an intended competitor to St. Louis, upstate. Near them lived another clan of Youngers that incubated three of America's most distinguished gun artists—Cole, Bob and Jim.

Prim Adeline Younger Dalton was related in some cousinly degree to these Youngers, who would get mixed up in merry brigandry with the James Boys and a gotch-toothed Missouri tart named Belle Starr. But no records have turned up to prove that she was the aunt of the Youngers who made history, or that any Younger tribe was any kin to the Jameses. Indeed, Cole Younger always denied more than a distant connection with the offspring of Adeline, who married that jovial chucklehead, Lewis Dalton.[3]

Those two met while living but a few jumps off the Santa Fe Trail. Lewis Dalton, making one of his rarely profitable horse trades, had opened a small saloon at Westport, now swallowed up by Kansas City. Adeline was living at Independence, where the Mormons had been run out not only for being polygamous but for being prosperous.

There probably wasn't much of a courtship between the big oaf of a man and the slip of a teen-ager who was many years his junior. No more, probably, than Mr. Dalton squiring Miss Younger to church a few times. Wooings often began quickly with the sharing of a hymn book and ended with an early march to the altar. Her family undoubtedly figured that her beau had settled down to a good, paying business, whatever they had heard about his previous bumming around western Missouri. Nor would they necessarily have held his trade of whisky-selling against him, it being an era when preachers cut their brimstone with corn liquor before mounting the pulpit, and the first temperance agitators were just beginning to trickle in from New England.

Adeline Younger might have hoped for something better than James Lewis Dalton, Junior. But the Mexican War had lopped the man crop considerably, and a girl took what she could get. By the records of Jackson County, she married him at Independence on March 12, 1851. Afterward, young Mrs. Dalton—she was fifteen, the groom thirty-six—went about the business of marriage.

Sex she accepted as dutifully as she did baking biscuits, because the act was commanded by the Bible. God might strike a woman dead for resisting a husband's natural wantings. But, essentially as puritanical as any flint-faced Down-Easter, Lewis Dalton's good wife undertook the salvation of her husband's soul.

She might as well have tried to make a parson out of a gypsy. Adeline demanded that her husband foreswear the jug. At least, he gave her a promise. Then she insisted that he close the saloon. It was the worst mistake she could have made. Tavernkeeping was the only thing he'd ever worked at steadily in his whole life. And never again would he labor at anything that brought in regular money.

She had hoped to turn him into a God-fearing farmer and a pillar of the community, as her father, Colonel Younger, had been. But Lewis Dalton had no use for plows—only for the nags that pulled them. For many years to come, his wife would live on a catch-as-catch-can basis, doing meager share-cropping in both states of the Buckshot Belt while Lewis gallivanted with horse traders, his visits home lasting only long enough to give her the next baby.

Each year saw Adeline's belly swell with new growth. Each year, Lewis Dalton kept bringing in slim money to support a family that was getting oversize, even by frontier standards.

Fifteen times, the poor woman gave birth. Fifteen times Lewis Dalton went on about his own happy-go-lucky affairs, leaving his wife and family to find their own bread. All the children were born in that bullet-pocked epoch stretching from the Jayhawker-Border Ruffian conflict of the 'fifties to the bloody sequel of Civil War campaigns waged in the border country. Sudden duels and bitter partisan clashes erupted near every cabin where Adeline Dalton came down with another babe, to get up with another burden.

Yet her first batch of youngsters was not warped by the

trouble that was their cradle. Adeline meant that none of her
brood should "take after" their father. The older ones among
the Dalton brood were a satisfying bunch, learning early to
do chores and being handier at it than was the lazybones
who had daddied them. When the Civil War began, she also
determined that none would copy her barely acknowledged
cousins, the Younger boys, now riding and raising hell with
William Clarke Quantrill.

It was just one more nail in a good woman's cross that
the second crop of Dalton sons would be marked by the gun
and start coming along the very year when North and South
passed the point of no return.

Five boys were of that bunch. The first was Grattan, born
in 1861, the year of Bull Run. His hatching place was near
Lawrence, Kansas. He would be two years old when Quantrill
would burn that abolitionist stronghold with the enthusiastic
help of Cousin Cole and his father's reputed first cousin,
Kit Dalton.[4] Out of some sentimental Irish quirk, Lewis
Dalton named the boy Grattan after a dead Dublin statesman. Grat had the heft of a bull calf and the disposition of
a baby rattlesnake.

Bill—William Marion Dalton, in full—came along in
1863, that midpoint of the Civil War when Grant's batteries
were pounding Vicksburg. He was the smartest of the quin-
tette, able to talk other frontier kids out of their homemade
playthings and himself "into and out of anything." He was
the lad who most deserved Ma Dalton's strap, but tasted it the
least. Some who knew him later felt that "he was the worst
of the Dalton boys."

Next came Franklin, or Frank, birthspot not definitely
known. He could cuss better than he could talk while still a
tot in gingham. Fighting was a business he took seriously,
but he was neither a bully like Grat nor a con artist like
Bill.

Bob, due to become the most celebrated, was born in
Adeline's native Cass County, Missouri, in 1870, five years
after the War. Robert Renick Dalton, he was baptized, Renick
being the name of a pioneer Missouri family to whom he may
have been related or who may have given the Daltons help
that they often needed. Bob blossomed out with the looks of
a little Rollo and the pluck of a Horatio Alger hero, tem-
pered with a saving caution so that he "usually knew
where he was going to land before he leaped."

Last came Emmett, named for an Irishman who had died
on English gallows, for nobler reasons than those which usually caused men to stretch hemp in the American West.

"Em," his brothers and playmates called him. A slavish imitator of Bob, his idol, he also had quick fists like Grat and a way of juggling the truth like Bill. He admired Good Women as much as his dad did Good Horses. To Em we owe much information—some that is accurate, more that is not—about the Daltons and their deeds.

There were also five "good Dalton boys"—tame Daltons who never pulled triggers except to pot table meat. Four of them—Charles, Ben, Littleton and Henry—grew to manhood. Simon—"Little Si"—frail and sickly, was born in Missouri around 1874, and died in Kansas at the age of fourteen.

Still two more children, name and sex forgotten, are said to have died in infancy. Besides ten known Dalton sons, we can account for three daughters—Eva, Leona and Nannie. Another girl, sometimes known as Minnie Dalton, was actually Minnie Johnson, an adopted niece, daughter of Adeline's dead sister. No matter how big your own family, you took care of your kinfolks' orphans in frontier America. Minnie grew up liking dashing boys, including her Cousin Bob.

It was a big flock for one harassed little woman to feed and raise, with a husband who felt more responsible for his colts than for his children. Her job was made rougher through decades of slaughter. The wonder of it was that Adeline Dalton was able to raise nine respectable citizens out of thirteen surviving sons and daughters, growing up in the most turbulent area of America since primitive Kentucky.

During the Civil War, the Daltons made out like other rootless nomads, keeping their wagons ahead of the shifting battlefields, with Adeline finding a majority of many refuges in Kansas. Lewis Dalton seems to have been a camp follower of the Union forces, tagging along safely behind combat lines and doing odd jobs for rations.

One of many handed-down stories has the Daltons living at Leavenworth, Kansas, after the grisly set-tos between Missouri and Kansas guerrillas forced them out of the Lawrence area. This border town, built around the Federal citadel of Fort Leavenworth, lay just across a river from Missouri and was a concentration point for Unionists expelled from that state.

Lewis Dalton would have liked the place for another of his sentimental reasons: the many horses of the Union cavalry outfits stationed there. He may have watered and curried the mounts of men brave enough to fight.

Two years passed, with a shiftless roamer enjoying the
war more than a lot of other Americans. Vicksburg fell and
the Confederacy was split right down the middle. Lewis Dalton found the market for Army horses skyrocketing, with so
many being lost in battle. And the elder Dalton could spot
a horse haven like a bee scouting a clover clump.

Around 1863, he rambled down to southeastern Kansas
where wild horses were still as plentiful as ticks, or so it
seemed. He pulled up on the Osage Indian reservation adjoining Indian Territory proper, in a stretch which, a few
years later, would be seized from the Osages to become Montgomery County. At that time, however, the area had no
settled white residents except those employed at the Drum
Creek Indian Agency in the Verdigris Valley.

It was pretty country, the prettiest Lewis Dalton had seen
since leaving the Scotch-Irish settlements of the Kentucky
Cumberlands to go vagabonding over the Buckshot Belt.
Three rivers drained the fertile surface of Montgomery
County. Flocks of prairie chickens fussed and fed on savan-
nahs still to be raped by the plow. Game, from bear to rabbits, frisked in the pleasant woodlands. A gray slime sometimes appearing on the top of waterholes would afterward
be identified as petroleum and make many a Kansan wealthy.

The Osages always had saddle-broken horses, or they captured wild ones to sell for money that would buy them flour
and firewater. Lewis Dalton was impressed by the scenery and
gratified by the sales.

In 1868 a town called Coffeyville was built on the banks of
the Verdigris River in Montgomery County. It became a trading center for a wide adjoining section of Kansas and for
the diminished Osage Nation, three miles over the line in the
Territory.

Coffeyville was a tough community in its early days, full
of bootleggers peddling illicit liquor to thirsty Indians and
saloonkeepers dispensing licensed stuff to farmers and cowpunchers. Billy the Kid lived here for a while as a youngster.
Not far from the town a woman named Kate Bender, who
pretended communion with guiding spirits, ran a tavern and
bordello where guests were robbed and murdered. Kansans,
finally losing their patience, strung her up, depriving the
West of one of its earliest mediums.

A bad, rough place was Coffeyville—one that just missed
attaining the notoriety of Tombstone and Tularosa. But
Lewis Dalton, the unstable wanderer, felt an odd affinity for it.
For the rest of his life he would keep returning to Coffey-

ville. It would become the only place that he could reasonably call his home town.

And by Coffeyville, three of his sons would be remembered.

2

JESSE JAMES'S HORSE

PEACE—of a creaky kind—came to America during the spring of '65. The Confederacy fell apart. An age stigmatized by slavery in the South had ended. A new one bearing the brand of outlawry in the West was just around a violent nation's next turn of history.

The roads were full of Southerners going home—whatever homes that might be left after four years of fights and foraging expeditions. Hungry men from crumbled battle lines were beating their way back to shattered states. Tired, disgusted warriors these were, with some of them already setting ragged boots west toward the long trail and the quick gun.

Fugitive families—solid folk and vagrants—were creeping out of temporary refuges in enemy territory. They also were rolling back to native haunts in squeaking covered wagons and shambling old surreys. Among those returning to Missouri was the James family, bringing with them from Nebraska a shot-up, moody young Quantrill veteran—son Jesse. From some other Quantrill hideout, embittered Cole Younger came back to Cass County, where his "connection" had moved before the war. To the same county returned the Daltons, with Adeline hoping to raise her young-uns right, as what mother in the Buckshot Belt did not?

From the best available accounts, Lewis Dalton and his family were living as squatters near the future site of Coffeyville when the war ended. There was much vacant land in southeastern Kansas, with so few homesteaders having been able to cross battle lines and occupy it. Some stories say that the Daltons waited till the early part of 1866 to repatriate themselves. That was the year when Cole Younger and Jesse James began talking about setting up in business.

Lewis Dalton was stone broke, the war's finish having temporarily knocked the bottom out of the saddle-mount market. Adeline's folks provided her with a tract of farm land near the little village of Belton. The pioneer code said that a

18

kinswoman and her children had to be looked after if her husband couldn't or wouldn't.

Times were hard. Slave labor was abolished. Tracts belonging to their former masters were being confiscated for unpaid taxes, then sold dirt-cheap to Yankee land speculators. A new Missouri constitution had barred all ex-Confederates from public office and saddled other disabilities upon them. Trigger fingers were restless in Belton and in Harrisonville, the county seat, where Cole Younger's clan lived. Dirty looks and muttered imprecations were cast in the direction of the Yankee-controlled banks and the crowing Missouri Unionists, making their jokes about old Jeff Davis, held in jail like a common horse thief.[1]

Resident Unionists started turning up dead in the thickets bordering the Little Blue River, the initial, ominous warm-up for western Missouri's long and bitter resistance to the victors. But there was one man, generally accounted a Yankee sympathizer, whom nobody ever touched.

That was lazy, jolly Lewis Dalton. You didn't see much of him around the farm at Belton, particularly not with his oldest boys, who were big enough to plow and shuck. Somewhere, as boot in a horse trade, he had picked up an old violin. Fiddlers, like preachers, enjoyed immunity from killing. Before long, he was in demand for country dances where each gent paid him a nickel a set. Not much money, but sawing a fiddle beat sawing wood.

Soon Lewis Dalton was on close terms with the James boys —Jesse and Frank—now often visitors to Cass County. Cole Younger became still another friendly acquaintance, although there was no family welcome extended to her cousin by Adeline, wanting no truck or no visits with any of the wild branch. In fact, there is no record of her sons ever having seen Cole Younger more than once, and nothing at all to show that they ever met Cole's brothers.

The Dalton farm was a pleasant spot. Once in a great while Adeline found time to sit down at the family organ and play hymns for the children she was trying to bring up in the redeeming fear of the Lord. Religion she considered to be the infallible antidote for all error, from crapshooting to man-shooting. Attendance at a Methodist chapel near Belton was a Sunday ritual. The young Daltons were expected to sit as patiently as their mother through two-hour sermons.

Unfortunately for the devout woman, there was scant peace even in the house of the Lord. Male worshipers sat with wary eyes peeled on windows for scalawag constables bearing warrants that charged mayhem committed on Unionists and Kansans. Six-shooters were in convenient, if hidden, reach for use against horse thieves roaming the county, ready to snatch ponies tethered at church hitching posts. Talk after services centered more about the legalized lootings by the banks and the expanding railroads than about psalm and text.

Such talk wasn't fitten for growing young-uns to hear, Adeline Dalton thought. It made her uneasy, what with those tots, Bill and Grat and Frank, showing more understanding of it than their tender ages warranted. Bob and Emmett hadn't yet been born.

Meanwhile resentment kept spreading, a festering pall, across the border counties. Barns of anti-Confederates were going up in flames; Northern-owned banks and railroads became inviting targets of the gathering counter-rebellion in place of the vanished Northern troopers.

Here and there a bank was robbed or a train stopped. Always the names of two sets of brothers—the Youngers and the Jameses—were whispered in talk about the hold-ups. People guessed that they were being sheltered by various ex-Quantrillites, now operating as a scattered underground resistance force, like the mushrooming Ku Klux Klan of the upper South.

Adeline Dalton saw that the crops were harvested and her children sent to a one-room schoolhouse. As for the mounting fury along the border—well, the worse it got the more she just "leaned on the Lord," backing up His commandments with switch and strap.

She gave her sons plenty of whalings for betting jackknives on colt races. Such antics with horses had been the ruination of their father, and Adeline didn't mean it to spoil her boys. "Dutiful, maternal, inexorably just she was"—maybe too much so.

Years went by, with western Missouri spinning its endless sequel to Appomattox. Cole Younger and Jesse James graduated from the coves and prairies of their homeland to become the best known outlaws of American history. Their names were in every paper and on the lips of every Missourian. Their pickings soared as more banks were opened and more railroads built west of the Mississippi. And in one more nod of fate, rail building brought still another vagrant craft to Lewis Dalton.

He became a barker for the circuses moving out across rural America, now that they had easy transportation to roll them here and there. Across the South and Midwest he traveled, luring customers in to see penned lions and troupes

of saucy girls kicking their legs high. When he wasn't spiel-
ing, he was moseying around at his old trade of horse swapping, trying to cash in on the fresh demand for ponies that
stemmed from the spectacular Texas cattle drives and the
booming new homestead migrations to the West. Coffeyville
was one of his supply sources for horses; Independence,
Missouri, where he had married Adeline, another.[2]

His older sons were growing up in the dutifully respectable mold of their mother. Those other five with the
wild streak, Adeline kept on praying for the Lord to change.
They showed every sign of having all the worst traits of
shiftless Lewis Dalton and hell-for-leather Cousin Cole combined.

At age sixteen Grat was as big as his daddy and willing
to take on, in eye-gouging combat, men still bigger. He had
whipped every boy his age around Belton, and could drink
more whisky than Quantrill. Nobody much liked him, but
everybody was afraid of him.

Bill was already talking about going out to the Western
gold fields and striking it rich in the diggings, but he always had a pack of forbidden playing cards in his pocket
when he was blowing. A smoothy, he might have saved old
man Dalton many a dollar had he been taken along for the
horse deals.

Frank, who seldom got into overt mischief, could out-cuss
any grown man in Cass County. Bob and Emmett, the two
tads born here in the county, seemed to have a downright
love of meanness for meanness's sake.

All five of them were proud to be pointed out at Sunday-
school picnics and crossroads stores as the cousins of Cole
Younger. Yes sir, they were kin to Old Cole himself. Wasn't
that a distinction for country boys? All of them, too,
showed an abiding love for fast guns, like Cole, and fast
horses, like their father.

How the boys loved to visit around the homes of people
who knew the Jameses and the outlaw Youngers personally,
soaking up legend and fact about those exciting land buccaneers. Sometimes an angry Ma Dalton would find them at
the country store of Jerry Robinson, where loafers sat around
on cracker boxes gilding the James-Younger saga.

"You had to be a fighting man to have folks palaver about
you around a grocery store," as Emmett Dalton said.

Grown men were saying too that the young Daltons were
learning how to shoot as straight and sure as Jesse and Cole
themselves. The compliment was cooling salve on the boys'
trigger fingers when they went hunting 'coons and possums

in the river bottoms. Good marksmanship was sure distinction in Missouri.

Under "drowsy hickory groves," away from the watchful eye of Ma Dalton, these five kept practicing what was becoming a Dalton art. Big empty snuff bottles made handy targets; the sharp tinkle of shattered glass was music to their ears. Sometimes while they were loading and aiming, bands of Missourians would go charging by in a tumult of hoof dust. Some other scalawag or some sneaking Kansan, they reckoned, had got what was coming to him.

Admiration naturally led to imitation. The brothers began learning how to shoot as they rode. All of them acquired their horses at an early age. They handled ponies as easily as their father did while looking after herds of them at county fairs.

Emmett, eleventh of the fifteen Dalton children, had acquired his first mount when he hit the promising age of eight. The horse was a bay mare called Katie, "highstrung, speedy," and with an "air that suited a Dalton." Katie had been brought by Emmett's father from a Cass County neighbor named Smoot, who had found that her past history made her too high-spirited for plow and wood cart.

According to Smoot—the story may have been just another Missouri windy—the mare had broken away from the James brothers during one of their plunder sprees. During their flight, the Jameses had run into the farmer, taken his pony and told him that he might have Katie as a replacement if he could find her. Smoot searched around till he found the bay mare. Emmett claimed her after she had been brought to the Dalton pasture, but all the boys took turns riding the celebrated nag.

They kept her sleek hide stuffed with "juicy roasting ears," curried her till she looked like "polished buckeye," and speculated on which of the James raids she had borne high-riding Jesse. Other country boys gaped at the Daltons in envy; and some of their parents no doubt dolefully predicted that these youngsters would turn out like the Jameses if their mother didn't come down on them harder.

And Emmett, Katie's master, had a brand-new hero to worship—Jesse James. The horse became a living tie between the professional outlaw and the worshipful country kid, although Jesse never knew about it. Some time during this period, barbershop literature like the *National Police Gazette* concocted the commonly believed tale that the Jameses and the Youngers were not only comrades-at-arms but own blood kin. Now the Dalton boys had something else to strut

about: they were kin of some sort to the Youngers, so that
made them cross kin to the Jameses. Such was the beginning
of another sub-legend; some Dalton descendants of today still
believe this bit of apocrypha.[3]

In August, 1879, the James-Younger gang was shattered by
embattled citizens of Northfield, Minnesota, who foiled the
bandits' raid on their bank with high-powered shotguns. The
Jameses barely got out of the state alive after posses chased
them across a string of murky swamps. One of the Youngers
died during the pursuit, with Jesse wanting to relieve him
from his misery by killing him. Cole and two other brothers
went to a state pen, far from their native range.

Then Lewis Dalton recalled to his family a pair of visitors
who had dropped by some years before.

Two men, identifying themselves as livestock buyers, had
stopped at the Dalton gate to chat with Lewis. Adeline Dalton
hadn't served them a bite, as was the custom in the easy
hospitality of Missouri. But the travelers who had gotten such
a short welcome had a bearing, a certain manner of speaking which had made Adeline's offspring forever remember
them.

"Those men you saw," Lewis Dalton now announced, "were
Jesse James and Cole Younger."

Adeline Dalton was upset. Her five wild sons had another
thing to brag about. They had seen Cole Younger and Jesse
James with their own eyes, heard their voices, spotted
the hidden bulge of guns at their waists.

SIX-SHOOTER ACADEMY

THE bitter decade of the seventies passed without much change in the picayunish fortunes of the Daltons. Adeline's womb became mercifully barren. Lewis Dalton, grim and beaten, started changing character, becoming glum and morose. Then came the chaotic eighties, which dislocated more native American poor whites than had the Civil War.

Jesse James died, back-shot by "dirty little coward" Bob Ford in 1882. Eleven-year-old Emmett Dalton must have gone out to the barn and shed some scalding tears. Future history would make the murdered outlaw ten feet tall.

Banks and railroads had the country's rural majority in a vise that squeezed. Factories in the brand-new industrial centers preferred to hire docile foreign-born laborers rather than unruly Old Americans with the Declaration of Independence in their blood streams. Recalling their ancestors, these turned their eyes west toward land to be had free as quickly as United States cavalrymen could make it secure from the resisting Indians.

The Daltons caught the moving itch. Each generation had seen some of them loading up for one or another promised land on one or another opening frontier. First of the connection to leave Missouri was cousin-in-law Johnny Ringo— correct name, Ringgold. Johnny found employment as a hired gunslinger in the grim Mason County, Texas, range war before drifting out to Arizona and making outlaw history in and around Tombstone.

Four of Lewis Dalton's grown sons pulled out of Missouri, where the cheap land was all gone. Charles, Henry and Littleton wandered around Texas and Montana, to wind up as ordinary farmers in the San Joaquin Valley of California. Bill, the smoothy, followed pretty much their itinerary, gambling whenever he had a poke, working as a miner in Butte, as a construction laborer sometimes, as a roving harvest hand in various agricultural sections. He was reaping wheat in California during the summer of 1883, when he married

Jennie Blivens, daughter of his employer, and started dabbling in politics.

Adeline Dalton wanted to stay put in Missouri with her kinfolks. But letters from the sons in California stirred the old wanderlust in the aging bones of Lewis. He kept remembering the days when he had seen the fleets of covered wagons headed west for Oregon and California. He could no more stay hitched than the wild horses he had once bought from the Osages to sell the federal troopers.

So, because he had to go, he went to the place that would be the least tiring to reach. The spot was Indian Territory, whose borders were already being breached by landhungry whites, whatever high-sounding treaties the government once had signed saying this would be redskin domain "so long as grass grew and rivers flowed."

He took a trip to the Cherokee Nation and leased acreage from one of the mixed-bloods who ran the affairs of that unique republic. The transaction had no validity under tribal law, which declared that the land itself belonged to the whole Cherokee Nation. Now, however, only the full-bloods back in the hills paid much attention to the old compact as more and more white squatters kept coming into the Territory.

The Daltons arrived in their own caravan of wagons in 1882, with Emmett helping drive the cattle and horses that trailed behind.[1] Rolling beautiful country the Territory was, with its great stretches of wild grass, "relieved by timbered hills and sweet-water creeks." The Cherokees were peaceful and literate, unlike the Arizona Apaches. Game ran thick in the woods; the yipping of skulking coyotes sounded accompaniment to the tinkling bells of grazing cattle.

It was inviting, mostly open country, where the Dalton boys found plenty of rabbits and prairie chickens for targets. All males, white, Indian, and mixed-blood, strode around with six-shooters in their belts at Vinita, where the Daltons bought hay and picked up mail.[2] The fall races, staged when crops were reaped, drew larger crowds than either the summer brush-arbor revival meetings or Dr. Blair's medicine show from neighboring Texas.

Horse racing became the ripe sap in the veins of the wilder Dalton boys. Emmett, while still in knee pants, acquired a short-lived reputation as a crack jockey.

He won dubious laurels at the Vinita races in 1883. Scott O'Drain, a mixed-blood Cherokee of near-by Prairie City, engaged the twelve-year-old to ride a fast mare called Dolly against a renowned Choctaw pony named Sitting Bull, slated to be ridden by an Indian of Emmett's age.

Before the match, O'Drain handed Emmett a buggy whip with a long butt end and whispered, "Don't let him pass you—understand?"

Emmett got the message. Piles of money had been bet on the race and the Dalton boy was due for a cut if he rode Dolly to victory. A starting pistol sounded. Dolly took the lead by a few paces. Sitting Bull edged up twice in the dead heat. Each time Emmett reached out to clout the horse over the head. Daltons never were much for rules.

He won the race easily but the foul almost set a mob after him. Six-shooters were flashing when he crossed the deadline in a long gallop; he showed enough good sense not to stop for any salute, and so made the first of all Dalton escapes.

Emmett and Bob already were getting reputations as hard cases in Indian Territory. Some of the neighbors were predicting that they likely would wind up on the celebrated gallows of Hanging Judge Isaac Parker at Fort Smith, Arkansas, center of federal jurisdiction for Indian Territory. Parker had wrongdoers strung up in batches. Emmett once heard a marshal of the court remark to another:

"That Dalton boy, he's going to be a tough man to handle when he gits growed up."

Emmett liked that, just as in Missouri he had liked being pointed out as kin to Cole Younger and Jesse James.

Grat also was doing a lot of strutting, along with a lot of fist-swinging, at Saturday-night square dances. White, Indian, or devil, he was ready to take anybody on. Frank was as handy with his fists as Grat, but he was not one to pick fights. Their reputation for courage got them their first jobs as lawmen.

More and more white squatters were coming into this second Cherokee Republic of Oklahoma, as drifters like them had inundated the original Nation back in Georgia.[3] The tribal legislature at Tahlequah ordered the establishment of a special Indian police force under the leadership of John W. Jordan, a courageous mixed-blood lawman. Jordan enlisted Grat and Frank Dalton, maybe because of the unproven story that the boys had inherited a strain of Indian blood through their mother.[4]

It was as "Cherokee" policemen then, that the Daltons made their bows as Western officers. Their service was creditable enough, within narrow limits. They did stop, at various tribal borders, a few caravans of Sooners heading in from adjoining states to help themselves to tribal lands. But for every prospective squatter that they stopped, ten slipped through at some unguarded spot. Others got off at various stations of the newly constructed Missouri, Kansas and Texas railroad, then stayed as unwelcome aliens in a theoretically sovereign nation.

Emmett, in his early teens, left home to go cowpunching. He hired out on the Bar X B Ranch, run by Oscar Halsell, a fervently religious Texan employing fiercely rough saddle hands. In no time at all, Emmett struck up close friendships with three other riders for Halsell—Dick Broadwell, Bill Powers and Bill Doolin.

This trio cronied with several men of their mettle and reputation for posse dodging, on the adjoining Turkey Track Ranch. Emmett, the red-blooded boy who loved outlaws, soon got to know them as Charlie Pierce, George "Bitter Creek" Newcomb and "Blackface Charley" Bryant.

These were all venturesome buckies, ready for anything and unimpressed by the strictures of law or morals. Doolin, the Arkansawyer with the drooping whiskers, thus far had escaped punishment for various scrapes through the lenience of federal marshal Bill Tilghman, who was often too considerate for his own good.

Pint-sized Newcomb got his nickname of Bitter Creek because he was always chanting a familiar song of the range:

> "I'm a lone wolf from Bitter Creek
> And tonight is my night to howl."

At times, Newcomb was also known as "the Slaughter Kid," having worked in Texas for John Slaughter, who was later to become the famous sheriff of Cochise County, Arizona.

"Blackface Charley" Bryant was so called because his complexion had changed from blond to a mottled dark as a result of gunpowder blasting him at close range. Moody and sardonic he was, ready to shoot at the drop of a tin cup.

Emmett's wages were average for cowpunchers—thirty dollars a month and board. But the "education" he got from his friends could not be overestimated for such an ambitious young man. As he once said, they taught him "to speak the language of the .45 with considerable accuracy."

Emmett never had been much for book learning in the one-room schoolhouses of Missouri and Indian Territory. But he enjoyed this semester of practical training, proving an apt pupil of such masters.

Soon he could outshoot Bill Doolin, the club's blue-ribbon marksman, and outbrag Charley Bryant, who had boasted of all the dust he'd raised in the faces of out-ridden posses. "Bitter Creek" Newcomb taught him how to outfox a man who was slow-trailing you with a Winchester. Charlie Pierce, an accomplished prairie Lothario, could have instructed him in another art, but by that time sixteen-year-old Emmett was in the first throes of Pure Love.

His heartbeat was a nester girl of the same age named Julia Johnson. Emmett said that he met her after hearing her heavenly voice floating into the Territory air from a church choir. Other sources assert that she was a hard little number with a constant yen for bad actors. Though sometimes attracted by competing trigger artists, Julia would remain in Emmett's life. So would his new partners of the range—spectacularly so.

Among these men, on ranges where law and order were despised brands, the Dalton gang was germinating.

FIRST KILL FOR THE DALTONS

BY degrees, the Daltons progressed from bearcatting to backshooting. They didn't suddenly pick up Winchesters and start puncturing Indian Territory, as writers of dime novels like "Harry Hawkeye" would have them doing.[1]

The process was much more subtle, much truer to the usual development of Western outlaws. It was a matter of an innocent lariat gradually spreading into a wide loop, of a pistol yielding to temptation when a poke was empty. In part, it was a matter of the boys being money-hungry because their father had so seldom been blessed with enough to buy them popcorn or winter shoes. Besides, they were pretty damn mean to begin with, as was said in the border country.

From his instructors on the Bar X B, Emmett first learned the techniques of bronc snatching. The ranch foreman, John McLain, sternly forbade rustling by his punchers, but he couldn't very well keep a close watch on every member of such a roistering bunch. From his chums on the ranch, the promising kid learned of the Southwest's biggest black market for stolen horses—Baxter Springs, where Missouri, Kansas and Indian Territory converged, with the savage land of the Arkansas Ozarks not far away.

Bob, the slick one, kept his nose clean during those early years, devoting his time to chasing girls instead of mustangs. Old-timers say that he swung a wicked leg. Bill was trying to make a splash in California politics after having been taken under the wing of Merced County District Attorney T. W. Breckenridge. Grat, always needing a dollar for a jug, may well have made his first slip by letting an occasional Boomer wagon slip through the Territory for a "fee" while flashing a star for the Cherokee Nation. Even this marginal operation would not have been undertaken, when Frank, a genuine man of law, was around.

Whatever the boys did on the side was kept from this strict brother, who would have jailed any of them for a slip of rope or gun. Because of his kinfolks, Frank Dalton has never been accorded his just due in the Territory's long struggle against outlawry. But he was brave and often as personally considerate as Bill Tilghman, though never Tilghman's peer in intelligence or social polish. Frank respected his badge and lived up to the obligations that went with it. It was not his fault that his brothers wore theirs as handy pegs on which to hang their orneriness.[2]

While Emmett had been learning the tricks of long riding on the Bar X B, Frank had graduated into one of the most courageous corps of lawmen ever to ride the borders of America. In 1884, while he was in his late twenties, the fancy-cussing Dalton brother joined Judge Isaac Parker's battalion of deputy marshals, riding out from Fort Smith. The work was rough; the pay was slow. A marshal got two dollars, sent him months later, for an outlaw he caught, and he had to bury at his own expense any man he shot fatally while making an arrest. Almost a third of Parker's marshals—sixty-five out of two hundred and twenty-five—died in line of duty. Even the Texas Rangers across Red River did not begin to have such a high fatality rate.

Indian Territory's outlaw population kept multiplying, not only by normal migration from neighboring Texas and Kansas but by an influx of hardcase fugitives from half a dozen new states farther west. Here they came as a developing Western society pushed them out. Here they rode and roistered, robbed and killed, on this last frontier, where Indian governments were weak and "there was no God west of Fort Smith."

Frank got a federal marshal's commission because of the way he had handled himself as a Cherokee tribal policeman under John Jordan. Each marshal was entitled to a posseman who functioned as general helper and to guard prisoners chained in wagons for transportation to Fort Smith; and Grat Dalton also left the Cherokee force to become his brother's aide. The big fellow aided Frank in the capture of many a roving bad man.

Then in 1887, Frank Dalton and Deputy Marshal Jim Cole were ordered to nab the Bill Smith band of whisky runners who were camped opposite Fort Smith in the Arkansas River bottoms of Indian Territory. Sale of hard liquor to Indians was forbidden everywhere by United States law, but here as elsewhere the statute was more honored in the breach than in the observance.

The officers rode to the Bottoms and flushed the gang, one of them a roving tart currently claiming to be "Mrs. Smith." Forty-fives boomed. Frank Dalton went down mortally wounded in the first salvo. Cole fired three consecutive shots which accounted in as many seconds for Smith, the gun-toting wench and an assistant bootlegger named Dixon. Then the deputy marshal threw down on the only survivor of the gang, a young criminal named Bill Towerly.

He missed, and Towerly aimed a final bullet into the heart of writhing Frank Dalton. After that sorry coup de grace, the killer fled into the Bottoms, one more gunslinger able to boast of "gittin' hisself a Judge Parker man."

The first Dalton had died with his boots on. He left a young widow of whom little is known except that she was an ordinary good girl named Naomi. Had his brothers lived by the sterling ethics of Harry Hawkeye, they would have avenged Frank's death by swearing eternal and implacable hostility to outlaws and outlawry.

They did just the opposite. Frank Dalton had made a bad thing of marshaling by taking it so seriously. His surviving brothers decided to make a good thing and an on-the-spot business out of it.

Grat was promoted to the marshal's job left open by Frank's demise. He, in turn, made Bob his posseman. Emmett left off cowpunching so he could ride around, uncommissioned, with his brothers and also so he would be free to do more harmonica serenading of his darling Julia.

Soon the boys showed that they had much better business instincts than their dad, who had made one last move to Coffeyville in 1886. They became the West's first grafting traffic cops.

Their earliest pickings were from the Boomers or squatters, who had no legal right in the Territory until 1889. How they greased their palms from poor people has been described by author Homer Croy in an account left by Frank Shufeldt of Lenapah, Oklahoma.

Bob and Grat would amble around on horseback till they spotted a prairie schooner. Then Bob would halt the driver, announce, "We're United States marshals," and start barking questions: "Where you from? Where you going?" plus enough other queries to scare a drifting ridge rat from Tennessee half out of his wits.

While this nonsense was going on, Grat would ride to the rear of the wagon and slip a bottle of whisky inside. The two marshals would take their leave with scowling good-bys, then rein up again a few miles down the road.

When the driver saw them for a second time, the brothers would move in for the reckoning. Using their authority as marshals they would "search" the wagon to come up with the whisky.

"Do you know what this means in Indian Territory?" they would thunder at the unfortunate Boomer.

The quaking "offender" generally paid off in a "fine" levied on the spot by the Daltons. After congratulating the "guilty party" on staying out of jail, the brothers would ride off, to look for more wagons.

So each ambitious Dalton boy always had a few dollars in his pocket. Most of their transactions would seem to have been of this order since very few formal warrants served by them are to be found in the archives of Parker's court.

But in fairness to the unfair, it must be stated that their form of graft was not exceptional in the West. Cow-town sheriffs and mining-camp marshals were often nominated by the gambling and liquor interests. Wyatt Earp and Wild Bill Hickok, no better or worse than the Daltons, used to drive hard bargains with cardsharks and saloonkeepers before they would condescend to preserve law and order for a community. A noted Texas Ranger captain was heavily involved with the Panhandle cattle barons and stood trial, during the Dalton era, for shooting a nester.

Grat did earn a whit of deserved glory for being wounded in a fight with a gang of horse thieves led by a bronc fancier named Felix Griffin. Nobody ever could accuse the big fellow of cowardice when gunplay was required. At the same time he never bothered any of Emmett's cowboy friends, though he must have known that four or five among them were wanted for stock theft in Kansas. Grat had less respect for Kansas, his native state, than did any *tejano* driving beeves from Laredo to Dodge.

During 1888, an honest opportunity came to Bob and Emmett. In fact, it could have been their best stroke of luck. Tired of being harassed by outlaws in the Osage Hills, the Osage Indians asked the federal district court in Wichita, Kansas, to organize a police force and send them an experienced officer as its head.

Bob put in for the job. Pawhuska, the Osage capital, wasn't too many whoops and hollers away from Coffeyville, where nubile Minnie Johnson lived with his parents. Near by on the Territory side dwelt Emmett's golden girl, Julia Johnson. No reliable evidence says that Minnie and Julia were any kin, though they were both sprouts from Kentucky.

Bob's application to lead the Osage force was helped by the record that Frank had made as a lawman for the Chero-kees. So peaceful Indians seeking recognition as "the Sixth Civilized Tribe" found themselves saddled with the dubious example of civilization presented by Police Chief Bob Dalton.

Bob, in the Dalton tradition, made Emmett his posseman. Both were supposed to work under the direction of the Wichita court, which also gave Bob a commission as deputy marshal. Grat continued to ride for the Fort Smith tribunal, whose jurisdiction had been reduced to the southern half of the Territory.

Bob recruited a dozen or more Osages into his corps of peace enforcers. Since he was not more than nineteen or twenty at the time, he ranked as the youngest police chief in Western history. However, he took the honor rather lightly, and spent more time inspecting horse herds than evidence left by long riders.

Emmett's post on the force was comparable to that of a sergeant. He thoroughly enjoyed ordering around Osage policemen twenty years older than himself, and he loved sticking pistol barrels into the ribs of prisoners being carried into Wichita. It was fun to stride down the streets of Pawhuska on Saturday afternoon, wearing his forty-five, showing off in front of the Indians and the white squatters coming in to trade.

For that brief period, these two Dalton boys were in clover. As usual, their official pay was slow. But by now they had learned all sorts of ways of picking up ready cash easily. They got along with the Osages by letting the tribal patrolmen do most of the work while they escorted their girls to church suppers and such traveling amusements as carnivals and tent shows. Emmett loved to serenade his Julia with harmonica renditions of *The Ballad of Cole Younger*, a number that had been neither written nor authorized by Cousin Cole, still sweating it out in the Minnesota pen.

In the meantime, Bob was finding Cousin Minnie accommodating. If the Dalton saga had been written as a tent-show script, Minnie would have been portrayed as Bob Dalton's road to ruin.

Fall of 1888, the season was. Minnie was then only about fifteen but what she knew couldn't have been put in a book for nice girls. Lewis Dalton had, by that time, been reduced to doing odd jobs such as cleaning yards and mending hen coops. Eight Daltons in all were now living at a shabby house in Coffeyville.

Bob, Emmett and Grat rode lickety-split to the Kansas town after receiving an urgent summons from Ma Dalton. Minnie embraced them all, but Bob was puzzled because she

gave him only the same kind of cousinly peck with which she
greeted his brothers.

Bob Dalton had the sexual intuition of a tomcat. Minnie
was bound to have taken on another lover. Otherwise why
should she be dressed in her "best Sunday clothes"—dolled
up as she'd never been on his visits? During a meager
supper, he kept trying to catch her eye and she kept shifting
her glance.

That night, Bob opened a familiar door into Minnie's bed-
room. The bed was there. The girl was gone.

Bob raised Billy hell and demanded from his parents the
name of his rival. Finally, at Lewis Dalton's prompting, Adeline allowed that Minnie had been keeping company with a
roaming Kentuckian called Charlie Montgomery.

Grat's slow mind began perking. "Charlie Montgomery?
Used to know a feller by that name peddled whisky all over
the Cherokee Nation. Was locked up in Fort Smith jail last
time I seen him."

Bob nearly hit the fly-specked ceiling. Their own brother,
Frank, had been shot down by whisky runners. Minnie taking
up with one was not only an insult to a marshal, but a
mighty bad reflection on the family that had raised her when
she had been left a squawling orphan. Obviously she had
slipped out to warn Montgomery not to come to the house
while her lawmen kin were there.

There was only one way to heal the wounded heart of
Bob and the bruised feelings of all the Daltons. Bob stood
up from his chair, then claimed his hat and Winchester.

"Guess I'll take a walk," he announced.

Emmett also rose. "I'll go along, Bob."

From the family the boys had learned that Charlie Montgomery was now working for Ted Seymour, a wealthy cattle
dealer living across the Santa Fe tracks on the south side of
Coffeyville. They hotfooted it to Seymour's big two-story
house, rousted that wrathful gentleman out of bed, and told
him that they had "a pressing message" for his hired hand.

Seymour directed them to Charlie's sleeping quarters in the
barn. They tramped on out there and started banging on the
door. Packs of disturbed rats let off munching Seymour's corn
to run in every direction, but the Daltons got no answer to
their knocks.

Charlie and Minnie were conspicuous by their absence
when the boys got the door open and rushed upstairs to a
loft furnished meagerly with a cot and a washstand. But
near the one window, Bob picked up a lady's red silk handkerchief.

"By God!" he roared. "I bought that for Minnie at the county fair."

She had contemptuously dumped the kerchief before eloping with no-'count Charlie Montgomery.

Bob stood dazed, like a man just buffaloed by the barrel of a forty-five. Then a locomotive bell rang from the Santa Fe tracks, a stone's throw from the barn, and Bob made a quick guess.

Flourishing his Winchester, he charged down the stairs and made off in a dead run toward the tracks. As the train was gathering speed after leaving the Coffeyville station, he saw Charlie and Minnie sitting together, loving arms around each other, in a passenger car.

Bob's congratulations were every bullet in the magazine of his rifle. The shots went whizzing through the open window of the coach. The couple inside screamed and ducked. No man took a woman away from Bob Dalton, by God!

Bob figured that Charlie Montgomery would be back for his belongings, left behind in the hurry of nuptial flight. He asked Kansas officers to keep a lookout for a hard customer whose record included horse stealing as well as booze peddling.

Seven weeks later, in the month of December, Bob got word that Montgomery had come back to Seymour's for a day. As part of what seems to have been a calculated frame-up, Minnie's bridegroom had been told that her ex-lover was miles away from Coffeyville and Indian Territory.

A lone bullet fired from behind got Charlie in the neck as he was leaving Seymour's barn with his belongings. Then Emmett helped Bob, the slayer, load the corpse into a wagon, which was driven to the establishment of old man Lang, the Coffeyville undertaker.

Lang noticed that the fatal wound was a backshot, but the guns of the Daltons caused him to make only discreet comment. He objected to burying outlaws on credit since they seldom had known kin who could pay burial costs. But he finally agreed to charge Charlie's laying-away to the federal court at Wichita, after requiring both Bob and Emmett to sign an acknowledgment of the debt.

The boys told Lang that they had shot Montgomery for resisting arrest. According to their story, they had caught him stealing horse gear from a stable that Ted Seymour owned on some ranch property in the Territory. Everybody in Coffeyville thought the yarn was fishy when Lang spread it around town.

GRAT TIPS THE GAME

APRIL 22, 1889 . . . a day of plunging wagons and popping whips—of men being bounced from saddles and pregnant brides out of buggies in a marathon of greed.

A sanctioned riot, that day was. A bawdy, brawling, eye-gouging, wheel-crashing span of twelve hours, which would be commemorated as the Homestead Run. Sixty thousand Anglo-Saxons and Scotch-Irish tore out at signals from soldiers' pistols to seize claims where they could sow corn and creeds and young-uns. Before nightfall, they would be starting towns and mapping streets across the burrows of suddenly evicted varmints.

Hungry Canaan seekers, these people were. Of "that gandernecked clan from which Calhoun and Jackson sprang. Jesse James—and Lincoln's people." [1]

From it also stemmed some folks named Dalton. Through the generations, Daltons had sought Canaans beyond rivers and ridges. With the others of their breed, they pushed out Indians living in harmony with the soil to leave the white man's landmarks of washouts and dust bowls.

Two Dalton brothers came back to the Territory during the homestead grab, not having been doing themselves much good in California. These were Charles and Henry. Bill stayed on in his adopted state, where he still hoped to break into politics, although he was neglecting his rented wheat farm.

The returning Daltons took up claims near Kingfisher in a severed portion of the Cherokee Nation. Afterward they found land in this booming nester community for the part of the family still living that squalid existence at Coffeyville. Simon, the youngest Dalton boy, had died. Ben, the oldest, who was then about thirty-eight, brought Ma Dalton and the others to the Territory.

But Lewis Dalton, now in his mid-seventies, decided not to make this one last move. He and Adeline had practically ceased speaking. None of his children had any use for a beaten old failure like him. For a while he hung around

Coffeyville. Then his hands got too feeble even for light casual work. So he went to the near-by village of Dearing, where a kindly family had offered him shelter. There, glum, bitter, neglected by his wife and children, he died, some time during 1890.

Kingfisher became the Dalton center. Adeline Dalton liked the brisk new town as much as she had despised Coffeyville. Respectable men began courting her girls—Eva, Leona and Nannie—with intentions all honorable. Minnie Johnson, who to Adeline would always be that hussy of a niece, had just disappeared after the distressing incident involving Charlie Montgomery. Church-minded Adeline no more wanted to claim kin with such a female than she did with the Younger brothers, penned up where black sheep belonged, in an iron fold of a prison.

Once in a while, the old lady worried about a pesty scandal involving the absent Bill. A woman named Mary Hughes claimed that he had married her ahead of Jennie Blivens and that he was the father of her ten-year-old son, Bill, Jr.— William Harmon Dalton, in full.

Ma Dalton had never seen this purported grandchild of hers. In fact, none of his Western kin ever knew him, his mother having gone off to Louisiana to give him birth.

Mary Hughes had kinspeople over at Hugo. They shot off a lot of mouth about Bill doing nothing for the son who bore his name, or even making a trip to see what the boy looked like. But the woman herself wasn't giving the Daltons active trouble, which was a sign that this was the way in which the Good Lord had willed everything.[2]

Adeline was concerned too about the letters Bill wrote her, bragging that someday he'd be governor of California. Such whopping hopes were bothersome, reminding her of all the talk that Lewis Dalton had spun about getting rich off horse trading.

The Dalton matriarch had no patience with the dreams of Dalton men. How could she, after having been married for almost forty years to that piddling dreamer who had sired them all? She would much rather have seen Bill driving a middle-buster behind a team of mules here in the Territory than capering around with politicians who, for all she knew, were unsaved men. And the same thing went for those stalwarts skylarking around with badges—Grat, Bob and Emmett.

What possessed these sons to be risking death bringing in bad men when there was plenty of good land to be had cheap right around Kingfisher? Why didn't Emmett marry

that flibbertigibbet, Julia Johnson, who needed a strong man
to tame her britches and put her at woman's proper business
of homemaking?

Privately, Ma Dalton somewhat resented Julia's dander.
But she was certainly a better girl than those jezebels that
Bob had been seen running around with in the new town
called Guthrie.[3] Bob's mother feared that the Lord had
made this born beau of the Dalton clan too handsome for
his own good.

And Grat! A deeply worried Ma Dalton prayed for him
hardest of all. Here he was, thirty-two years old, with no
thought of pledging his sinning soul to the Lord or his reckless life to some virtuous woman. Grat, so happily unre-
deemed, wouldn't have known a Bible from a poker deck or
a pure church girl from a Guthrie street slut.

Ma Dalton's prayers followed her four maverick boys but
never quite overtook them. The lads obviously loved their
mother with filial devotion. But they loved something else
a degree or two better. That something was money, which
talked to them louder than did any preacher.

Banks, bulging with a tempting crop of green, were appearing in this newest nester land. To get at that crop, you
needed more complex tools than granger hoes and hay
rakes. Railroads kept extending tracks across Indian Territory, which was a natural passageway from the Midwest to
the Southwest. Everyone, and most certainly marshals, knew
that express cars carried piles of cash from one point to
another. Land speculators, flying like hawks to chicken
flocks, were cleaning up as more and more home hunters
moved across the line. Lots in Guthrie, that prairie Sodom,
once could have been bought for twenty dollars, and that
paid out on tick, a dollar or two at a time; now you couldn't
buy them for two hundred.

Since the covered-wagon invasion, men were getting rich
overnight. But the ambitious Dalton boys were still working
for two dollars a prisoner and six cents per mile traveling
expenses, with the pay always delayed and thirty-five per
cent of it going, under court rules, to the chief marshal in
Fort Smith or Wichita.

It irked the brothers to see so much easy cash floating
around when theirs came so hard, although they were still
nicking off every quick dollar they could. The Daltons ought
to get a bigger cut of the Territory's fast-circulating currency.

So three hustling young men decided to enter the horse

business—but to hold onto their steady jobs till the new enterprise got going.

Soon the contraband horse market at Baxter Springs was receiving more ponies of finer grade from Indian Territory. The law badge, of course, gave its three wearers more freedom to scout around for supply sources than that enjoyed by old-line, well-known horse thieves. Plenty of middlemen could always be found around a "Springs" joint operated by Annie Walker, an ex-mistress of guerrilla-chief Quantrill.

Once delivered, stolen ponies would be placed in various local pastures owned by shady operators calling themselves "ranchers." Brands would be altered if they had not already been changed in the Territory. Buyers in the know would arrive from Denver or Kansas City, make their selections and afterward move the stock in small lots so that lawmen would not become unduly suspicious.

For some months, the unlicensed firm of Dalton Brothers, dealers in horses, prospered. Bob was the unofficial president. Grat the outside man scouting for merchandise, and Emmett, now with plenty of money to spend on his girl, a sort of junior executive. Where their father had failed in the hoof trade, the boys seemed bound for success.

Skilled labor came easy, with so many cowboys out of work after the sodbusters had done their worst with huge tracts of the range land. Preference in employment naturally went to Emmett's old buddies of the Bar X B. Weren't they men of experience who had learned the trade up and down the Chisholm Trail? Bill Doolin, hating plows and hoes, seems to have been the first to throw in with the Daltons. By Territory legend, those bitter anti-agrarians—Blackface Charley Bryant and Bill McElhanie—were also on the brothers' string of piecework helpers.

The pay, of course, was figured as so much per pony, delivered to other Dalton intermediaries driving remudas to Baxter Springs. An ordinary much-used saddle bronc was probably worth only from two to five dollars in the accounts that Bob Dalton kept in his shrewd head. But frisky two-year-olds might bring their finders from five to ten.

America was in need of lots of horses in the great expansion of Western agriculture that followed the wholesale dispossession of the Indians, from 1880 to 1900. Profits were satisfactory, if risks were great. Now more money—plenty of money—jingled in the pockets of the Dalton boys.

Shrewdly the partners covered their side business by continuing to bring in minor offenders for trial at Fort Smith, Wichita or a third United States District Court, which Congress had established at Fort Scott, Kansas, not far from the Missouri border. To keep the deception going, Bob and Emmett kept grumbling, loudly and publicly, about their irregular pay as policemen of the Osage Nation.

Everything was as smooth as a two-year-old's hide till Grat tipped the play. Bumptious Grat, who didn't have horse sense, let alone man sense, let himself be found prowling, in broad daylight, the pastures of a rancher named Charles McLelland.

The rancher's cowpunchers would have strung Grat up then and there had he not been a marshal. You had to accord him the presumption that he was looking for horse thieves who had been helping themselves to the broncs of an honest citizen. Nevertheless, the affair cast suspicion upon all three of the Dalton brothers.

Grangers and punchers began adding up all kinds of conclusions about them. That trick of planting whisky bottles in wagons to collect "fines," for instance. The dubious slaying of Charlie Montgomery also came to mind. Gossip around Coffeyville kept saying that Bob Dalton hadn't given Montgomery the chance of a suck-egg dog. If a marshal wanted to gun-fight a man over a girl, he ought to take off his badge before drawing, and fight face-to-face instead of backshooting.

One conspicuous thing, too: why were so many respected Territory officers always so broke, while the Daltons could ride into Coffeyville or Guthrie at any time with plenty of money to lay down on bars and gaming tables?

Murder was getting out—and so was graft. The Daltons had pinned on badges when their residue of good will from the martyred Frank ran high in the Territory. Now some citizens of the Territory were boldly saying that his brothers were living disgraces to his name.

Then their main front of respectability—their connection with the Osage Nation—began crumbling. Leading Osage families might bear colorful names such as Black Dog, Tallchief and Baconrind. But, increasingly literate as a result of mission schools, the tribesmen were anxious to cancel any impression that they were primitive Indians harboring white criminals.

Indians were becoming more civilized; whites like these Daltons, less so. More and more schoolhouses were being built by the numerous tribes of the Territory. It is doubtful that Emmett Dalton had at that time ever read anything except dime novels purportedly telling the adventures of Jesse James and Buffalo Bill. Of these he was an avid fan. Grat did well to write his own name legibly. Bob's interest in the printed word was limited to the study of reward posters.

Through still other ways, a fateful margin of history was narrowing the chances of the boys to make a permanent good thing of their chosen trade. Congress was considering a bill to organize that truncated western section of Indian Territory into the new commonwealth of Oklahoma. Which would mean that very soon there would be a county courthouse every twenty miles or so, and county sheriffs' posses to bedevil wrongdoers.

Every time the boys went to Kingfisher, Ma Dalton pleaded with them to settle down on farms. The old lady had a point, but it wasn't one that Bob and Emmett and Grat ever could quite comprehend.

6

THE BOYS LOSE THEIR BADGES

THAT geo-political conglomerate called Indian Territory
was nearing its wind-up. So was the tenure of the Territory's most controversial lawmen, the brothers Dalton.

Branches of the Farmers' Alliance and the King's Daughters now convened on sites where, not long ago, the Indians
had gathered for solemn councils and pagan love sprees.
Little post offices, in corners of frame cabins, delivered cor-
sets and boots and churns ordered from the Montgomery
Ward catalogue. Watkins and Raleigh salesmen rolled
around in their big hacks distributing extracts to granger
wives and lotions to granger girls. In raw young towns,
mixed-blood Indians were more often reading *Leslie's Weekly* than the *Cherokee Advocate*.

It was an era of blending. Smart redskins were uniting
with foes who couldn't be licked. Sons of chiefs and stomp
dancers joined the Masons, to wind up as Past Worshipful
Masters, or the Woodmen of the World, to become Consul
Commanders. White skin or copper skin, or fusion of both,
you swam with the tide or risked being washed under.

The Daltons never joined the Woodmen, or anything else
except the crap games in the back rooms of barber shops.
Change was to them merely the opportunity to pull off bigger coups by tried and true methods. Otherwise, they would
have abandoned their pattern of range larceny to start legitimate businesses or rent out their guns to the expanding
railway systems that were seeking capable guards.

By this time, Bob had added Grat to the top command of
the tribal police force.[1] The appointment pleased the full-
blood moonshiners of the Osage Hills, but not the nearly
white civic boosters of Pawhuska.

For some months the Daltons maintained their curious
triple role: they were marshals of the federal courts, ram-
rods of a tribal police force, and the reputed bosses of the
Territory's most efficient horse-stealing ring. A parallel that
comes to mind is Montana's crooked sheriff, Henry Plum-

mer, who was hanged by the Alder Gulch vigilantes after being exposed as a chieftain of stagecoach robbers.

But in the end Pawhuska's pre-Rotarians got the Dalton boys off their backs, if not quite out of their hair. Tribal tradition says that influential merchants pulled wires to ease out the three brothers. The parting might have been more cordial if the merchants had passed the hat to settle back wages that Bob had coming, but they didn't. And as Emmett later would comment in one of his truthful statements:

"It was a debt for which, among other things, Bob Dalton eventually took compound interest in vengeful retaliation."

The boys still retained their commissions as marshals. With experienced men so hard to get, the federal tribunals were reluctant to fire any officer unless he was caught red-handed in some breach of the law. Till the heat could cool in the Osage country, the Daltons transferred operations to Claremore, in the heart of the Cherokee Nation.

The Cherokees remembered Grat as having been an efficient officer under their law enforcer, John Jordan. His brothers were therefore accepted, whatever the scandals that had followed them from the neighboring Osage Nation. It was not long, however, before they landed on the no-good roster of a second Indian tribe.

A Claremore citizen, Alex Cochran, who was seven-eighths white, got drunk one day, pulled a trigger and severely wounded the lawman who was trying to arrest him. The victim was Marshal George Cox, who would later become an implacable foe of the Daltons. Now the three brothers were bound to bring the gunslinger in.

They started looking for him in the prosperous Indian town. From speakeasy to speakeasy and store to store, they sought the murderous drunk. Finally they entered a business place whose proprietor spoke slyly to the head Dalton:

"If you want Alex Cochran so bad, Bob, why don't you take out after him? He was in my store a few minutes ago buying a box of cartridges."

The storekeeper walked to the door and pointed toward a man riding away from the town. "There he goes down the road, taking it kind of slow. I'd know him anywhere by that old roan mare."

Bob rushed outside and borrowed somebody's horse from one of the hitching racks. Grat and Emmett also helped themselves to waiting mounts. The three brothers then took off in pursuit of the lone rider.

They got within a hundred yards of the figure on the

crowbait roan. "Halt!" Bob yelled. The man responded by putting spurs to the mare for a sudden burst of speed.

Bob jumped from his mount and fired three swift shots from his Winchester. At the third blast, fired from a distance of 200 yards, both horse and rider went down. On foot, the Daltons advanced cautiously to inspect.

"That'll settle the old 'breed's hash," Bob was gloating. "He won't go shooting no more federal marshals."

They reached the "old breed"—who turned out to be Cochran's young son. The boy was as badly shot up as Marshal Cox had been.

The Daltons would have been mobbed if the town hadn't been afraid of them. Emmett always insisted that the young Cherokee had been "an innocent victim of the merchant's ghastly notion of a practical joke on the marshals."

Maybe so. But now two ugly scandals about the brothers were being projected in gossip from the Kansas line to the border of Texas.

"Did you hear about the Daltons shooting an Injun young-un over at Claremore?"

"Yeah, like they bushwhacked that poor feller, Charlie Montgomery, in Coffeyville."

Then came a spate of gossip circulating around country stores and the shanty post offices:

"You know them Daltons was born with bad blood. Hear they're Cole Younger's cousins."

"Yeah, and kinfolks to Jesse James too."

"I been told they're kin of that old bitch, Belle Starr."

Actually, the Daltons were no more related to Belle Starr, six months dead, than they were to the Jameses. But Belle's daughter, Pearl Younger, a professional prostitute, was their somehow cousin, Cole Younger having been her father. The legend may have given the boys some protection against Cherokees indignant over the shooting of the Cochran boy. Belle Starr had been a Cherokee citizen, through her marriage to Sam Starr, member of a clan which had been a rowdy one even before the tribe's removal from the South to Indian Territory.[2]

But the Daltons were completely discredited as marshals after the Cochran shooting. According to Glenn Shirley, "They made their last trip as officers for the Fort Smith court" on June 20, 1890. This is confirmed substantially by records in the National Archives, showing that Bob and Emmett served on a posse during that month of 1890.

The same source—Record Group 60 of the General Records of the Department of Justice in the archives—shows that Grat Dalton ceased being a marshal during May, 1890. This was the dramatic month in which all Indian Territory except the waning republics of the Five Civilized Tribes became Oklahoma Territory. Again the Daltons had a chance to mend their ways, for all their pleadings that they were "forced" into outlawry by slow pay and "bad treatment."

New towns and counties were begging for experienced officers in an era of rampant lawlessness unparalleled in America since the California Gold Rush, three generations before. Guthrie, the roaring territorial capital, might have been a more peaceful place if the Daltons had sold their guns and experience to the side of justice by enlisting in its outnumbered police force. Or, if they had wanted to put away their guns, the opening up of so much good Oklahoma land for homesteading offered opportunity for honest citizens.[3]

They could have found employment on the great unscarred ranges of the Texas Panhandle, as did many other Oklahoma spur-and-saddle men who spurned the sorry emblem of the hoe and the dull ways of living it brought. Anywhere, the Daltons would have been hired as top hands for their abilities with six-shooters as well as with branding irons. But that wasn't the Dalton style.

Oklahoma celebrated its creation with barbecues and prayer meetings and with gunpowder-loaded anvils exploding over the mushrooming new communities. The Daltons had a different way of commemorating one of the major events of Western history.

In June of 1890, they left Fort Smith, no longer wearing badges to cover their illicit operations. Defiantly they moved on to Claremore, which hated them, remaining there until July the Fourth. Then they went back to the Osage Nation, now a part of Oklahoma and already being pressured by whites greedy to acquire its land.[4]

They capped their homecoming—if one may call it that —by stealing seventeen broncs and "a pair of fine mules" from a resident of the Osage belt. With nobody interfering, they drove the catch to Wagoner, on the border of the Cherokee and Creek Nations, about a hundred miles northwest of Fort Smith.

Grat was left to mind the stock. Bob and Emmett rode brazenly into Fort Smith, where everybody knew them, looking for buyers.

They made the rounds of local livestock dealers, offering to make delivery either at Wagoner or in the Arkansas River bottoms of Indian Territory that lay opposite the city. No sale. Stock buyers had their own grapevine, and the messages tapped over it said that merchandise gotten from the Daltons might be of the brand-burned kind.

On a sweltering July day, the two bright Daltons rode away from Fort Smith. It was the last time they ever would see the city they had helped make hell on earth for lawbreakers. Now they were leaving it as men irredeemably outside the law.

As they crossed the river into the Cherokee Nation, the kittens in Cousin Pearl Younger's cat house would be getting dolled up for the day's business.[5] Around the saloons, the word would be going around that two well-known ex-marshals had come into town trying to peddle some ill-gotten merchandise.

Not that the Daltons would give a damn. They hadn't done any business, but there was one satisfaction they could boastfully share with Grat.

They had hustled for orders right under the very shadow of Judge Parker's gallows, and had come out with whole necks.

That was really squaring things with the old so-and-so!

THE BIRTH OF THE DALTON GANG

THE two Daltons had their little triumph in Fort Smith, but it was an empty one. All their posturing hadn't brought in a copper cent to replenish their gaping pockets. And the boys would rather be six feet under than be short of cash.

They sped back to Wagoner, where brother Grat had been left with the stolen stuff and a jug of Ozark 'shine to keep him happy. The mules were sold for needed ready cash to an unquestioning Cherokee farmer, Emmett Vann. But offering the ponies to other tribesmen might entail an uncomfortable risk in the shape of the somberly prosaic militia known as the Cherokee Light Horse.[1]

Those unimaginative troopers could not be expected to appreciate the frolicsome high-heartedness of three young men carrying on such a dashing trade. Besides, the Daltons preferred Cherokees as suppliers rather than as customers.

Kansas was the indicated market for the Dalton line of goods. There, Cherokee horses, generally called "Indian ponies," always brought good prices. At a town in the Jayhawk State, the boys disposed of the stock for a fancy sum. Then, money bulging their jeans, they rode back to the Cherokee Nation for more merchandise.

Boldly, the unwelcome ex-residents camped near Claremore, where everybody still hated them because of the shooting of the Cochran boy. Their return was, in a way, a studied insult to that eminent Cherokee dynasty—the Rogers-Adair "connection"—which ran this town as the Ross family dominated Tahlequah, the Nation's capital.

Handsome Bob Dalton showed off before the pretty quarterbreed girls whose parents scarcely considered him an eligible beau. Emmett wrote lyrical letters to his Julia. Grat, out of the running, consoled himself with whisky. But, industriously, the boys were also getting together another remuda to drive to Kansas.

This catch was to be a cautious one—two or three ponies stolen from each of a number of prosperous Cherokee ranchers. Thus each victim, thinking that he had lost a few

47

horses by straying, would not raise any big fuss. The industrious thieves levied upon the Musgroves: an old and upright mixed-blood family. They picked off other broncs here and there.

Finally, the brothers had a herd of twenty or thirty good horses for the next trip to Kansas. Unfortunately, they made needless trouble for themselves when they raided the pastures of Bob Rogers. This Rogers was a tempestuous, fiery Cherokee who claimed collateral descent from the Texas firebrand, Sam Houston.

He missed several of his ponies after the boys had set out with their haul to Columbus, Kansas, eleven miles northwest of Baxter Springs, in a county coincidentally named Cherokee. The angry Indian gathered together some neighbors, tired of being victimized by poor-white no-goods, and started out after Rogers ponies and Dalton scalps.

The lot of broncs brought the boys $700. A Columbus stock buyer named Scott wrote them out a check after they had given him the names of well-known Indian Territory citizens as references. Scott drove the stock to one of the boarding pastures at Baxter Springs. The Daltons cashed the check, endorsed it with their proper names, and rustled still another bunch of horses on the Territory's edge.

Jauntily they herded this string down the main street of Baxter Springs. Their boots were shined, their spurs were jingling.

The Daltons rounded a corner with the mustangs, Bob riding ahead, Emmett minding the middle and Grat bringing up the drag. A party of mounted men approached them—just about the last people the boys wanted to see.

Bob Rogers had the gleam of hemp in his eyes. Siding him were other Cherokee mixed-bloods, no longer afraid of Daltons. It was the last Indian invasion of Kansas.

Bob Dalton yelled a command to his brothers. Abandoning the stolen ponies, he and Emmett lashed their mounts to tear out in one direction. Grat raced off the opposite way, heading toward their camp a couple of miles from the town. Bob Rogers paused long enough to reenforce his posse with some local citizens so that the pursuers would have some standing on Kansas soil. Under the command of a Baxter Springs officer, the combined group then took up the chase. For five or six miles, Emmett and Bob managed to keep distance between themselves and their pursuers. Then Emmett's horse played out and Bob had to slow down too: you couldn't leave your brother to the mercies of redskins and Jayhawkers.

The boys looked around wildly, scanning the sparse thickets that bordered the road. Those scrubby groves were too scant for protection.

They could hear the oncoming hoofs of the possemen. Things looked mighty bleak for Bob and Emmett. Then they saw a farmer driving a wagon, heading in their direction. They headed straight to the vehicle, pulled their six-shooters and demanded the best-looking horse of the man's team.

The granger gave them no lip. Hurriedly the boys un-hitched the horse, leaving in exchange the jaded bronc, with Emmett's coat still tied to the saddle. The Daltons "were being so closely pressed that they had no time to transfer the saddle from one horse to the other."

Emmett leaped on the fresh mount and dug his spurs into its side. He and Bob rode off to safety. A minute later, the posse stormed up to halt at the wagon and recognize the coat. And right then who should come bumbling along but Grat, leading two spare ponies from the camp.

He had arrived too late to help his brothers but in time to get himself arrested. The Kansas officers must have stopped the Cherokees from staging a necktie party after guns were drawn on the big fellow. His place of capture apparently was across the Indian Territory line because he was taken to jail at Fort Smith, the center of federal jurisdiction for the Territory. There he was thrown in Judge Isaac Parker's jail, to await convening of Parker's grand jury.

Somehow he managed to come clear, after a stay of some weeks behind bars. An Arkansas newspaper, the *Fort Smith Elevator*, reported on May 8, 1891, that he was released because there was "no evidence implicating him in the horse stealing business."

It was pious twaddle covering up some sort of maneuvering, as the newspaperman must have known. Grat had been caught redhanded with his brothers at Baxter Springs. His endorsing signature was on the check given by horse dealer Scott at Columbus. Another explanation is required.

Somebody in Fort Smith must have feared that too big a scandal would shake two outlaw-ridden territories if the culprit were tried for stealing horses after having been so recently a marshal. A federal prosecutor must have asked the grand jury to no-bill the oldest Dalton, then ordered him to get going.

Sometime in the early spring of '91, big Grat, always the luckiest and unluckiest Dalton, rode away from Fort Smith.

This would also be the last time that he would see "Parker Town," as other outlaws had named it.

Now the Daltons could claim nothing else but the name of outlaw, whatever poses they had struck as champions of justice in the past. The Cherokees had called their number, and called it publicly. Printers already would be striking off reward posters bearing their pictures, to be tacked on the walls of new courthouses still fresh from paint in new Oklahoma counties and to be kept in the saddlebags of sharp tribal policemen. Their past services to the law would not help them if they got caught again.

The changed status of the Daltons must have been plain even to the dim wit of Grat as he rode to join his brothers, holed up in one or another sub-range of the western Ozarks —probably the Cookson Hills, still one of America's main incubators of bad men.

But major decisions had to be made once the three brothers met for a reunion in some cove or canyon. Warrants were out for Bob and Emmett after the incident at Baxter Springs. Bob, with that agile mind, may have figured that Grat had been turned loose in the hope that he would unintentionally lead them to his brothers. It was Bob who was making the decisions, and this time he came up with one that was crucial.

The close family combination had to expand in order to survive. For the present—anyhow, till official heat began to cool—a safer base of operations must be found than the two territories.

Emmett's cowpunching period had been the nascent stage of the future Dalton Gang. Those war councils in the Ozarks were its season of molting. The next time that the Daltons rode out from the red hills, it would be as leaders of a full-fledged brigade of bandits.

Recruits were not hard to find. Emmett had only to contact the old cowboy chums with whom he had kept in close touch while serving as a lawman. But Bob, the organizer, decided to make haste with reasonable caution. Too many men would attract too much attention when the band was just getting under way.

Only three men were chosen at the outset. They were Bitter Creek Newcomb, Blackface Charley Bryant, and Bill McElhanie. Grat wanted to pay a visit to Brother Bill, now living near Paso Robles, California. Bob didn't stop him— best to have the bumpkin out of the way while the organization was being formed.

Five men thus constituted the original Dalton Gang. A

number big enough to be effective, yet small enough to be handled easily. So far as Bob was concerned, no drifting amateur highwaymen would ever be added to the roster. Jesse James had been far too lax when he enrolled one tyro, Bob Ford, and had wound up backshot for being so careless.

Next came the question of where best to locate the budding enterprise. Nebraska? That would be like putting a bur to a bronc's tail. To get there the gang would have to cross Kansas, where horse-stealing warrants were out for all five of them. Also, it was a state where its erring son, Mr. Newcomb, was particularly well known. Although he generally claimed to be a Texan, his family were wealthy residents of Fort Scott.

Texas was suggested as a possible base of operations. Mr. Bryant shuddered at the idea. That was *his* home state, where too many countrymen were waiting for him to come back and give battle. What was Mr. McElhanie's choice? He passed.

California? Bob Dalton emphatically vetoed that one. No use crimping Bill's ambitions. The family—and particularly its three present mavericks—might some day need a successful politician as kinsman.

One possibility remained: New Mexico, as happily lawless as Indian Territory had been before the damn grangers had come to spoil it with courthouses.

Then the Daltons remembered that the marshal of New Mexico's toughest municipality, Silver City—Ben Canty— had been their neighbor back in Missouri. Lawman Canty saved his job and his neck by being tolerant of the town's gamblers and fancy women.[2]

Bob got more and more interested as they talked it over. Women were his weakness, as whisky was Grat's. A place where the girls were free and easy and the head lawman disposed to be tolerant made an enticing combination.

Not much later, five men rode west toward the line of New Mexico Territory. They were going, as Oklahoma Marshal Chris Madsen would comment later, "to spot out the lay of the country." Silver City would be a good place to roost while they did it.

Long before they hit the boundary, Bob and Emmett, the managing partners, had made a resolution befitting their new prospects:

No longer would they steal horses as a main business.

That was traffic for two-bitters like the ones they formerly had caught and delivered to Judge Parker.

There were bigger pickings to be had, bigger deals to be swung, bigger jobs to be pulled.

Emmett and Bob meant to grab their share.

"RAIDER'S MATE"

SILVER CITY was Babylon-on-a-pithead, a place of florid squalor, with money heaping the varnished keno tables and burro dung littering the bawdy streets. Temporary millionaires awoke to find themselves paupers after heady all-night tourneys of blackjack where the earth was the stake—or whatever chunk of the earth that the loser had annexed with pick and shovel and pan.

Grifters and con men roamed the unswept sidewalks looking for tenderfeet who could be bilked into "buying" nonexistent town lots and salted mines. Silver City was a great roulette wheel. The civic spirit was chance. Civic virtue was getting everything you could out of the other fellow before he got it out of you.

The population was heterogenous, the talk polyglot. Welsh diggers cursed each other in raucous Celtic and pinned onions on their shirts in celebration of St. David's Day—April the First. Other countries of Europe—England, Italy, Greece, the Slavic lands—sent their quotas to the mines owned by Yankee satellites of the Goulds and the Astors. Chinese, now barred from prospecting and railroad labor, evened scores by bootlegging the slow poison of opium in their network of laundries. Mexicans peddled firewood and chili peppers and the marijuana extracted from a profitable weed grown in shanty backyards. A man could enjoy any dissipation, if he had the dinero to pay for it.

Of the native Americans, two elements stood out from all the rest. One was the post-Confederate Missourians, strayed from the Buckshot Belt but always of it. Strapping big hulks who could have drunk dry the adjacent Gila River had somebody spiked the channel with corn juice to kill the flat taste of water. Lethal, casual men who loved to shoot and brawl, some telling each other hopefully that Jesse James hadn't really died at St. Joe but had gone into semi-retirement after substituting a stand-in to be downed by Bob Ford.

Paralleling the Missourians was that feared élite of pow-

53

der and lead—the ubiquitous gents from the Lone Star State. Truculent, belligerent, almost uncontrollable when high on tequila, the Texans moved in to dominate local six-gun circles as they did wherever they found refuge from the Rangers back home. They hired out for high wages as guards in gambling casinos or as professional sharpshooters for New Mexico's cattle royalty, protecting their pastures against nesters and sheep raisers.

Every nationality despised the Indians. All but gone, they were now, except for a few threadbare derelicts begging *centavos* and crumbs of smoking tobacco. These outcasts from shattered tribes were the lowest in the pecking order of Silver City. The town had been securely established only after its original promoters had offered bounties of $250 apiece for the scalps of evicted Apaches, and a good many prosperous citizens had thereby gotten their starting capital. Now the Apaches were through, following the surrender of their last great chieftain, Geronimo.

Here, during the summer of 1890, the ambitious Dalton gang interned in big-scale outlawry before going on to practice it. Whatever instruction they had missed in Indian Territory was more than made up for in a community drawing the old grads of Tombstone and Butte and San Antonio and a hundred other such higher institutions of wrongdoing.

Around the casinos, these five eager newcomers met inspiring buckies who had fought Kansans with Ben Thompson from Austin or matched aces with Wes Hardin in El Paso. One Texan sometimes in town was said to be Frank Jackson, sole surviving lieutenant of Sam Bass and the only member of the Bass gang to get away from that big shooting scrape at Round Rock.

By still another coincidence, Billy the Kid had once lived in Silver City, as he had at Coffeyville where the Daltons had done much of their earlier helling. Here, the story went, Billy had killed his first man, when he was twelve. Silver City was nothing but a robbed purse and a likely hole in the head for greenhorns and tenderfeet. Silver City was Christmas and Fourth of July and joyous romps in bawdy houses for those so naturally attuned to it as these roisterers wandering in from Indian Territory.

If the Daltons and their three partners could have put in for a town made to order, cut to their jib and styled to their manner, this burgeoning haven of sin would have been the result. Marshal Ben Canty's friendship opened all the proper—or improper—doors for them. The Daltons were careful not to abuse his confidence, not only because he was a sidekick from good old Missouri but also because he could be counted on to give them due warning if an extradition warrant came through from Kansas or Indian Territory.

Canty let it be known that the Daltons were kinsmen of those noted Missourians, Johnny Ringo and the Youngers. It was a subtle hint to some of the Silver City gun gentry that their prestige would end with their lives if they challenged Emmett or Bob. The brothers loved the reflected glory: what maverick Dalton ever ducked a limelight?

Up and down the noisy streets men pointed out the two Daltons, stopped them in front of saloons and offered to set up the booze, it being a mark of prestige to have drunk with kinfolk of the legendary Youngers. Deserved respect also went to their saddlemate, Charley Bryant. You could tell from his Texan brogue and his gun-blistered cheeks that he was a real bad man from the real bad state. Accepting various compliments, Mr. Bryant was still somewhat standoffish. With commendable caution, he kept a keen eye peeled for old foes who might show up from his native terrain.

Bitter Creek Newcomb, hiding his Kansas identity, now most often liked to be introduced as the Slaughter Kid. It implied that he was either from Texas, where John Slaughter had started ranching, or Arizona, where he was sheriffing. It didn't make much difference, as long as nobody took him for a Kansan.

Nobody paid much attention to Bill McElhanie, except to observe that he always tagged the rest of the Dalton crowd. He shone only when the bunch went "across the Arroyo" to visit the scarlet sorority of the cat houses. Not the least of Silver City's attractions for men with sap in their limbs and hair on their chests was its sin center, bordering the long creek that bound off the girls from their customers.

If you possessed the cash for value received, you could have just about any kind of woman you wanted in Silver City. Mexican and Negro girls sold themselves at cut rate, being of races held in contempt. Hard-faced, higher-priced floosies with French accents, sometimes simulated, came from the crib houses of New Orleans. Country girls, new at the game, were not long away from farms in Texas and the Midwest.

Here beyond the Arroyo, Charley Bryant could drape his jeans over the foot of a girl's cot and forget, for a few minutes of happy frenzy, his moody, disfigured face. It is likely that Emmett Dalton lost, in one or another Silver City red-light shack, that chastity which he had been saving for his

Julia. Emmett may have had a Galahad fixation in his larcenous mind, but, a virile frontiersman, he sometimes just
had to give in or bust.

And, like blooms flowering on the prickly pears, love
came again to Bob Dalton—came in a cathouse idyll that is
a droll aside in the Dalton saga.

Our knowledge of Bob's dream girl comes from two men,
both of whom knew her but saw her through different eyes.
One of these was Emmett Dalton, who painted her in Came-
lot colors. The other was Chris Madsen, who described her
as a hard-bitten bitch.

Emmett disguised the girl under the name of "Eugenia
Moore." Blunt old Chris Madsen knew her as "Tom King,"
as did most of Oklahoma Territory, but was also aware that
she often paraded under the Moore alias.

Her real name was Florence Quick, and she grew up in
Cass County, where the Dalton brothers were partially
reared. An exceptionally bright girl, she migrated west, put
on cowboy chaps and became an outstanding lady bandit,
one converted into a fallen angel by the romanticism of
the youngest Dalton.

She was in her early twenties when she became Bob's
sweetheart. He found her to be much more his kind of a
woman than that faithless little peasant, Minnie Johnson.
Emmett Dalton has declared that she and Bob met through
Marshal Canty in Silver City. There is a possibility that the
Dalton boys had known her as a child in Cass County or
had become acquainted with her when, as "Tom King," she
was also directing a horse-stealing ring.

According to Emmett, she was "as spirited as she was
attractive, and tenaciously vital despite an encroaching malady . . ."

The belle of the Dalton Gang had no "malady," unless
it was her infatuation for Bob. Early she learned that easy
morals brought easy money. Her love of male garb and her
preference for a male monicker suggest a strong lesbian
streak which she probably expressed through her florid
pseudo-masculinity. In our epoch, she might have been a
sexy fashion executive or a high-class call girl. By definition,
she could not have favored a forty-dollar-a-month cowhand
in her century or a forty-dollar-a-week clerk in ours. To the
bold belong the bold.

She may have once been a schoolteacher, as Emmett
claims. For she could parse a sentence and cipher by all the
rules in *Ray's Arithmetic*. It is highly questionable that the
Cass County Flo was ever a telegrapher in the professional

sense, as Emmett Dalton made her out. Yet she did acquire a working knowledge of the Morse code by hanging around railroad stations and ogling telegraphers.

Sex she used ruthlessly as a weapon, as her high-geared type of woman is wont to do. But of all her companions, transient or otherwise, she loved only Bob Dalton.

Bob Dalton was *her man*. The rest were mere men.

Pleasantly, it can be recorded that Bob loved her with the same deep, if unorthodox, devotion. Now and then he might hire a partner for a night from one of the cat wagons operating out of Muskogee or Fort Smith. But, in an observation we can believe, Emmett said that Bob "was a one-woman man in his heart, notwithstanding his easy friendship with many."

As a romantic, Emmett naturally had to endow brother Bob's girl with frail health. Ladies were always swooning in his pretend-world. In his book, he brought her back to Indian Territory, then shipped her out again to Silver City, where the sun heals sick lungers.

She left Indian Territory for her health, all right, but she did so even before she teamed up with Bob Dalton. Chris Madsen has hinted why the Territory became so ominous for "Tom King's" well-being:

"She was the greatest jailbreaker that I have ever known. She would be on the streets at Guthrie, dressed in a fancy buckskin suit, and after dark you would find her out in the country dressed up in a pair of overalls spotting horses for the rustlers."

By the blunt testimony of an honest peace officer, Bob's inamorata broke out or somehow got out of jails in Guthrie, Oklahoma City and El Reno. Several times Chris himself arrested the girl who had been behind bars more times than any other female outlaw in the Territory, not excepting Belle Starr. Each time there would be this inevitable dialogue between them:

"Who is the jailer where you are taking me?"

"Why do you want to know?"

"Just so I'll know what kind of medicine I'll have to use on him."

Understandably, Emmett, being a romantic, was inspired to do a whitewash job on his all-but sister-in-law. Yet sometimes the truth broke loose from his guarded pen. She was, he admitted, "no tame, spineless creature of soft conventions." In his words, she was "fit to be a raider's mate."

Eminently fit.

FIRST HOLDUP

THE money they had brought from Indian Territory was all but gone, lost on the gaming tables of Silver City. Because of their soiled reputations as federal officers, Ben Canty couldn't hire Bob and Emmett as deputy marshals. Bryant, McElhanie, and Newcomb had no qualifications for this sort of employment. Then and there, the five original members of the gang again had the chance to blaze a straight trail. Mine labor wouldn't have hurt them, though laying down six-guns for shovels might have maimed their spirits. They could have hired out on almost any big ranch there in Grant County. Any cattle baron would have gladly bought the services of men who rode and shot so superbly.

None of that for these virtuosi of the gun, however. The five were determined to keep their wills unfettered, their talents unmortgaged to humdrum society.

The best place for creative, free-lance accomplishment seemed to them to be a Mexican mining camp halfway between Silver City and Grant County's other major town, Santa Rosa. The hamlet wasn't much—a few diggings and a dozen or so false-front business houses strewn along its one street. But it did have a prospering gambling den where pesos from the pockets of dark-skinned diggers piled up in tempting sums.

Robbing a blackleg joint wasn't the worst crime in the West's roster of sins. Pillaging Mexicans was the very least of offenses in that long list. Mexicans on the northern side of the international boundary still looked upon themselves as compulsory citizens of the United States. Anglos—particularly Texans like Charley Bryant—held them in contempt as members of a conquered race.

With pockets low and hopes high, the five set out on a scorching desert evening toward the village. The two Daltons, Newcomb and Bryant rode four abreast. Bill McElhanie tagged slightly behind, leading a pack horse with one hand and guiding his own bronc with the other. The junior member of any ensemble was generally given this assignment, and McElhanie was younger than nineteen-year-old Emmett Dalton. The presence of the pack animal suggested two things.

The Daltons intended to be away from Silver City on a scout for some time. They expected the robbery of a place run by despised Mexicans to be something that could be accomplished without too much fuss. A laden pack horse could be a hindrance in a flight.

Bob Dalton had worked out with his new girl the practical details of this first foray in New Mexico. The gambling house would be tapped. The gang would then withdraw to what would be a paradise of future operations, a great quadrangle bounding portions of Texas, Kansas, Colorado, and Indian Territory, a piece of America appropriately called "No Man's Land" because Congress had originally failed to include it within the bounds of any state or territory.

Finally it had become incorporated within newly formed Oklahoma Territory. But legal institutions were still elemental on its ridges and prairies. Bands of outlaws continued to use it as handy headquarters for excursions across borders.

"Tom King" and Charley Bryant both had connections within No Man's Land. The girl was to go there and establish a hideout for the gang. Starting capital was to be gained from the robbery of the Mexican mining-camp deadfall.

Dusk had fallen when the five men rode into the place. The gang ate supper at a Chinese restaurant, then proceeded to the dive. As they entered, by Emmett's description:

"A Mexican orchestra was setting a tempo for the hectic life of the place—a rootin' tootin' bedlam of miners, cowboys, professional gamblers, and professional women. . . . Stacks of gold and silver glinted in the gaming racks. Revolver butts shone from holsters. The light flashed from the teeth of smiling señoritas and their paler sisters."

The visitors decided to buck the faro game. Bob Dalton, Bitter Creek Newcomb, Bill McElhanie and Charley Bryant played active hands. Emmett acted as lookout, "having previously paid the price" for what a novice "knew about faro."

Even a greenie could see that the game was rigged. That was what the Daltons wanted it to be, for crooked plays would give them the justification for what was coming.

Emmett's partners lost the small sum of money they had expected to drop. Then they leisurely walked away from the faro table and halted at the bar.

Nobody paid much attention to them. Customarily, men

had swigs to bolster spirits when gambling luck had been bad.

The bartender asked these losers to name their poison. The only response was that of five pistols drawn simultaneously, with the synchronization of instruments in a band. Then one voice spoke, loudly:

"Hands up—*everybody.*"

The dealer jumped to his feet. So did the proprietor of the joint. So did all the forty-odd customers. The Dalton Gang raised their forty-fives higher. Every hand in the place was lifted to the ceiling.

"*Bandidos! Bandidos!*" someone yelled fearfully.

Covered by the Colts, one of the gang cleaned the faro table of its winnings and stuffed the money in his pocket. Bitter Creek Newcomb noticed that some of their girls were stuffing money and jewelry into "ladies purses"—their stockings.

"No need o' that," he said courteously. "None of us fellers sports any rocks."

Bob added righteously, "This will show you how to treat strangers."

Keeping their guns covering the crowd, the boys walked backward to the door. Once outside, they sprang to their ponies, with McElhanie grabbing the line that held the pack horse. Their pistols roared in a salvo as a discouragement of pursuit. The exodus from town was swift. Once away from its blinking lights, they slowed down. Why worry about the possibility of lowly Mexes giving chase?

All night the gang rode along toward No Man's Land. Dawn came. Just as a routine check, they looked back in the direction of the mining camp.

They saw a swift cloud of dust which they mistook at first for an approaching sandstorm. Then the cloud rumbled with a thunder that men of their kind instantly identified.

Posse thunder! The Daltons had picked the wrong Mexicans.

The gang headed their mounts toward a deep arroyo. The possemen spurred their horses in an attempt to gain on the fugitives. As the pursuers came nearer, Bob Dalton made out seven men, all but one or two wearing the high-crowned straw sombreros of Mexicans.

The boys unsheathed their rifles and found refuge in the far side of a timber-matted canyon. The posse paused for a council. Apparently they had counted on a running battle, not on the gringos forting themselves up.

Rifles were checked in the canyon. Maybe the posse

would give up the chase rather than face determined resistance from a well protected position.

The decision was made by the Mexican deputy who was leading the posse. *"Vengan, hombres*—go, men!" he yelled. *"Alla estan*—there they are. *Muerte los*—kill them."

Possemen charged, shooting. Bob ordered his henchmen to hold their fire till the attackers drew nearer. The Daltons hurriedly dismounted. With the distance between pursuers and pursued rapidly diminishing, the first shots came from the outlaws, answered by more from the attackers.

A bullet from Bob's rifle narrowly missed hitting the chief deputy's mount. The pony reared on its haunches. In the next exchange of volleys, a Mexican's bullet struck a frying pan in the bundle of stuff strapped on the pack horse. The shot ricocheted and plowed into Emmett's arm.

It was first blood from the Daltons, but the possemen hesitated instead of charging further. Then Bob Dalton ordered a counter-offensive.

The outlaws remounted and charged, firing, toward the officers. One of Bob's rifle bullets dropped a horse. Its rider scurried away afoot as the posse scattered.

Bob looked to Emmett's hurt arm. It was only a flesh wound. The bullet could be cut out with a sharp knife, the anesthetic being swigs of whisky. Emmett would bear the scar for the rest of his days.

Money the Daltons had again. Glory, too, for having whipped a posse. But underestimating the Mexicans had wrecked their plans.

It would be dangerous now for the band to ride en masse to No Man's Land. Emmett's wounded arm would be a giveaway of what they had been up to and draw unwanted attention from Oklahoma officers. Nor could the gang return to Silver City. Somebody from the mining camp would surely recognize them, and even Ben Canty would be forced to undertake arrests.

After a conference, with Bob making final decisions, it was agreed that he and Bill McElhanie would go to California and stay with Bill Dalton till the commotion about the mining-camp h'ist quieted. Emmett Dalton and Charley Bryant would hole up on the isolated ranch of Big Jim Riley, sixty miles southwest of Kingfisher. Bitter Creek Newcomb would go back to his homestead claim not far from Guthrie.

To Guthrie also would return "Tom King," the queen bee of the gang, for certain purposes which she could inimitably fulfill. The escaping desperados found some way of sending her the message.

How much the gang got in the holdup has never been revealed. The important thing was that the Daltons had committed their first armed holdup. They felt a tang in their veins and entertained hope—great hope—for the future.

It would have been better for Bill Dalton if Bob hadn't changed his mind about going to California.

THE SP'S MR. SMITH

BOB and Grat arrived in California, with no gunfire having contested their way, to visit close kinfolks. Their sisters-in-law, the wives of Littleton and Bill, were less than joyous about their children meeting the two notorious uncles, not to speak of that third veteran of the dry gulches, young Mr. McElhanie. But jovial Bill Dalton was proud to welcome the boys, and his fellow settlers of the San Joaquin already were proud of Bill.

To date, Bill's eloquence had given signs of paying off. He was the up-and-coming champion of the common man against the Southern Pacific Railroad and its president, United States Senator Leland Stanford, a statesman obsessed with a downright passion for every dollar in any pocket. William Marion Dalton had his sights set on a seat in the legislature at Sacramento (he never actually served in it, as some writers have stated).[1] He had helped elect a fiddling, ferret-faced friend of his, Ed O'Neil, as sheriff of Fresno County; and he was a valued member of the anti-railroad political machine which included O'Neil and that barb-tongued scourge of the Eastern monopolies, Lawyer Breckinridge.

Bill's great mistake was in letting his brothers hang around. They made quick impressions on California, especially Grat, whose impact added up to something very different from the one already registered by popular Brother Bill.

Grat didn't spend much time at Bill's ranch in the Clovis community near Paso Robles. Jennie Dalton's respectability was just too much for a man more at home with a whisky cork than a napkin. He moved on to Fresno town, a few miles from Paso Robles, to set up as a professional gambler in an anything-goes hostelry called the Grand Central Hotel. Unfortunately for Grat, the Grand Central was the lodging place, as well as the headquarters, of the gentleman who was the main guardian of the Southern Pacific's humming rails.

This was its chief of special detectives, William Smith.

The railroad's head man hunter was big and brawny, with a face disfigured by the sores of incipient cancer.[2] Smith's job was to watch anybody who might harm the Southern Pacific and its vast properties, whether by a speech on a political stump or by a six-gun jabbed into the ribs of an express messenger. Naturally, Smith kept a wary check on Bill Dalton, whose persuasive folksy influence extended over three or four counties of the San Joaquin Valley.

Still plaguing Smith, a blotch on his standing in the SP Security Division at San Francisco, were two unsolved train robberies that had been committed in the Valley. One at Pixley, on February 22, 1889, had cost the SP and the Wells Fargo Express Company $12,000, with the Modesto County sheriff having been wounded while trying to foil the two bandits involved. In another at Goshen, on January 24, 1890, the loot had amounted to $20,000, a haul also made by just two bandits. In 1886, settlers had fought a pitched battle at Mussel Slough with marshals and railroad police trying to evict them from land to which they once had been promised title, so a good many grangers hoped that even more SP trains would be held up.[3]

Soon after Grat began operating around Fresno, Will Smith learned of the Younger-Dalton kinship. Men who knew their outlaws made much of the Daltons' blood ties with the Youngers, who had been past masters at train-robbing. Other straws and wisps of gossip began adding up to something in the police-dog mentality of Smith, for whom a bark was as good as a bay.

Rumor laid it that Grat and Bob Dalton were renegades from the law badge; they could be doubly dangerous to the Southern Pacific from knowing the operative techniques of both outlaw and lawman. For some reason, possibly a slight facial resemblance, Smith believed Bill McElhanie to be Emmett Dalton, sporting an alias. Emmett, who actually had made a trip to California several years earlier, also was numbered among the defectors from the star. Right now, though, he was hiding out on a remote ranch in Indian Territory.

Smith, who was thorough if nothing else, extended his surveillance to all the California Daltons, even to harmless Littleton, who was running a ranch not far from Brother Bill's. Their cousins also fell under his scrutiny, particularly one named Sam Oldham, with whom Bob Dalton and Bill McElhanie were boarding, near a country trading center called Kingsburg.

Smith was no man to spoil a prime hunt by a sudden flush,

however. After all, the main quarry was not a trio of roving
rowdies, who might or might not give trouble, but their respectable brother, who already was giving so much. Meantime, though, the officer kept his sharpest eye on Grat.

That wasn't hard to do. Often Smith stalked into the
gambling room of the Grand Central to eye the big fellow
as he plied his questionable trade. Grat, not paying Smith
much mind, was engaged in remunerative work that didn't
tax even his limited mental capacities.

He would strike up a conversation with some yahoo in
the lobby, invite him first to the hotel bar for a sociable
drink, then to the poker table, a few handy feet away. Brother Bob sometimes lent a hand to help with the shearing,
but not often. Grat could always count on assistance from
other members of the gaming fraternity, hanging around
Grand Central for a share of the pluckings.

If the sucker contested the payoff, Grat's big fists settled
the problem. Generally, he didn't have to use them; the
trimmed mark would take one look at Grat's glowering mug
and do a quick fadeaway.

Yes sir, Grat liked Fresno, liked the way a man really
could be a man here. A spanking fine town, he thought it;
a fine town for Daltons.

Even if Smith and the other railroad dicks watched him
more closely than they did the other wolves, who gave a
hoot? Everybody knew that Sheriff Ed O'Neil wouldn't be
holding office if Brother Bill Dalton hadn't managed his
campaign—and O'Neil was an SP man.

The poker chips thumped. The fleeced lambs bleated.
The pretty girls ogled Bob, but high-hatted Grat. He didn't
give a damn, as long as Fresno had plenty of redeye to swill
and garden-variety strumpets to bed.

For several weeks, Bob and McElhanie managed to keep
their noses clean while staying with Cousin Sam Oldham.
Whatever Will Smith's suspicions may have been, no proof
exists that Oldham was consciously sheltering fugitives or
that he knew anything about the boys' battle with the New
Mexico posse. Cousins were kinfolks, and you took kinfolks
in. Their friends also could claim your hospitality. The little wheat-growing community accepted the two boarders
without question, although having some private reserva-
tions about Grat when he came visiting. Any family was
apt to have a black sheep or two. And when you met Bob
Dalton, or let him come sparking your daughter, he always
behaved like a gentleman. How he behaved with the girl

when the old folks weren't around was something the pair kept to themselves.

The favorable first impression didn't last, though. Bob and Grat spoiled it by making one of those social errors that Daltons often committed.

On a Saturday night, the brothers went to a dance at the Brick Hotel in Kingsburg. Accompanying them were Bill McElhanie and a couple of local boys, Charles Flewelling and Eugene Curtis, teamsters who hauled wheat and other farm products to Fresno and neighboring towns.

During the first few sets, people noticed that the Dalton boys were swinging the pretty girls stiffly, as if they were carrying rocks in their pockets. After the dance, the town found out why.

The brothers had been carrying guns inside their breeches —so reported Flewelling and Curtis. Before the end of the evening they had stepped outside and hidden the pistols under the hotel's front porch.

"We want our guns where we can find them in a hurry in case we need them," Bob Dalton had remarked.

That incident ruined the social standing of the two brothers and their partner, Bill McElhanie, around Kingsburg. The code said you never carried a gun, loaded or empty, inside a house. The tale checked, in the ears of local residents, with spreading rumors that the boys were bad men on the scout. The neighborhood girls began to give them the cold shoulder. Within a few days, Bob and McElhanie moved themselves and their trappings from the Oldham place to Bill Dalton's ranch.

Even then, Bill failed to see the shape of things to come. His friends and political allies did, however, and disliked what they saw. The two maverick Daltons were getting to be as notorious in this California valley as they had been back in the Oklahoma hills. Bill's close acquaintances tried to make excuses for these unwelcome migrants, meanwhile silently wishing they would get the hell out. Yet they couldn't violate frontier etiquette by even hinting to Bill that he should send his own brothers packing.

Bill's foes, personal and political, had a different kind of comment to make about the Daltons who didn't belong: "A pair of tough men, these Oklahomans; but if it's trouble they're looking for, they'll get it right here."

Back in Fresno, Grat kept on swigging rotgut and winning acclaim as rough-and-tumble champion of one dive after another. Bob joined him there occasionally but he seems to have managed to stay out of scrapes. Bill continued to move

around the Valley, building his political fences and hoping
he'd be nominated for the Assembly on the Democratic
ticket to buck Leland Stanford's Republican candidate in
the next election. If not, he would just as soon run as the
choice of the emerging Populist party, whose wealthy California spokesman, Adolph Sutro, had published a pamphlet
denouncing the Southern Pacific as "a giant octopus holding
in its tentacles five states and territories." [4]

That was hyperbole that Bill Dalton knew how to em-
bellish with his flavorful rural demagogy when he chatted
with settlers buying flour and overalls at country stores.

Weeks rolled by. Bill's wife was becoming increasingly unhappy about her brothers-in-law, who kept blowing in every
now and then to upset the God Bless Our Happy Home
atmosphere she was trying to maintain for the benefit of
her children. But there was nothing a poor woman could do
about the strong family loyalties of her husband.

Then loyalty suddenly turned into a deadfall. On February 6, 1891, three men robbed the Southern Pacific Express at Alila, in Tulare County. More than a few people
began whispering that Bob and Grat Dalton were bound to
have had a hand in the job. Will Smith's sensitive ears
quickly picked up those insinuating rumors.

By the most reliable accounts, the Alila robbery followed
the general pattern of the preceding hauls at Pixley and
Goshen. Except—and this was something for Will Smith to
chew on—three bandits had been involved in this operation
instead of two.

The train, listed by the Southern Pacific as the Atlantic
Express, was on a regular run from San Francisco to Los
Angeles. On the evening of February 6 it was filled with
passengers en route to the health resorts of the Los Angeles
area. Alila, a water stop, was an isolated village settlement
in the hilly southern section of Tulare County. The county,
largely settled by emigrants from Dixie, was a focus of op-
position to the railroad. Here had been fought the battle of
Mussel Slough. Here, Bill Dalton was a popular figure
among the farmers and small ranchers.

It was nine P.M. when the engineer paused for what ordi-
narily would have been a very brief stop beside the water
tank on the railway's right of way. Three masked men,
with the rough look of the Daltons, jumped on the coal tender and then advanced into the engine cab with drawn revolvers.

Engineer Charles C. Harwell wasn't going to let bandits
rob his train unchallenged. He grabbed a gun and fired four

shots at the robbers. Neither he nor the bandits were injured in the ensuing exchange, but a bullet, which may have
come either from his weapon or one of theirs, hit Fireman
George W. Radliff in the abdomen. The express messenger
also put up a fight. The unwelcome visitors fled, without a
red cent to show for their trouble.

If the Daltons actually had perpetrated the robbery, they
behaved out of all character with their later reputation.
Dead shots such as they were could have mown down in a
minute, at such close quarters, the engineer and the messenger. Nor was it in keeping for the boys to abandon a job
empty-handed.

Radliff died the next day, not instantly as some writers
have recorded. Then followed a strange sequence of events
—one that has not been analyzed by anyone who has dealt
with that aborted holdup in the tiny hamlet which has long
since disappeared from the map.

Modern policemen would have suspected a connection
between the marauders at Alila and those who had previously boarded engines at Pixley and Goshen. Intensive checks
might have been made of Bob and Grat Dalton and Bill
McElhanie, who was believed to be Emmett. But logic and
sense also would have taken into account the fact that the
two earlier crimes had been committed before any Dalton
brothers with outlaw background had shown up in the state
of California.

Amazingly, the first move of the lawmen was to charge
the SP's own courageous employee, Engineer Harwell, with
the shooting of Radliff, the fireman.

Why? Perhaps the railroad was trying to evade a financial
settlement with Radliff's heirs, making the dubious charge
against the engineer in an attempt to establish legally that
the fireman's death was due to the "negligence of a fellow-
servant" and was no fault of the Southern Pacific. Such a
defense was permissible under the compensation laws of
the Grover Cleveland-Benjamin Harrison era.

Engineer Harwell had fought for the Southern Pacific and
Fireman Radliff had died for it. Perhaps some division road-
master nourished personal spite against one or both of them.
Or, perhaps, there was some other reason for the farcical
proceeding against Harwell.

Southern Pacific Special Officer W. E. Hickey of San
Francisco supervised the investigation that followed the
crime, with Will Smith, still operating from Fresno, serving
as his chief assistant. Wells Fargo detectives also participated in the hunt, since every sortie against an express car

also jeopardized the express company. On February 26, 1891, Hickey issued a special circular letter, addressed to California law-enforcement officials, offering "a reward of $5000 for the arrest and convictions of all parties concerned in the attempted robbery."

Five thousand dollars was a lot of money in those days, a tempting plum that caused many mouths to water—including the thin-lipped one of Bill Dalton's friend, Fresno County Sheriff Ed O'Neil, who had been elected on the anti-railroad ticket.

The full details of what happened during that curious month of February have escaped most writers of popular books about the Daltons. All of them have accepted the repeated statement that it was the rambunctious brothers who stopped the train at Alila. One prominent writer who has raised serious doubt about the whole thing is Carl B. Glasscock, who still skims only the surface in an otherwise very good book, *Bandits and the Southern Pacific*.

A more plausible chain of events is given by an unfortunately obscure local historian, Kathleen Edwards Small, in a little-known history of Tulare County, published in 1926. Mrs. Small was the daughter of a pioneer family in the San Joaquin Valley and a newspaperwoman in Visalia, the county seat, at the time that her work was published. She not only had access to official court records and newspaper files of the nineties, but she could tap the vast store of oral legend about the Daltons among old-timers who remembered the brothers as well as the turbulent warfare between the settlers and the Southern Pacific.

Let it be noted, however, that Mrs. Small was just a good reporter, not a trained historian. She, herself, does not question the assertion of the Daltons' guilt, but she does supply otherwise unrecorded background information that makes that assertion look pretty limp.

What does emerge from her methodical research is the sedulous building of a campaign by California newspapers and badge wearers to create a climate of suspicion against the brothers, with Bill Dalton being the ultimate target. Bill was too big game to be flushed immediately. First his wily antagonists had to knock down those clay pigeons who were his kin.

Some time during February, 1891, according to Mrs. Small, Special Agent Hickey arrested in Fresno "an all-round gambling man and a sport by the name of Dalton." Who was this "Dalton"? Naturally it would seem to have been Grat, the two-fisted cold decker from Oklahoma. But other items in the same account suggest otherwise.

The suspect, "Dalton"—or whatever his real name may have been—was hauled off to Tulare and purportedly questioned about the job at Alila. Mrs. Small supplies no other facts except in an additional press quote to say that the man "admitted he had been rambling through Tulare County on a gambling tour that took him to both Tulare and Visalia." Then she quotes an unnamed reporter for still another unidentified newspaper as saying:

"The express company will not bother him [Dalton] on the charge of gambling."

Who was this Mr. Dalton of no given name? Was he somebody unrelated to the Daltons that powerful interests wanted to get? Or was he simply some drifter picked up and tagged with that name as the first step in pinning suspicion on Bill Dalton?

Why wasn't the full name of this vagrant given to the press? Why didn't some reporter demand it, even if California newspapers were generally sympathetic to the Southern Pacific because of advertising that came their way?

Yet we are confronted with still another taunting question. What became of the roving tinhorn called "Dalton"? Did he serve his purpose, to be given a train ticket for greener pastures elsewhere—or did he wind up inside a box tailormade from California pine?

Quein sabe? The last old-timers who might answer the question are dead and gone. But the detention of this alleged "Dalton" set a precedent for another probably phony arrest.

This was of one "Cole Dalton," reportedly arrested by Sheriff O'Neil. The name under which he was booked indicates a crude attempt to remind the public that Bill Dalton's family were kin to Cole Younger, now sweating out a sentence for train robbery in the Minnesota state prison. Underscoring the whole procedure, a news dispatch of March 3, 1891, quoted by Mrs. Small, declared that "the Daltons were said to be cousins of the Younger brothers, notorious outlaws."

To make the whole thing look more plausible, Sheriff O'Neil, now boldly and openly on the side of the Southern Pacific, arrested a real and acknowledged Dalton—Grat—and somebody called "Jack Parker" when he made the pickup of the apparently bogus "Cole Dalton." No evidence so far unearthed has turned up any Dalton named "Cole" or any Dalton ally known as "Parker." There is no proof that

Grat Dalton ever had known or heard of these two fellow suspects.

According to Mrs. Small—her press source probably was the San Francisco *Examiner*—Grat and the other two prisoners were first taken to San Francisco, the city that the Southern Pacific ran as completely as any textile firm ever did a Carolina mill town. Again—why? Probably because there the railroad investigators might have easier and safer access to them. Safer, anyway, than in Tulare County, where the tears had been shed for George Radliff rather than for his employers.

After a few days, the prisoners were surrendered to Tulare County authorities, who began grilling them at Visalia. At this point, "Cole Dalton" and "Jack Parker" vanish into thin air, like the no-first-name "Dalton" before them. Where they went, if they really existed in fact, is anybody's guess.

PINNING IT ON THE DALTONS

MR. ROBERT RENICK DALTON decided to terminate his vacation in California, where the climate was healthy but not the atmosphere. He and Bill McElhanie started east on a pair of fast broncs after a Tulare County grand jury had obliged the Southern Pacific by voting indictments that would land Bill, the politician, as well as Grat, the card sharp, in the county jail at Visalia.

The SP had called the game. Will Smith had flashed the aces. The play is best described in a circular issued by the railroad's security division on March 26, 1891, which read:

$3600 REWARD

Supplementing circular letter of W. E. Hickey, Special Officer Southern Pacific Company dated February 26th, 1891, wherein is offered a reward of $5000 for the arrest and conviction of all parties concerned in the attempted robbery of train no. 17 on the night of February 6th, 1891.

The Grand Jury of Tulare County have indicted Bob and Emmett Dalton as principles [sic] in said crime, and William Marion Dalton and Gratton [sic] Dalton as accessories; the two latter named being now in jail at Tulare County awaiting trial.

The Southern Pacific Company hereby withdraws said general reward in regard to Bob and Emmett Dalton, and in lieu thereof offers to pay $1,500 each for the arrest of Bob and Emmett Dalton, *upon their delivery to any duly authorized agent or representative of the State of California, or at any jail in the States or Territories of the United States.*

In addition to the foregoing the State and Wells, Fargo & Co., have each a standing reward of $300 for the arrest and conviction of each such offender.

In flight across the sweltering Mohave Desert, Bob now

was beating his way back to Oklahoma with McElhanie, who would have been tried as "Emmett Dalton" had the two been caught. Grat had been charged after having been released, then picked up and grilled several more times by Will Smith; he was nabbed for the last time on a citizen's arrest made by Fresno saloonkeeper Patrick J. Conway, whom Grat had been foolish enough to regard as his friend.

Putting up no resistance, the big fellow had obediently followed when Conway's finger beckoned him toward the county jail. If Grat actually had been guilty of the Alila crime, it seems unlikely that he would have submitted so tamely to arrest by such a nobody, without police help. It wouldn't have been in the Dalton pattern.

Bill Dalton's judas had been the man who owed so much to him politically—Fresno County's sheriff, Ed O'Neil. Suddenly and brazenly, the "anti-monopoly" lawman had teamed up with the railroad's Will Smith to harass the whole Dalton contingent in California, including Brother Littleton and Cousin Sam Oldham.

Bill of course was the big fish that the Southern Pacific wanted to land. Now he was in the net, the principal evidence against him being a pair of spurs, claimed to be his by the lawmen, which had been found in an abandoned camp of Bob Dalton and McElhanie, the two fugitives. Meanwhile, railroad-controlled newspapers were already trying Bill and Grat in print, and condemning them. They claimed that Bill had been "captured" at Paso Robles; actually, he had surrendered peacefully when Detective Smith showed up with a warrant, although the arrest had been a severe jolt to his ego.

Bill and Grat now were in the custody of Sheriff E. W. Kay, of Tulare County. On April 6, 1891, the two defendants were brought before Judge Wheaton A. Gray, a decent jurist who was as sympathetic to the Daltons as he dared to be.

Both brothers pleaded "not guilty" before the court of this man, who was Bill Dalton's personal friend and political ally. Appearing as attorney for the Daltons was Judge Gray's brother-in-law, who was also Bill's old political sidekick, Lawyer Breckenridge. With such seeming odds in his favor, Breckenridge should have been able to get Bill Dalton, a citizen of good reputation, released on his own recognizance.

Instead, bail was set at $4000, which Bill could not produce. So he went back to jail with Grat. The trial of the brothers was set for the 18th of May. Then began a series of strange maneuvers by the law.

When May 18 came, Judge Gray postponed the trial till a later date in June. It seemed that Sheriff Kay had received word that Bob and Emmett had been seen in Oklahoma Territory. "This was the signal for the sheriff to leave the county," wrote Kathleen Small. "He was away thirty days. During his absence, his deputies were busy unearthing evidence to be presented by the state when the cases were taken to trial."

While Bill and Grat Dalton were lodged uncomfortably in the calaboose, Sheriff Kay was probably in Oklahoma, looking for Emmett and Bob. It would have been a real coup to bring back two more Daltons to face what was currently passing for justice in California. Moreover, legal procedures made it difficult to convict alleged accessories— mere helpers on a job—unless you proved the main facts against the principals.

One of Emmett's stories indicates that he and Bob were indeed trailed in Oklahoma during this period but identifies the pursuers as Heck Thomas and Burrill Cox, both United States deputy marshals; Tiger Jack, an Indian scout; and Will Smith.

Anyhow, Sheriff Kay came back to Tulare County empty-handed during the last week of May. A few days later, on May 28, according to Mrs. Small:

". . . came word that the two missing men [Bob and Emmett] had been captured in Indian Territory after a desperate fight to retain their liberty had gone against them. The battle lasted nineteen hours. Indian scouts were given much of the credit for ascertaining the place where the fugitives had hidden out. Bloodhounds also played an important role in trailing the pair to their hiding place in a cave."

This preposterous yarn, at the time widely believed by credulous people, went on:

"A sheriff's posse of nine members which threw its lines about the bandit rendezvous, found it almost impregnable and decided more men would be needed to bring about their capture. Half a hundred United States soldiers, used to Indian fighting and the life of tracking criminals upon the frontier, were pressed into service. The Daltons, unabashed by the vastly superior odds against them, decided not to give up without a desperate fight and, as a result, one of them, Bob, was slain. One of the soldiers also gave up the ghost. Another soldier was wounded. When it became evident to Emmett that the pursuers had every avenue of escape blocked, he decided there was nothing left to do but surrender."

No one bothered to explain why, if Emmett had "surrendered," Sheriff Kay hadn't brought him back. The purpose of the story probably was to cover up the sheriff's inglorious failure as a man hunter. Bill and Grat must have had a good laugh over it in jail. So must have Bob and Emmett, when the story finally got to them.

Now the scene was set and the props were in place for the dime-novel plot being enacted by the authorities of the sovereign state of California. There was the original situation of the "daring" train robbery. Grat and Bill had been drafted for the villain roles. Will Smith was handling well the part of the sharp-eyed Nick Carterish detective. Two heroic tin-flashers, Sheriffs O'Neil and Kay, were in the cast tearing around like a pair of Keystone cops. There had been the cyclonic, if strictly faked, battle with the younger Daltons in Oklahoma. One element, however, was still missing: you couldn't produce a Grade-B Western without a couple of Grade-B broncs.

The horses were supplied by another lawman, getting into the act belatedly: Deputy Sheriff Witty of Merced County, where lived some wealthy in-laws of Bill Dalton. He came jogging into Visalia leading a couple of plugs that looked as if they had long been pensioned from the plow. Witty swore they had been the getaway mounts in the Alila robbery.

The Visalia *Weekly Delta* published eight separate stories in as many issues on the big doings. It was quite a bonanza for a country newspaper, used to recording such humdrum events as county fairs and Methodist church suppers. Clippings must have been sent to Senator Stanford, who was properly attentive to everything published in the California press.

The authorities, worried by public reaction in favor of Bill, decided to try Grat separately. It was arranged to have the case heard before a judge who was a Southern Pacific man instead of before Gray, a known critic of the railroad.

The trial began on June 18, 1891, in the audience-packed Tulare County courthouse in Visalia. Grat was brought in handcuffed to face "justice" on one of the counts preferred against him: "assault with intent to commit robbery." The jurors had been carefully handpicked. Will Smith was present, sitting in the courtroom, gloating as Grat sat down beside his lawyer, the Honorable Mr. Breckenridge.

Somehow, another prominent attorney who was a friend

of Bill Dalton managed to speak with the defendant before the proceedings opened.

"You're being jobbed, Grat," he warned.

Grat couldn't believe him. Wasn't Breckenridge a close family friend? Hadn't Bill, his brainy brother, told him to trust the lawyer implicitly?

But as the trial progressed, the prosecution thundered and raged while Lawyer Breckenridge put up a pro-forma defense for his client. As Emmett Dalton wrote, this time correctly, "examination of defense witnesses and cross examination of prosecution aids was most perfunctory." Breckenridge should have moved for quashing of the indictment on grounds that were unquestionably clear—the absence of principals in the dubious case. For as Emmett also indignantly observed: "Convicting an accessory before the fact while no principal had even been arrested was something new in jurisprudence."

Breckenridge also should have grilled every prospective juror to assure Grat the best possible panel instead of letting twelve political antagonists of Bill Dalton be sworn in. Instead, he left his client to the mercies of a dozen men whose minds were already made up.

During the first day of the trial, Grat started getting restless. Familiar with legal procedures from having attended many courtroom set-tos as an Oklahoma marshal, he began suggesting some simple defense moves to the placid Mr. Breckenridge.

The lawyer tried to soothe him: "Don't worry, Grat. When we get through we'll move to dismiss. The court will have to grant it."

Later the lawyer turned suavely to the desperate man: "If you've got anything to break jail with, you'd better give it to me. I'll hand it back to you after the trial if they convict you."

"*If they convict you.*" Right then, Grat should have seen through the whole hoax, stood up in his own right and asked the court for a change of legal representation. He just wasn't that astute.

"No danger of their convicting me," he replied. "Ain't I proved by the Grand Central register and the testimony of twenty reliable witnesses that I wasn't in a hundred miles of Alila when them fellers pulled that holdup?" He laughed: "And you've said you're certain you're gonna get me free."

On the second and third days of the trial, the prosecution put Smith and other detectives on the stand. They swore, under oath, that Grat had been "badly bruised" dur-

ing the Alila holdup by a fall from a horse. Other witnesses
were produced to identify one of the plugs brought over
from Merced County by Deputy Witty as the mount.

Lawyer Breckenridge did little to challenge this "evidence," did not raise the question of absolute identification
of any horse after nightfall, did not demand that the jury be
taken to the livery stable, where the ponies were being held,
for direct inspection. Nor did he probe deeply into the detectives' testimony which followed, linking Bill with the
robbery through his brother.

"Through a chain of circumstances," including the dis-
covery of the spurs, they claimed that they had traced Grat
from Alila to Bill's ranch. Any reasonably able attorney or
any trained newspaperman could have demolished this
"chain," link by link. Breckenridge, one of California's
eminent trial lawyers, let it be wrapped around his client.

Next, engineer Harwell was put on the stand. The reason
for that original charge against him should have been clear
even to Visalia's village idiot: make the trainman buy his
own freedom by testifying against a Dalton. This, also, was
a vital legal point which Breckenridge should have invoked
for a mistrial or a dismissal. Again he let dubious, uncertain
evidence pass unchallenged.

Both Harwell and the Wells Fargo messenger, assigned
to the held-up train, testified that Grat's "general size and
outline corresponded exactly with those of the robber left in
charge at the engine." Once more Breckenridge made little
effort to discredit evidence unworthy of a case over a ten-
dollar dog. There was no positive identification of Grat as
the bandit. Plenty of big, powerfully built men corresponded to that description.

During the third week of the trial, on July 7, the jury
found Grattan Dalton guilty as charged. The judge fixed the
time of sentence as July 29—twenty-two days away. Breckenridge announced in a perfunctory manner that he would
take an appeal to California's supreme court.

The general belief in Tulare County was that Grat would
get twenty years. Nobody seriously believed he would be
turned loose by a state supreme court allegedly dominated
by the Southern Pacific and the Leland Stanford crowd.

The SP's chief bulldog, Will Smith, hadn't the slightest
doubt that Grat would wind up converting boulders into
pebbles. As soon as the jury announced its verdict he sauntered over to Grat and said tauntingly:

"I told you I'd land you."

Grat couldn't concede anything. "You haven't landed me yet, Mr. Smith," he said.

On July 29, Grat, trussed up like a circus panther, was marched back before His Honor. But the court reporters pleaded for a delay in the sentencing so they could prepare the transcripts necessary for Lawyer Breckenridge's appeal. The judge granted a postponement until September 21.

Grat went back to jail. Bill was still locked up, awaiting trial. At this juncture four Merced County citizens, friends of his father-in-law, stepped forward to provide the $4000 bond. Bill Dalton went home, pending trial, defiantly telling all who would listen that it would take the entire California state militia to transport his brother to prison.

After Grat's conviction, the uproar subsided for a while. Those who wanted to scalp Daltons felt it wise not to stir up more public comment till Grat should be sentenced and safely tucked away in the pen. A full account of the trial's ending appeared in the Visalia *Delta* for July 9, 1891, but the Fresno daily newspaper of July 8 devoted just one sentence to the verdict, though the entire city was talking about it.

Before September 21 Bill Dalton was brought to trial—and freed, despite all the efforts that Will Smith had made to send him up with Grat. This verdict, in a sense, was a confirmation of Grat's innocence. On the basis of the total evidence, both brothers were either guilty or innocent.

Grat Dalton stood condemned. Bill Dalton stood ruined—ruined politically, which hurt him most of all. Lawyer Breckenridge was revealed as a paid hireling of the Southern Pacific when everything came out in the wash.

Now it was time to ring down the curtain on the show, time for Will Smith to step out and take his bows for a production well done. Then, however, came an epilogue not called for in the script, one that played hob with the plot.

On September 16, 1891, two men robbed a train at Ceres, California, 200 miles from Visalia. Once again, lawhounds swooped down on Bill Dalton to accuse him of being a co-culprit. Bill was taken back to the Tulare County jail, but lodged apart from Grat, who was awaiting sentence.

The Dalton name was now automatically linked with train robberies in California. The holdup at Ceres would mean that the vengeful judge would throw the book at Grat. It was enough to make him break out in a cold sweat.

On September 18, three days before he was due to be sentenced, Grat escaped with two other prisoners from the jail, to find refuge in the wild hills of Fresno County, where the ranchers hated the Southern Pacific.

By this time, Bob Dalton had been back home in Oklahoma for several months. He and Emmett were meeting their mother often in clandestine reunions at the Negro settlement of Dover. Bill McElhanie, for good reasons, had resigned from the gang and gone back home to Arkansas.

Not a mile of Southern Pacific track ran across Oklahoma. But two railroads that did span the Territory would pay for the SP's actions in California—the Santa Fe and the Missouri, Kansas and Texas.

A KIND OF REVENGE

RAILROADS had been the downfall of four Daltons, who reacted to hard luck in three different ways. Bill Dalton tried to handle everything legally while giving as much sub-rosa help to his brothers as possible. Grat broke out of the jail where the Southern Pacific had put him. Bob and Emmett went into bold and acknowledged train robbing.

Revenge spurred their determination to even scores with the rail lines. A train was a train, whatever its brand. A railroad detective was a sworn foe, whoever hired him. An express safe was an express safe on any track.

Their first train job was, in the bitter words of Emmett, "blind striking back at all corporate interests in any way related to their troubles."

Bill and Grat were still awaiting trial in California on that night of May 9, 1891, when Bob and Emmett, with Bitter Creek Newcomb and Blackface Charley Bryant, rode toward Wharton, a whistle stop on the Santa Fe, in the Cherokee Outlet, some sixty miles south of the Kansas border. They hitched their ponies near the stockyard, just south of town. The four stood by the Santa Fe tracks while Bob hurriedly reviewed the information passed on to them by his girl friend, Florence Quick, who, disguised as a man, had cased the spot by posing as a telegraph officer and pumping the local express agent.

The train would be carrying a large shipment of cash and currency for one of the banks in Guthrie, or so Florence, who had returned to the territorial capital, had informed the boys while they lay denned up in Bitter Creek's homestead shack. At ten-thirty the train, known as the Texas Express, would pause for a brief stop in Wharton.

Ten-ten, by Bob Dalton's heavy gold watch. "Remember, boys," he warned them; "no killing less'n you have to do it or be killed. No holding up passengers. We can't afford bad names with the grangers. And tear out quick once we get the cash."

The powder-smudged face of Charley Bryant frowned at

these orders. Suffering from a "ravaging disease"—probably a neglected venereal one—he had been declaring that "he wanted to go out in one minute of smoking action." And this promised to be a pretty tame robbery if it went the way Bob Dalton had planned it.

At a signal from Bob, Bryant and Emmett took up their positions alongside the track. Bob and Bitter Creek then walked toward the depot, a stone's throw from the stockyards. Friction between townspeople and the railroad had caused the Santa Fe to locate its facilities away from the half a dozen shanty stores that passed for a business section.

The distant stores were dark when the two strangers entered the depot. Wharton, since renamed Perry, was a nine-o'clock town. Behind his cage sat a young citizen who doubled as station agent and telegraph operator for the Atchison, Topeka and Santa Fe. Occasionally the youth, whose name has been forgotten, would look up from his desk to swap banter with the handful of loungers who gathered nightly at the depot.

"Hear them Daltons have been seen up around the Osage reservation," a loafer commented, spitting into a cuspidor.

Another got up, yawned and stretched, "Reckon not. Daltons ain't fools. Everybody knows 'em up there. So long. I gotta be hittin' the hay."

He almost collided with Bob and Bitter Creek as they stepped through the station door. " 'Scuse me, gents," he said and passed on.

Nobody paid much attention to the pair of strangers, looking like ordinary cowboys in their rough chaps and twisted red bandannas. Bob quickly scanned the faces of the men in the waiting room but saw nobody he could identify as a lawman. But a reward poster hanging on the wall offered substantial sums to be paid for the apprehension of Emmett and himself.

The Dalton name was everywhere by now, blazoned on huge cards like these in every station of every railroad throughout the Southwest. Blood money, the posters were offering.

Ten-twenty-two. Satisfied with their check-up, Bob and Bitter Creek hurried out to take posts on opposite sides of the tracks.

And in its tracks, they stopped the Texas Express, halting it with commanding shots from revolvers and Winchesters before Bob Dalton and Bitter Creek Newcomb leaped into the locomotive cab. Hearing the volley, the station agent doused all lights in the depot.

A tall gentleman wearing a white sombrero dived from the platform of the smoking car into a thick patch of bushes near the rails. He was United States Deputy Marshal Ransom Payne, the least courageous and the loudest-mouthed of the federal lawmen who ever crossed trails with Daltons, although he would later inspire the first of a string of cheap books about them. Payne was returning to Oklahoma after delivering some prisoners to the court at Wichita, Kansas, his home town. Now he lay quaking in the bushes, probably wishing that he'd stuck to peddling real estate in Wichita.

With drawn guns, Bob and Bitter Creek escorted the engineer and fireman from cab to ground, then ordered them to halt by the express car. Emmett and Charley Bryant kept the two covered while their partners boarded that car, looking for loot. But, according to the *Fort Smith Elevator* of May 15th, 1891:

"When the robbers boarded the train, the messenger was looking out the door of his car, and seeing what was going on, immediately closed and locked the door and commenced to hide the money and valuables in his keeping."

The Daltons had run up against the shrewdest messenger of all the trains they were destined to ransack. Bob demanded that he open the safe. The express-company employee stoutly insisted that he didn't know the combination.

Bob Dalton knew, through Florence Quick, that this was a lie. "Word had been circulated by the express company that these through money vaults were always closed and set at Gainesville, Texas, and in Kansas City, and the combination wired to the terminus, so that not even the messenger could open them en route. The same report had been broadcast regarding all trains going through the Indian Territory. It was designed to reach the ears of outlaws and to give messengers greater immunity."

But by adroitly quizzing some informant—maybe while sleeping with him—Florence Quick, calling herself Eugenia Moore, had learned that this was a "ruse."

Bob let his pistol slide downward. "A stimulating shot" whizzed by the messenger's brogans. That gentleman became more cooperative—but within limits.

"All right," he sighed. "Reckon I'll have to accommodate you and open the safe."

He tinkered a minute with the combination. The safe door swung open. The messenger handed Bob a large wrapped package which the outlaw's hungry eyes judged to be greenbacks. Bob tossed the package to Bitter Creek Newcomb, who dumped it into a burlap sack. Other members of the train crew and "the more inquisitive passengers" were getting what Emmett, in masterly understatement, called "restive."

As tranquilizers, a volley of shots rang out from the guns of Emmett and Blackface Charley standing guard by the tracks. Bob fumbled inside the safe to come up with a smaller packet. He winked at Bitter Creek Newcomb, then hurled it into the bag.

It looked like a good night for neophyte train robbers, a night that would give the Daltons the name as well as the fame of being engine boarders. And wouldn't Will Smith—that old so-and-so—split his gizzard when he read about it in California?

Satisfied that all the loot had been scraped up, Bob Dalton ordered an exit. The four bandits quickly unhitched their horses from the stockade and rode away as the train began moving upon orders from Conductor McTaggart. Grabbing it on the fly was Ransom Payne, the cautious lawman.

At the very moment when the robbers were passing the depot, the young agent turned on the lights. As he stood silhouetted in the glow of the big kerosene lamps, Charley Bryant drew a .45, fired through the window and dropped the lad as callously as if he had been a partridge.

"No bloodshed" had been the command of Bob Dalton. But Bryant had committed wanton murder in their first actual railway robbery.

What Bob had to say about such disobedience has gone untold. Bryant was a psychopathic killer if there ever was one. Maybe even Bob Dalton would not have wanted to face him down. But the unjustified homicide would bode no good for the Daltons and their followers in the future. Nor did they emerge with much for their labor after that first express-car haul, although Emmett would claim that it amounted to $14,000.

Twenty miles or so from Wharton, the bandits stopped to divide the proceeds. Bob ripped open the large package the express messenger had handed him. There fluttered to the ground canceled waybills, yellowed copies of telegrams and other such useless papers. Not one solitary dollar bill.

Bob looked pained. The other three started swearing like cavalrymen balked by Comanches. They had been taken in by a common trick of railroad and express companies to fool larcenous invaders.

Bob opened the lesser package. Small consolation: it did contain actual currency, but only $500 worth. The divvy would amount to $125 per man, less than the winnings of one good poker game.

Only later did the outlaws learn where the real money had been hidden. The minute the messenger had seen them from the express-car window, he had put the funds for the Guthrie bank in the empty stove.

Drab little Wharton had something big to talk about. The station agent was decently buried. Charley Bryant looked more than ever like a sick sidewinder on its last crawl.

The express company gave its quick-witted messenger a gold watch, probably worth fifty dollars, wholesale.

THE BATTLE OF TWIN MOUNDS

THAT murderous business at Wharton did nothing to help the precarious position of Bill and Grat Dalton in California. If anything, it made certain that Grat would get the bitter medicine. As for Oklahoma, authorities there didn't waste their time in involved political shenanigans. They cinched saddles, loaded forty-fives and set out on the pressing business at hand.

Less than twenty-four hours after the robbery, carrying John Doe warrants, they were in pursuit of the bandits, whose identities had not been established. That very first group of federal marshals to chase Oklahoma engine boarders included George E. Thornton, Frank Kress, Joe P. Jennings, George Orin Severns, Ed Short, a tough ex-sheriff from Kansas, and the ludicrous Ransom Payne.

In that hair-raising farce, *Eyewitness*,[1] Payne claimed to have been the "trusty" lieutenant of Chief Marshal William Grimes, who, he alleged, telegraphed him "not to spare any effort to overtake the assailants of the Texas Fast Express and to gather in those well-known members of the gang who did not happen to be present at the time of the Wharton outrage."

Payne did not head the posse, and it was not sent out "to assist Payne," as he would have had his readers believe. Probably he was riding drag.

After the holdup, Bob Dalton and his crew took to the thickets between Wharton and a mean little hellhole called Orlando. This was terrain that Bob and Emmett knew well, having marshalled across it. Within its briary stretches lived their buddy, Ol Yountis, sometimes spelled Yantis. Mr. Yountis, who occupied a homestead with his sister, rated merely as a local bad man; but he had ambitions.

The Yountis acres were largely uncleared woods, Ol being an indifferent kind of farmer. His "estate" offered a refuge where the gang hoped to lie low till excitement died down.

Ol and his sister would bring them grub. Water could be had from a convenient stream called Beaver Creek. Then,

according to Bob's original plan, the four would retreat to
their main hideout on the isolated ranch of Big Jim Riley,
sixty miles southwest of Kingfisher.

It was planning that reflected the preliminary field work
of Florence Quick. When Florence had set up the robbery,
she had also arranged for the hideout with Ol Yountis. Mr.
Yountis gladly rendered the favor in the hope of certain
favors in return from Miss Quick, who proved indefinitely
slow about extending them.

But this time Miss Quick had slipped up. She had picked
a neighborhood of Missourians who were law-abiding and
therefore acutely self-conscious about such native prodigals
as the Daltons. Hard-working, church-going nesters were
these folk, brought in as emigrants by two brothers, George
and William T. Starmer; but they were also, when necessity
required, hard-riding and hard-shooting. Like Bob and Emmett Dalton, their anti-types, they were sons of the Buckshot
Belt.

For two or three days, the gang lounged in a patch of
timber connected with the Yountis premises by the dimmest
of foot trails. All four of them were disappointed in the
take at Wharton, but all agreed it had been "a good shake
run" that would provide valuable experience for the future.
If anybody expressed remorse about the murder of the station agent, nobody has set it down. After all, he was just
another railroad flunkey, and hadn't they declared unlim-
ited war on all railroads?

At their shack, Ol Yountis and his sister kept a wary
vigil for marshals who might come sniffing around on the
trail of their guests. The sister is said to have been sweet on
Bitter Creek Newcomb, but there is no evidence that Bitter
Creek gave her a tumble. The outlaws diverted themselves
by playing poker and blackjack with a deck spread on a
blanket under a handy tree. Charley Bryant's health seemed
a bit improved from the tonic effect of killing a man. Bob
and Emmett did a bit of boasting about avenging the pil-
lorying of Bill and Grat in California.

Soon the four began getting restless. They were men of
action. This kind of fooling around was bad on whatever
souls they had. Idle hands began straying toward minor
mischief—toward the one diversion, aside from cards, in
those dull surroundings.

That was horse stealing—the fine art of which the Daltons were old masters. Temptation came in the form of fine,
broken brones wandering past their camps, wearing the

brands of the Starmers, the Thompsons and other Missourians who farmed along Beaver Creek.

Putting a Dalton next to a horse was like putting a hungry rabbit next to some lettuce. The pull of so much loose horseflesh became irresistible. At Bob's direction, the gang appropriated ten of the best ponies on the local range. That theft got a quick reaction.

Under the leadership of Starmer and William Thompson, the Missourians mobilized and searched the area till they spotted the gang's hideout on the Yountis property. The boys, detecting their approach, retreated farther into the Beaver Creek wilderness.

Soon the chase became a grim game of one-sided tag, with Bob Dalton outgeneraling and outfoxing Thompson and Starmer, who was some kind of an officer, at every turn. Bob's genius at this kind of frontier warfare should have discouraged the pursuers and impelled them to a wise decision to let the horses go, what with Missouri-imported mares steadily foaling fine new colts. But it had no effect on these pioneers, whose literal minds and stern honesties showed the Buckshot Belt at its best. Their horses had been stolen. Decent, Godfearing men didn't let go unanswered that kind of challenge flung by mangy wide-loopers!

So they let the gang draw them into a widening trap. Volley after volley the settlers fired at opponents who remained unseen and who responded with not one answering blast. Rod after rod they advanced into the brakes as the gang abandoned one position after another.

Bob Dalton knew exactly where he was leading this pack of cloddish hoemen: toward a pair of strategically placed Ozark hillocks called Twin Mounds, a mile or two from the banks of Beaver Creek. He had stopped there many times while he'd been a marshal to rest his pony or boil himself some coffee.

Some of the Missourians must have caught on to his scheme as the fox-and-geese contest went on. Some must have protested to Starmer and Thompson, realizing that they were being made the geese. Yet not one man would turn back unless all did.

Their hands were bleeding from thorns and burrs. Their pants were ripped. Little pods of the pernicious growth called "stick-tight" clung to their cotton socks. Wood gnats got in their eyes.

But the nesters kept crawling and crouching through the morasses of underbrush, kept plowing through the swarms of insects, unwittingly helping the retreating thieves, kept firing those futile shots to keep their spirits up.

The desperados reached Twin Mounds ten or fifteen minutes ahead of the hoemen. Piles of dead timber in front of the hillocks gave the gang even more security. Bob Dalton was ready to spring the trap. He did so with a literal bang.

Four shots thundered as the Missourians arrived to face the barricade—two from the guns of Emmett Dalton and Charley Bryant, concealed behind the left-hand mound, two more from those of Bob Dalton and Bitter Creek Newcomb, aiming from the pile on the right. Then came a continuing hail of lead as the boys punished their foes.

William Thompson, leading the front rank of the Missourians, reeled to the ground, his hand clutching his chest, his blue calico shirt turning scarlet. With bullets buzzing around them, the settlers picked up their wounded neighbor and withdrew to take scant cover in a low-lying brush heap fifty yards away.

The battle should have ended then. Other men didn't count themselves cowards for retreating when the odds so favored the Daltons, including posses of commissioned lawmen. But these men held on. Bill Starmer, after attending to Thompson's wounds as best as he could, announced his intention of going in after the outlaws alone.

A burst of fire greeted him as he crawled into the underbrush outside the Daltons' "fortress." Then, for a tense moment, all firing stopped on both sides, after which the Missourians heard the scuffling thud of retreating boots. The bandits were getting out. His companions did not see Starmer returning. The settlers sent a long-range volley whistling across the mounds, hoping to wing an outlaw on the fly.

"They got away, damn 'em," one of them conceded. "We'd better go look for Brother Starmer."

Brother Starmer was a dead neighbor when they found him in the brush. There were three bullets in his lifeless body.

The score of the Wharton spree now stood at two men dead; one man wounded; five hundred grabbed in cash; ten broncs snatched; and something that in time would plague the victors of the battle of Twin Mounds.

That was the bitter anger of another Missourian named George Starmer. Soon afterward he would sign up as a federal marshal. This brother of Bill Starmer would make plenty of trouble for Bill Doolin and Ol Yountis, years later.

14

THE DALTON HIDEOUTS

AFTER Beaver Creek, Oklahoma's marshals and allied lawmen spent days searching for the murderous gang that was
prowling the Territory. They climbed mountains bristling
with Russian thistles and frequented by copperheads. They
scoured ravines and kicked around the ashes of abandoned
camps, hoping their boots would turn up something dropped
from the Wharton robbery. They followed horse-hoof tracks
which led finally to legitimate corrals or were blotted out by
the fresher tracks of deer.

Let a Dalton loose in Oklahoma and who could find him?
You might as well have tried to handcuff the wind. At that
time, no positive identifications had been established for the
Wharton bandits. They had worn masks at the holdup. The
Missourians of Beaver Creek had got only fleeting glimpses
of them in their transient hideout before that ambush at
Twin Mounds. Ol Yountis and his sister had lied nobly to
investigating officers, expressing shocked surprise when told
that four bad hombres had camped on their homestead.

Ol Yountis was richer by twenty dollars that Bob Dalton
had slipped in his pocket, for a stake in one or another of
Orlando's round-the-clock crap games. That was more than
his sister got out of it, her crush on Bitter Creek Newcomb
unrequited. They were a singularly unattractive pair, the
sister's lips ringed with snuff, the brother's yellowed teeth
protruding past his upper lip so his face seemed set in a per-
petual snarl. But they knew how to keep secrets, looking innocent, pointing to their scraggly cotton patch and their
skinny milch cows to show that they were just struggling
grangers.

Nobody in Oklahoma except the Yountises and artful
Florence Quick could have said positively that the Dalton
gang had pulled the Wharton job, with its brutal sequel.
Yet most people guessed that the Daltons had been mixed
up in the business. Robbing and shooting—such goings-on
were in keeping with what Oklahoma already knew about
Bob and Emmett and the absent Grat. Elements like the

trashy Yountises said hooray for them. Their kind had also cheered Sam Bass in Texas and the Jameses in Missouri.

But thoughtful tax-paying Oklahomans were worried. How would this new rampage of outlawry affect the reputation of the two-year-old territory? What would it do to land values? How would it affect the growth of towns and the development of business? How long would it postpone the expected merger of Oklahoma and Indian Territories into a state of the American Union?

Worried, too, was Oklahoma's first territorial governor, George W. Steele, although he did little to cope with the challenge of the gang's depredations. The main burden of curbing Dalton outlawry fell upon Chief United States Marshal William Grimes, a resident of Kingfisher, where the peaceful branch of the notorious family lived.

Grimes suspected the Dalton hand in that murderous double tragedy of Wharton and Beaver Creek. He enlisted as informer a member of the clan itself—Kingfisher meat-market proprietor, J. K. Whipple, an unctuous, greedy character who had married one of Adeline Dalton's daughters. He staked out operatives to watch the mother's home, hoping that Bob and Emmett might be unwise enough to pay her a visit.

It showed how naïve even such a sharp lawman as Bill Grimes could be. Bob and Emmett, foreseeing such an obvious move, gave Kingfisher a wide berth. But as frustrated officers kept searching, Marshal Ed Short was guessing at two basic elements in the gang's strategy.

After a crime, they scattered, with each man on his own, pending on agreed reunion at one or another hideout in the protecting Oklahoma hills. And they maintained a network of counter-espionage never equaled by the "intelligence systems" of any of the older outlaw combines of the West.

After the battle of Twin Mounds, the gang divided, subject to the call of Bob Dalton. Bitter Creek Newcomb returned to his homestead claim near Guthrie, to go through the motions of being a peaceful farmer. Charley Bryant sped to Hennessy, near Kingfisher. In this remote community, twenty-five miles from a railroad, Florence Quick and Bob Dalton had set up an undetected love nest. Bob gave his partner a few days' head start, then cautiously followed. Emmett, judging it unsafe to visit Julia Johnson on Caney River, rode without stopping to the Dalton central headquarters: the dugout on Jim Riley's ranch.

The earthen den had been the young man's first venture in home-building, though it wouldn't be his last. From the account he left of it, Emmett couldn't have been prouder of the construction if it had been the capitol building at Guthrie.

The gang had needed an assembly point which would be both refuge and citadel, a place spacious enough to shelter the ten men comprising the total roster, although they seldom were all there at any one time. Jim Riley's spread, made to order for an outlaw operations base, was located in that rugged branch of the Ozarks called the Gloss Mountains. It was country where, in the words of Marshal Chris Madsen, "every breeze of air would cover the tracks of man or beast with deep sand." It was country sparsely populated by shiftless white nesters who had been outraced for the best claims in the great Run of '89; by ranchers like Jim Riley, partial to hired or volunteer guns for private armies; by cadgy Indians such as those who had given big Jim his wife.

Festering country it was, a fit haunt for outlaws. To it, the Dalton staff had drifted in, one by one, to report for duty, after Bob and Emmett had escaped from California.

Charley Bryant was first to answer the whistle. Then came Dick Broadwell, and Bill Powers; Bitter Creek Newcomb, still singing that identifying song, still holding on, for policy's sake, to his claim at Guthrie; Charlie Pierce, who had originally come to Oklahoma as a professional racehorse man; and, last of all, Bill Doolin, forever suspicious of Daltons but always involved with them.

Emmett Dalton and Charley Bryant had already scooped out a burrow whose sustaining wall was a bank of red clay in the dense timber bordering the South Canadian River. This permanent hideaway was a rougher one than any of the transient lodges ever occupied by the more fastidious Jameses and Youngers. But it was a safe headquarters, if brush poppers ever built one.

Thick high grass grew in front of this outlaw warren, almost concealing its door, from an aperture in which the freebooters could detect any movement on their "lawn" and figure whether it was made by moving man or prowling beast. Matted willow brush grew along the sides of the den and could be reached "in a few strides from the door." Portholes for rifle barrels were cut over the double-deck bunks along the clay walls that were bolstered with stout posts cut and trimmed by the gang. Thick sod, raftered up by heavy branches lopped from trees, served as roof. Eighteen feet square the interior was.

Emmett afterward referred sentimentally to this subterranean shack as "the brave little hut amidst the cedars of the wilderness." Not far away from their hole, the bandits threw up a small corral of brush whose branches were intertwined with stout ropes in lieu of wire. Within this improvised pen, the gang "always kept several horses ready for flight or foray." The Dalton remuda consisted of from twenty to thirty swift ponies that ran on the range with Jim Riley's broncs. The nearest neighbors were the hospitable, closemouthed Rileys themselves, and they lived fifteen miles away.

Everything else fell into a convenient pattern for men on the dodge. Water, tasting slightly of gypsum, was to be had from a bubbling spring just below that dugout manse of the Daltons. The fireplace served for both heating and cooking, with the usual five or six occupants alternating as "old lady" or grub wrangler. Emmett became a master of the culinary art, although there wasn't much "art" needed to satisfy the tastes of men living in such rugged simplicity. Even Bill Doolin, the "plains epicure," liked it.

Meat—deer, stray calves, and wild turkeys—were to be had on hoof or wing. Extra chuck—canned stuff, flour, baking soda, salt, beans, bacon—was ordered by the case or sack through Jim Riley, from the nester settlement of Taloga, some twenty miles off. With such fixin's, Emmett whipped up meals that Doolin praised as tasting "sweeter than a wildcat's ham rolled in meal."

Fingers were nature's forks. Pocket knives carved up steaks and turkey gizzards. The favorite beverage—whisky raw enough to burn even Bryant's cast-iron guts—could be bought cheaply and in quantity from nesters making out for cash money through moonshining.

No rent to pay: this was public land which the obliging Daltons had occupied to hold its grass against homesteaders for Jim Riley. No taxes on a promising, if risky, business. No dolefully respectable wives to turn rovers into hoemen and prayer-snorters—a dismal fate that brought more hardy buckies to heel than all the marshals who ever held commissions. The company of one's peers, accented by the glib brag that outlaws swapped. Target practice, with bullets bouncing cans from stumps. For extra diversion, a decrepit fiddle, played by Bill Powers on evenings when the coyotes yipped and the brown jugs gurgled.

A secondary hideout, duplicating the facilities of the first, was located in the black granite crags of the Ouachita (Washita) Mountains, where Indian Territory joined Arkansas in that common wilderness of the Southwest's great Ozark subregion. From this area had come one of Judge Parker's marshals, pious Jim Peters, destined to turn Baptist preacher;

and Parker's hangman, saturnine George Maledon, now hoping that neighbor Peters would fetch him a Dalton to swing.[1]

Emmett had his own private treasure, joyfully used during every stay at the shack. He had acquired a set of field glasses which became a part of the gang's stock equipment. Standing by the cabin, he would put the glasses to his eyes and survey everything that moved for miles around till Bob's holler told him it was time to start the cook pot.

Right after the meal, Emmett would grab his plaything and start peeking again, watching deer, bear, wolves and the trailing smoke from the cabins of Indian full-bloods who didn't talk much to marshals. Emmett couldn't have been happier over that very first orange ever tasted by Julia Johnson, the one he'd bought her at a Fourth of July blow-out on Caney River after they had ridden the mule-powered merry-go-round together.

Many other sites in Oklahoma are reputed to have been squatting places for Daltons. Similarly, New Mexico abounds in "hiding places" of Billy the Kid, while Texans claim every canyon along a certain route to have been a refuge of their own Mr. Bass.

But Daltons were never at a loss for a hideaway afforded by nature or man. They knew Oklahoma far better than their forerunner in train robbery, Sam Bass, ever knew Texas. They had more friends than he ever numbered in the Lone Star State because—except for Grat—they had more sense and, usually, better manners.

Bob Dalton, the gang's boss, "worked on the theory that if one hideout was discovered and they were forced to vacate, they should have another in which to move."

It was a good theory, one which in practice kept the Dalton band riding high across Oklahoma's red hills.

15

MR. BRYANT MOVES
TO BOOT HILL

FOR forty days Oklahoma officers searched for the ugly band which they figured was bound to strike again. During that time the Daltons lay low. One reason was, of course, Bob's honeymooning need to see a lot of Florence Quick. Another, though it dawned late on the Oklahoma brothers, was the plight of Bill and Grat in California, for the newspapers there had recorded the Wharton holdup as the work of Bob and Emmett. This time, they had been right.

Gradually, during that frustrating summer of 1891, the marshals had to give up the chase for the murderers of Bill Starmer and the Wharton station agent. Chief Marshal Grimes had too many other fish to fry, as bad men from all over the West kept drifting into Oklahoma, attracted by its juicy pickings.

Yet one lawdog kept his nose to the trail. He was an officer as fast on the gun as any Dalton, as lacking in sentiment as hard-bitten Charley Bryant or brutal Dick Broadwell, as eager for a fast dollar as any of the assorted banditti roving the young territory.

Ed Short was "the fearless gunman," as the *Daily Oklahoman* called him in a commemorative feature some years ago; big, blond, domineering, deadly, he was feared as much as Wild Bill Hickok had been by everyday Kansans. Almost, by unvarnished legend, as mean as Hickok, Short was innately more courageous.

Short was an Easterner, originally, with an imperious air of innate violence about him. Nature had given him a profession—that of gunman. For years he had drifted around as a free-lance pistol toter, protecting his employment with one or another transitory badge.

Before the spectacular rise of the Daltons, Short had been hired to lead the armed forces of Woodsdale, Kansas, in its tussle with a neighboring community called Hugoton over which should be the county seat of Stevens County. His backers had invested him with the title of city marshal to legalize a lot of necessary shooting. The rival factions had fought it out, not on the soil of Stevens County but on the adjoining terrain of No Man's Land, that odd enclave which was under the government of no state or territory.

Marshal Short had spilled his expected quota of blood in the fight. Afterward, by inevitable civic retribution, he had become unpopular in Kansas. Knowing no trade but the gun, he had drifted into Oklahoma, where his kind of labor was in demand. There Bill Grimes had been more than happy to hire him.

He was the one born detective of the federal force; with the possible exception of Chris Madsen, its one outstanding investigator. This somber man of the law no doubt had subconscious affinities with the outlaws he hunted—something like the kinship a spirited hound has with the wolves he bays, perhaps.

It was Ed Short who uncovered the first clues to the identities of the Wharton robbers. While other marshals were following one or another futile "lead," Short questioned the engineer and fireman of the Texas Express, who had witnessed the killing of the station agent. The marshal asked if they could recall any distinguishing marks on any of the holdup men.

The bandits had been masked, they said, but a small portion of the face of one, visible under the twisted bandanna, had been deeply smudged, as if by gunpowder.

"Did he say anything during the holdup?" Short asked the trainmen. "What kind of a brogue did he have?"

Both railroaders declared that the killer had said little, but that it had been uttered in "Texas lingo," recognizable throughout the West. Short went back to Guthrie and the office of his superior, Chief Marshal Grimes.

In the primitive files of those days, he found a record on a Texan with a smudgy face named Charles Bryant. Bryant was known to have punched cattle with Emmett Dalton on the Bar X B. Both had been frequent visitors to the close-by Pawnee reservation, where they had raced and swapped ponies with the braves.

Most of Blackface Charley's family were believed to be still living in Wise County, Texas, but a brother named Jim Bryant was homesteading at Mulhall, in the same general area as Kingfisher. Further probing indicated that Charley was a sick man, with not many more months to go.

Sooner or later, figured Ed Short, the ailing desperado would have to crawl from some hideout and go to his brother's shanty for help. Through local officers, he established a watch on Jim Bryant's shabby farm. Then, in a calculated

move, he set up an office in the wild little town of Hennessy
on the western border of Hell's Fringe.

There Charley Bryant had a reputed sweetheart, though
the exact relationship of the two has never been clearly
established. The girl was Jean Thorne, kid sister of Ben
Thorne, a former cattleman who now ran the Rock Island
Hotel in Hennessy. Moreover, the move put Short in a better
position to watch out for Daltons, right in the heart of enemy
territory.

Hennessy lay approximately halfway between Kingfisher,
where Adeline Dalton lived, and the Negro town of Dover,
where she made surreptitious visits to her boys when they
were on the run. All three communities were within the
bounds of Kingfisher County, so christened for a prominent
Cherokee family of that name.

For some months Short hung out in Hennessy, doing routine chores for the second Oklahoma judicial district, comprising the counties of Canadian, Kingfisher, Washita, Roger
Mills, Day and Beaver, the last of which had been No Man's
Land before Congress incorporated it into the territory.
These, as Chris Madsen observed, were "the counties where
the outlaws had their best protection in the West. because
there were no railroads." Kingfisher County, however, had
recently been reached by an extension of the Rock Island
railroad.

Marshal Short kept a sharp eye on the Rock Island Hotel
and its pretty hostess, Jean Thorne. Not once did a gent
with a charred face step in to sign the register, but Ed Short
was a patient man who knew how to bide his time. That
quality also showed up in the way he handled a gun: he
always got results even though he always seemed to fire so
deliberately.

Patience began bearing its fruits. Before too long, the
marshal began hearing of another Bryant, one who didn't
check with the complete list of the family sent him by the
Wise County sheriff in Decatur, Texas.

This Bryant was a lady, and a dazzling one. Daisy, she was
called, and she was the purported sister of Blackface Charley
She also called herself after a husband whom she claimed to
have divorced in Dakota Territory. Her neighbors felt that
she must have gotten a settlement as handsome as herself,
for she had made some expensive improvements on a place
she had recently purchased.

Her "estate" was an abandoned homestead in a sparsely
settled section twenty miles or so west of Hennessy, seven
miles from a cow camp called Buffalo Springs. A large house

had come with the property. This dwelling, commanding a view of the country for miles around, had been painted and repaired by nesters who welcomed the generous cash with which Mrs. Jones, allegedly née Miss Bryant, seemed to be well supplied.

Some girl Charley Bryant was laying up with and calling his sister to keep the nester women from gossiping—or some wench from a whorehouse in Muskogee or Fort Smith. Such were Marshal Short's first estimates of the reports buzzed to him by suspicious dowagers in sunbonnets.

At first, those reports didn't cause Short much concern. After all, he wasn't out to correct Charley Bryant's morals but to get Charley's neck. Then the marshal began re-examining those constant siftings about the glamour girl living in the foothills of the Gloss Mountains. Where would a whorehouse alumna get all that money unless she had managed a highly improbable shakedown of some wealthy customer?

Nor did her kind hole up in coyote diggings once they had gotten a stake through blackmail. Neither were they likely to join fortunes and flesh with a diseased, perennially broke no-account like Charley Bryant.

No sir! That type of woman went to more lucrative fields once they got in the chips. To Kansas City, where they could grab off wealthy beef packers. Or to Denver, where the girls did right well by entertaining silver magnates at the gaudy Windsor Hotel. Or they opened their own temples of sin, like Pearl Younger, Belle Starr's daughter and cousin of the Daltons, in Fort Smith.

Who was this mysterious woman, getting to be the talk of all the scandal-ridden little towns, brazenly admitting to being both a divorcée and the sister of an outlaw? Ed Short wondered, like everybody else. But, playing it cool, the marshal didn't consider it expedient to take a bronc ride and find out. Ed Short, like a fox, knew when it was best just to stand under the vine and let the grapes fall.

At that time, Mr. Bryant's health wasn't showing much improvement, though he was getting plenty of fresh country air. He was living with fellow cowboys in a camp at Buffalo Springs and they were doing their limited best for him. His reputation as a bad actor didn't faze them.

They didn't share the cautious qualms of the invading granger hoemen, who were even planning "local option" elections to vote out the saloons! Hell's fire, did the damn jaspers expect grown men to guzzle milkshakes in their measly little confectioneries?

Now and then Blackface Charley managed enough energy

to swing a stirrup and visit the pleasant home of Miss Bryant, seven miles from the camp. There he could always be sure of meeting some of his bosom friends, slipping out from Jim Riley's distant ranch for a little sociability.

Dick Broadwell sometimes stopped by. Good old Dick was still grieving over a nester hussy who had eloped with him to Fort Worth, then disappeared with both his roll and his ring. What the hell did a long rider want with a wife? Look at what had happened to those who'd gone soft and attached themselves to spouses. All the lead gone from their guns. Wearing overalls instead of chaps, by God! Mr. Bryant was forever reminding Mr. Broadwell that he'd been lucky to be spared.

Emmett Dalton was often around to shake hands with Charley, his old mentor in outlawry. A promising boy, that Emmett. Might even outclass Jesse James if he didn't tie himself down to that man-hungry Julia too soon. All women— the gamy ones like Julia Johnson, the demure ones like sweet little Jean Thorne in Hennessy—spelled trouble to Mr. Bryant.

The wasting bad man also saw a lot of Bob Dalton around the pleasant big house, turned into a free hotel for road agents. Bob was there often, of course.

Marshal Short must have gotten grapevine reports on the doings in this outlaw roost not far from his nose. Why then did he not summon help, ride out and bag the Dalton gang en masse, including the woman who ran the joint?

The answer is that Short would have been bucking a lawless strip of malcontents who didn't even acknowledge the authority of a precinct constable. Had he led a posse to this outpost of freebooters, bullets would have blazed from behind every rock, not all of them fired by enrolled members of the Dalton band. Even had officers made it to the home of the mysterious woman, they might have found all the birds flown; Hennessy was full of Dalton sympathizers who kept the gang informed of every move made by the marshal. Short was nobody's coward; neither was he anybody's fool.

Late in July, 1891—more than two months after the Wharton haul—Bryant became violently ill at the cow camp. None of the common folk remedies gave him any relief. His cowpuncher friends began insisting that he see a doctor.

There was a physician at Mulhall, where Charley's brother, Jim Bryant, lived; this medico was rated as pretty good when he wasn't drunk. Charley hoped he could stay under cover at Jim's home, have the doc make a house call on him there, get straightened up and then head quietly back to Buffalo Springs.

The road to Mulhall went through Hennessy. At that time, Charley did not know the marshals suspected him of complicity in the Wharton incident. Maybe he was too sick to care. At the town where Short maintained headquarters, Bryant stopped at the office of a physician who immediately ordered him to bed.

Naturally the community had no hospital. There were not a dozen such institutions between Fort Smith and Denver. Bryant checked in at the Rock Island Hotel, since he and proprietor Ben Thorne had known each other on the range. Jean Thorne volunteered to take care of the suffering man, as she would have offered to do for any ailing guest.

The date was August 1, 1891, not long after the conviction of Grat Dalton, in California. Short soon learned that Bryant was at the hotel, and on the second of August, he stormed into the outlaw's room at the Rock Island. Either Jean Thorne betrayed the wanted man to the law or Short slipped in behind her as she entered the room with a tray of food.

At any rate, Short pulled a six-shooter and informed Blackface Charley that he was under arrest. The outlaw fumbled for his own weapon, concealed under his pillow; then, realizing the marshal had the drop on him, he surrendered.

Ed Short had got his man. Now the question was what to do with him. Hennessy, like most of the towns in the brand-new counties of Oklahoma, had no jail. The nearest place of confinement was the federal lock-up in Guthrie, but there the prisoner had many friends who could be counted on to attempt a jailbreak. Wichita, Kansas, where the federal court sat, seemed to be the safest place of durance for Blackface Charley. So on August 3, at five P.M., Short escorted outlaw Bryant aboard a northbound train. There was no demonstration of outlaw sympathizers at the station, but the marshal was troubled by rumors that a delivery would be attempted along the way. It would be best to keep the prisoner out of sight.

Short deposited the handcuffed man in the baggage car rather than in a passenger coach, keeping him company with small talk and a loaded Winchester. As the two chatted, Bryant noticed a row of pigeonholes used for sorting mail dropped off at post offices along the route. One of these slots contained a Colt's pistol owned by the baggage agent.

"Ed, you got these bracelets on too tight," Bryant complained. "They're hurting my hands."

Marshal Short obligingly loosened the cuffs without removing them, feeling he had to show some consideration to a sick man, even if he was a bandit. The train was now reaching its first stop before the Kansas border—Waukomis, thirteen miles north of Hennessy, on the edge of the Cherokee Outlet. Here, Short reasoned, was the likeliest place where friends or supporters of the prisoner might try a rescue.

As the train neared the village, Short ordered the agent to stand watch over the prisoner. Taking his Winchester, the marshal stepped to the car's platform to do some cautious reconnoitering. His back was barely turned when the manacled hand of the prisoner dived into the pigeonhole and grabbed the pistol.

The agent began quivering. "Keep quiet or I'll blow your head off!" the outlaw warned. A moment later, Ed Short turned to see Bryant standing behind him, the weapon pointed toward the marshal's skull.

His rifle at hip level, Short fired again and again. Six shots—the revolver's capacity—roared back from the agent's gun in Bryant's hand.

Lawman and outlaw both were mortally wounded, but Short managed enough strength to help carry his foe back into the car and there stretch him out on a cot.

Both of them were dead when the train ground to a stop at the Waukomis station, two minutes later. Blackface Charley's spine was severed; Ed Short's vital organs were punctured.

Subsequently, Bob Dalton and Florence Quick, alias "Miss Bryant," abandoned their love nest in Kingfisher County.

16

THE DALTONS' BIGGEST HAUL

THE Dalton hideout, that September forenoon of 1891, was the scene of duding-up. Razors were being sharpened on whetstones, mustaches waxed with tallow, scuffed boots shined with blacking. Bill Doolin was trimming his drooping whiskers with scissors borrowed from Mr. Jim Riley. Charlie Pierce was giving himself a manicure with a jackknife.

All seven of the hideout's current tenants had donned neckties for a major event. Bob Dalton was wearing his blue serge suit and a white silk shirt freshly laundered by Emmett, the gang's housekeeper. Every few minutes Bob looked into a cracked mirror above his bunk for a fresh self-inspection.

"You'd think we wuz dykin' out for Chris Madsen," Bill Powers quipped.

The outlaws guffawed. Stocky, plodding, Danish-born Madsen was a new, hard-shooting deputy United States marshal. Dick Broadwell spoke with a Texan's contempt for the lesser breeds:

"Hellfire, boys, we took care of that damn Yankee, Ed Short. Reckon we don't aim to be scared of a sawed-off son-of-a-bitchin' furriner like Chris Madsen."

Bob Dalton frowned. "Don't take Madsen for any tinhorn. I knew him when he was supply sergeant for the army over at Fort Reno." The young bandit gave his boots a final swipe with a rag. "No cussing, you fellers, when Florence gets here. No barbershop jokes." He grinned. "And no trying to beat my time, Bitter Creek."

Bob's followers nodded. Florence Quick might not be a lady within the parlor definition of that term, but you never treated a partner's sweetheart with any less respect than you did your own sister or mother. Besides, Bob had hinted that Flo's visit might mean a lucrative journey for broke, cramped-up freebooters. At that moment the boys were low in pocket and awfully fed up with so much close confinement.

Flo had been at Wagoner, 200 miles away, when she had sent word by some lawless drifter that she could be expected for a personal call on a certain date. The name of the town had brought up certain associations for Bob and Emmett: it was where they had left Grat with those stolen broncs after their final visit to Fort Smith. More to the point, the place was an important stop on the Missouri, Kansas and Texas Railroad.

It was midday when Florence Quick, resplendent in Spanish chaps and a brand-new sombrero, reined in before the dugout. All seven of the slicked-up desperados were waiting outside to meet her. She jumped from a fine stallion, stolen along the way, and joyously rushed into Bob Dalton's arms for a long embrace. Then she gave Emmett a sisterly peck on the cheek and asked solicitously when he'd last seen Julia Johnson. Afterward the honor guest shook hands warmly with Bitter Creek Newcomb, Charlie Pierce, Bill Doolin, Dick Broadwell and Bill Powers.

"Big news, boys," she laughed. "But first give a girl some grub."

Emmett had prepared a planked deer steak. The day was warm and Indian-summerish. Outlaw queen and her devoted subjects decided to eat under a big tree with saddle blankets serving as seats. There at this jolly picnic, the Dalton gang plotted what would be its biggest job.

The railroad to be honored with their attentions was the MK&T—"the Katy." The place chosen for the hist was Leliaetta, a tiny flag stop four miles north of Wagoner, its sister community in that sparsely settled section of eastern Oklahoma. The pickings looked promising, for the train, a regularly scheduled express, would be carrying the proceeds of the summer's cotton-crop sales to banks in Texas.

Besides the immediate need for cash, ulterior motives were prompting Bob and his mistress. One was revenge that Florence had nurtured for the shattering of her hearthstones in Kingfisher County. Now there was an added element that they had discussed recently at a furtive half-hour meeting in a little granger town called Woodward.

A stake that would take them clear out of the United States, with its officious marshals, to set them up on a ranch which they hoped to find in Mexico. Maybe they'd take Emmett and Julia with them—and Grat, if he could be located. It would be a quiet, peaceful, happy ending for the Dalton Gang. It was a standard dream for freebooters of the Southwest, who habitually foresaw themselves living in prosperity and peace across the Rio Grande.

It was sundown when the seven men and the girl finished conferring on the impending job. When evening came,

Bob's six comrades spread their blankets in the woods so that he and Florence might have the dugout in privacy.

The projected holdup had been planned with extreme care. They expected it to go off better than the haphazard Wharton job, which had yielded so little cash and such a disastrous aftermath. This time there would be an adequate corps of train boarders instead of a mere four, as at Wharton. The gang would scatter for a future reunion as soon as the loot had been divided. And, emphatically—Bill Doolin bore down on it hard—there would be no wanton killings, like Charley Bryant's cowardly murder of the Wharton station agent.

Florence left the next morning, her eyes looking as dreamy as Bob's. The outlaws saddled their best horses for what would be a four- or five-day ride across back country to Leliaetta, a spot where nothing exciting had ever happened.

Shortly after dusk on the evening of September 15, seven men dressed in the rough garb of cowhands rode down the MK&T tracks that led to the village. They halted their ponies cautiously when they saw an elderly couple shambling along the rails.

"Looking for something?" Bob Dalton called out.

The man gazed innocently at these strangers. "Yeah," he whined, "me and the old woman thought we might find us some coal dropped off the train so we can warm up our camp, over there by the siding."

The travelers glanced around to see a crude squatters' shanty across the track. The old man spoke again, plaintively.

"You fellers don't happen to be wantin' a man to do a job of work, do you?"

Bob laughed. "Nothing you could handle, stranger. But if you'll wait up the track a piece, you might find some coal after the express goes through."

The bandits flipped their bridles and rode on. The old couple shambled away, pausing now and then to cast backward looks at the wayfarers who had made such an odd promise.

Within a few minutes, the gang reached the settlement. Light from kerosene lamps glowed in the few houses. Dogs had begun their nightly chorus of raucous barks and keening howls. Leliaetta's general store had closed for the day, and no idlers lounged on the benches of its broad front porch. Another light flickered in the depot. Barring some hitch along the line, the express would come rattling through any minute.

At a sign from Bob, the outlaws quickly halted their horses. For a tense moment, their eyes fixed on the depot semaphore. Leliaetta was a flag stop, where trains paused only when passengers were waiting to board it. Even then, a station agent, warned in advance, might signal the engineer to keep moving, thus leaving earnest outlaws with nothing but a mocking cloud of steam for their troubles. Also, a quick tap of a telegraph key could send posses thundering after surprised freebooters.

There came the sound of approaching iron wheels. Hastily, Bitter Creek Newcomb and Emmett Dalton took up positions on one side of the track, Charlie Pierce and Dick Broadwell on the other. Fingers caressed cold metal.

Four shrill blasts sounded from an engine whistle. From the railroad safety code taught them by Florence Quick, the bandits knew that the engineer was signaling a question to the station agent: Was the line clear of those who might have other business with a railroad than buying tickets?

The semaphore bobbed yes. Relieved, the boys exchanged knowing smirks. Money was coming. Coming on wheels, just for them.

The train passed the semaphore and slowed to a crawl. The engineer was getting ready to pull the throttle when Bob Dalton and Bill Doolin leaped into the cab, covering him with loaded rifles. Bill Powers ran to the express car. A salvo of intimidating gunfire roared from the weapons of the four men on "outside duty."

"Holdup! The train's being robbed!" shouted passengers in the coaches. Some dived between seats; others piled outside, hoping to save their valuables if the robbers made the rounds of the cars.

The station agent ran to the door of the depot, got an eyeful of what was happening and vanished. None of the train crew showed any signs of fight, but the messenger inside the express car at first refused to open the door. With engineer and fireman both cowed, Bob and Doolin ran back to the express car.

Bill Powers called out a threat to use dynamite, which would have blown both door and man behind it to kingdom come. By way of punctuation, the outlaw fired a "hurry-up" shot or two outside the door.

The door slid open and the messenger's hands swung up as Doolin leveled a rifle on him. Bob climbed into the car and ordered the custodian of the funds to unload. In a few minutes the messenger had a meal sack full of silver dollars, greenbacks and non-negotiable bonds.

"Jump out," Bob Dalton commanded. "Put that sack on the station platform."

The messenger stumbled past the locomotive crew, who by now had been marched into the express car. He jumped to the platform and laid the bag down on the boards. Bob, watching him from a window, saw that the mood of the passengers who had fled the coaches was becoming threatening. Their voices buzzed in angry protest. Many of them certainly were carrying pistols and might be tempted into a counter-offensive against the train robbers.

Bob yelled to the passengers to get back aboard. A few obeyed. Many more ignored the order. Bill Doolin lost his temper.

"Them jaspers make me tired," he shouted. "Watch me chase 'em."

"Stick where you're ordered," Bob Dalton snapped, not wanting to provoke a battle against such odds. But this was Doolin's chance to flout a Dalton command and he took it.

Yelling like a cowhand on a Saturday-night drunk, he jumped from the car, mounted his horse and charged the length of the train, shooting into the air as he rode. The passengers piled back into the coaches.

The job was about finished and done to a Dalton's satisfaction. Newcomb, Emmett, Pierce and Broadwell gathered around for any last-minute help that Bob, the director of operations, might require. Bob escorted the crew back to the cab, told them to get going and said to the engineer:

"When you get down by the siding light yonder, you slow down and have the fireman heave off a few shovels of coal. Don't be too stingy about it, neither, or you might run into some more trouble."

The engine started chugging. A triumphant phalanx of seven, the Dalton gang roared out of Leliaetta, the bag of loot swung across Bill Doolin's saddlehorn. At a siding light a little piece out of town, the outlaws paused a minute to witness a heart-warming scene: an old man and an old woman picking up a quantity of coal dropped off by the fireman, courtesy of the MK&T.

Friends, as well as money, the band had made from this invasion of a hamlet whose sole distinction would be the Dalton visit. The two elderly squatters would tell others of their kind that "them Daltons made the railroad give us some coal when they robbed the train." Poor folks across the two territories would spread the story, with embellishments, giving the Boys the appearance of kindly knights of the highways. The marshals, consequently, would find more blocks along the twisted trails of the Daltons.

All night long the bandits rode, laughing and joking, toward the hideout on the Canadian. Like country kids coming into two-bit windfalls, they speculated joyfully on the ways in which they would spend their respective shares of what looked like a mighty big haul. Bob Dalton reckoned he would first buy a ranch in Mexico, taking Emmett, Julia, Grat, and Florence Quick with him. What a menage that would have been!

Bill Doolin figured he'd just go back to Arkansas and start raising apples, after raising so much hell in these two territories. His courtship of a preacher's daughter, Edith Ellsworth, apparently was giving him an itch for respectability. Bitter Creek Newcomb, getting sweet on a nubile tot, Rose Dunn, was more cautious, declaring that he never counted his chickens before they hatched. Bill Powers, fluent in Spanish, allowed that he'd also buy himself "a fancy *hacienda* in Old May-he-co."

Finally Doolin got irritated by all the jabber. "Here," he growled, "you fellers that's doin' all the spendin', do your part of the carryin'! My goddam legs are plumb stiff from this load."

He placed the bag on the saddle of a comrade. It was a mistake that he always regretted. It didn't mend his shaky relations with the Dalton brothers but shaped events for one of the internal crises that persistently beset the outfit.

For with the divvy, made either on the trail or in the dugout, came disenchantment. Emmett Dalton always claimed that the Leliaetta take amounted to $19,000. Best estimates indicate it was about half that—ten thousand—in greenbacks and silver dollars. The railroad claimed it was only three thousand.[1]

Once the loot passed out of Bill Doolin's hands, however, the share for the five Dalton employees amounted to just $300 apiece. By some kind of juggling, about $8500 of the total ended up in the pockets of Bob and Emmett. It was a radical departure from the classic outlaw code: share-the-risks, share-the-take.

Through bitter hours, employers and employees argued, with recesses for shaving, eating and the repair of riding gear. A six-gun affair might have been the answer to a short pot, if the hired help only had stood united.

But runty Bitter Creek Newcomb could always be counted on to stand by his tall and admired leader, Bob Dalton. In a showdown the split would have been only four to three in favor of the employees, an uncertain margin with none of them except Bill Doolin matching the Daltons in nerve and gun skill.

Even so, six-shooters might have been cocked had Bob Dalton not hit on the obvious solution of many firms beset with labor trouble: he suddenly announced that he was dissolving the business.

"Boys," he declared pompously, "Emmett and I are through."

Even Bill Doolin, the spokesman for the gripers, was flabbergasted. "Through?" he protested. Why, the express company tied up big wads of money with ribbons, all nice and dainty-like, and threw it right into their hands. And the brothers wanted them to bust up and forget it. The big Arkansawyer's laugh was like the grind of a buzz saw:

"Some folks just ain't got no financin' sense."

Emmett said nothing that might interfere with his brother's play.

"I don't care what you boys think," Bob said firmly. "Chances are too many against us. Nobody's going to take Emmett and me alive to chuck behind any bars. This is where we call quits—and you can tie to that."

Disgruntled, the others saw nothing to do but hit the trail. Completing the double cross, the Daltons rode off with them, making believe that the dugout was being abandoned. Few words were spoken among that sullen seven who had been so jubilant after the successful strike at Leliaetta, hardly forty-eight hours before. An early wind-blown snow stung their taut faces as they rode.

All night the tense ride continued, with Bob Dalton keeping a particularly keen eye on festering Bill Doolin. At dawn, with a pale sun doing nothing to warm the parting, the seven pronounced good-bys that were stiff and formal.

"So long," said Bob. "I'll let you boys hear from us later on." The protocol of the minute required that the leavetaking not appear to be final.

"So long," chorused the others doubtfully. Bitter Creek Newcomb was looking like a tad whose candy had been snatched. "If you fellers are sure-enough through," he said plaintively, "guess the rest of us'll have to go back to twistin' the old Longhorns' tails and livin' on sowbelly and beans."

He and the other four scattered to go their separate ways. Bob and Emmett headed for a certain farmhouse near Guthrie, knowing that this new lawdog, Chris Madsen, wouldn't be looking for them right under his own nose.

There Florence Quick would be waiting to get a first-hand report of what had happened in a haul that had been a proud sequel to her planning.

It isn't often that a career man can get along with a

career woman, particularly when they are engaged in the same craft. But Florence would be proud of her man and co-worker.

He'd gotten off with eighty-five hundred dollars, minus something that would have to be given Emmett. And money sweetens a woman's heart like love. Her man had really started bringing home the bacon. Now she could start fixing up another love nest.

Most females are beset by incurable domesticities. Even the free-lance ones like Flo Quick yearn for the vine-covered cottage.

BILL DALTON COMES HOME

BOB DALTON failed to notify the government's representatives that he had liquidated the Dalton enterprise. The hardheaded marshals hardly would have credited such a story anyway. Dispersal after a robbery was a common tactic. Three of the nation's great railroads—the Southern Pacific, the Katy and the Santa Fe—now claimed to have been victims of one set of brothers named Dalton. This mattered to American law-enforcement officials far more than the intramural disputes of outlaws. Three bad Daltons—Bob, Emmett and Grat—were running loose, despite all the lurid reward posters and all the newspaper furor. Then, to cap the situation, the SP's own big domain of California set a fourth one free.

Shortly after the nationally headlined robbery at faraway Leliaetta, a California trial jury had acquitted Bill Dalton of any complicity in the Alila robbery. By the same token, Grat should have been freed in the earlier proceedings.[1]

Meantime, evidence indicated that the later holdup at Ceres had been the work of the Sontag-Evans gang.[2] Certain facts also suggested that the three previous train hauls, in the San Joaquin Valley, including the one at Alila, had been staged by this previously unidentified band, lying low and letting the Daltons take the rap. Under the circumstances, it was politically expedient for the giant corporation to change its tactics toward Bill.

Bill walked out of the Tulare County jail, crowing like a cock of the walk. Yessir, by God, he'd licked the Southern Pacific! Pinned down Leland Stanford's ears like no other California farmer ever had before. Put the Dalton brand on the Iron Horse and made Will Smith look like a stray pup with the colic. Or so it seemed to him.

Conceivably, the SP might have forgotten Bill if Emmett and Bob hadn't started playing with trains back in Oklahoma. Or if somebody had providentially shot fugitive brother Grat. Or if Bill had given some sign that he would stay out of politics instead of continuing to try to beard the ruling dynasty at Sacramento.

Soon it was pretty obvious why he actually had been freed. The authorities hoped he would lead them to Grat; they started following him everywhere. Bill decided on some counter-strategy of his own.

Six weeks after the Leliaetta robbery, the SP's detectives and Oklahoma authorities decided on a combined operation against Daltons. They hoped that a joining of forces and a pooling of evidence might result not only in the capture of Bob and Emmett in Oklahoma but also in the nabbing of Grat. They believed he was still hiding in Tulare County, where, suspiciously, Bill had remained after the trial.

Deputy Chris Madsen was assigned by Chief Marshal Grimes of Oklahoma to go to San Francisco and confer with Southern Pacific detectives, including, presumably, Will Smith. Madsen, then stationed at El Reno, was given a railroad pass good for transportation to the California city. His route lay through Kingfisher, where the train stopped for a few minutes. There at the station the marshal sighted none other than William Marion Dalton, who greeted him with a casual "Hello, Chris."

Madsen tried to hide his amazement at seeing Bill Dalton on the soil of Oklahoma. When the devil had he gotten back, and how? In some way, the tricky Bill had managed to slip past the continued surveillance of the Southern Pacific's keenest operatives.[3]

The question was still plaguing the marshal when he reached California. His first stop was at Visalia, where Sheriff Kay showed him $3,000, stowed in a safe as a reward for whoever might kill or capture Grat Dalton.

Madsen then went on to San Francisco, where he was scheduled to confer with the railroad's general attorney. Only then did the lawman spring his bombshell:

"I saw Bill Dalton in Kingfisher, Oklahoma, just a few days ago."

The lawyer jumped out of his chair. "That can't be, Mr. Madsen! Bill Dalton's right down in Tulare County. Our detectives have him spotted every minute."

Chris grinned. "Better buy your detectives some eyeglasses, then."

The attorney was getting angry. "Are you sure that the man you saw was Bill Dalton?" Then, in the manner of a prosecutor grilling a witness: "Would you know Dalton if you saw him?"

Madsen laughed. "Mr. Lawyer, I know every Dalton of the

name. Bought beef from his brother-in-law to feed my soldiers when I was the supply sergeant at El Reno. I even talked to Bill a few minutes at Kingfisher."

The railroad man was mightily upset. "We'll verify that assertion of yours!" he stormed. He called in a secretary and ordered telegrams sent to the SP operatives in Tulare County.

Soon enough came the answer. Bill Dalton had left Tulare County two weeks before. During that period, he had fooled detectives by getting another man to dress in his clothes and drive around with Bill's wife in a buggy.

It was a slick job, for sure. But then Bill Dalton was the brainy one of the family. He had proved it again.

Before going, he had arranged for Grat to get a fresh horse in furtherance of his brother's escape. Undoubtedly he had managed meetings with Grat, after using one dodge or another to shake off nosy sleuths. Naturally, the authorities would have trumped up some charge to hold him had they suspected he was planning to leave California.

But now he was back in Oklahoma, a free man, strutting boldly around with no legal complaints of any kind against him. Not long afterward, Littleton Dalton would also return, to farm peacefully at Kingfisher.

Marshal Grimes's deputies weren't worrying about Littleton. Bill was somebody to watch, though. If they still hadn't heard of the dispute which had followed Leliaetta, their fears soon proved well founded. Bill Dalton's return meant that the Dalton Gang was back in business.

Bill left his wife and six children in California while he got the lay of things in Oklahoma. He instructed Jennie to write to him under various names at remote post offices. Too many frontier postmasters were tipping marshals about who got mail from whom. They were, of course, violating federal rules about the privacy of communications, but many of these officials also ran general stores whose tills might be temptations to outlaws.

It would have been futile, however, as well as dangerous, for Bill to have gone under an alias in Oklahoma, where he was so generally well known. He had to establish a respectable identity that would let him move freely around Oklahoma while keeping in contact through devious, law-proof ways with his fugitive brothers.

Often he was around Kingfisher, where his family lived. What was more natural than that a dutiful son would come often to visit his aging mother?

Poor Ma Dalton! Many were the uses that her prodigals made of her, even to touching the harassed old lady for

money during their frequent spells of being hard up. Bill now
was utilizing her motherly love as a screen through which he
could watch the marshals always hanging around this dusty
county seat, made so uncomfortably prominent by Daltons.

Officially, Bill's residence was Bartlesville, Oklahoma, next
county seat across the border from his old home town of
Coffeyville, Kansas. Prodigals pine for familiar pastures,
especially when alien ranges have turned into so much scrub
grass. At Bartlesville, Bill set himself up as a land trader.

Some of the proceeds from the haul at Leliaetta may
have gone to stake Bill in that new start. The need to help
a returning brother may have been a main reason for Bob's
having short-potted his followers. Bill had lost everything, including his reputation, for his brothers out there in California.
They had to put him on his feet again and everybody else
be damned.

Conveniently, too, Bartlesville was near the Osage Hills,
where Bob and Emmett reportedly had been seen. Some of
the initial conferences of Bill with his brothers may have been
held in the isolated shack of some full-blood, given an ap-
preciated couple of dollars for playing host.

Bill began prospering as a realtor. Homestead relinquish-
ments could often be bought from discouraged nesters for as
little as five or ten dollars—house, well, land and everything
else going in the deal. Then the equity could be resold at
many times that amount to some sucker lured west by the
gaudy advertising of land bureaus set up by the railroads.
Through comparable methods, Florence Quick had acquired
the love nest she had shared with her Bob at Buffalo Springs.

Indirectly Bill Dalton was profiting from the railroads which
he so despised. There were other ways in which he meant
to collect from them, too.

After a while, the people around Bartlesville and Coffeyville
uncrossed their fingers about Bill. They remembered him as
trifling Lewis Dalton's son, who had gone roaming farther
west without a dollar or an extra pair of pants. His brothers
having gone wild was another blemish in the eyes of the
respectables who nodded casually when they saw him, then
passed on. Everybody knew, too, that he had been im-
plicated in some trouble with the boys out in California.[4]

But now they saw him paying cash for his purchases in
local stores, glimpsed wads of greenbacks in his wallet when
he opened it to pay. Old man Dalton had always owed everybody. Bill could play a fiddle sweet and tell a yarn as well
as his dad, but unlike his sire he always had that dollar in

his pocket. Folks began to believe that one of Lewis Dalton's sons had amounted to something, after all.

But Bill Dalton had come back to Oklahoma with one central purpose in mind, a purpose that was an obsession well concealed. He was going to get even with the railroads, as his brothers already had done so effectively. The gang they had organized gave him the ready-made striking force he needed.

18

THE DALTON
INTELLIGENCE SYSTEM

SERENE months passed for the Dalton boy now so busily "making good." Bill showed up at country church services and at public displays of righteousness staged by such worthy organizations as the King's Daughters and the Royal Neighbors of America. He read the weekly *Kansas City Star*—fifty cents a year, with a free thermometer as a premium—and agreeably sawed the fiddle for Saturday-night breakdowns.

How could anyone believe that such a charming gentleman would be involved in looting and long riding? Bill Dalton was wearing a mask far more effective than the ones his brothers wrapped around their faces when they went out on a train job.

Easily, plausibly, playing his cards close to the vest, Bill Dalton had established the public identity he needed in his private war against the railroads. Untouched by precinct constable or federal marshal, he proceeded to build a strong foundation for the gang's future operations.

He helped his brothers forge the most efficient intelligence system enjoyed by any gang, up to its time, in American history. Assisting him was Florence Quick, who functioned as the band's inside gal while he was its outside man.

In fulfillment of her duties, the lady had added still another name to her long list of monickers. She was now calling herself "Mrs. Mundy," having shacked up with an eminently honest citizen bearing that handle. Her responsibilities were to keep the band provided with broncs, since the Daltons themselves had become somewhat allergic to horse-stealing after that escapade at Twin Mounds, and to continue doing specialized jobs of spying.

Florence also was message bearer for Bill to his brothers, whom he saw only at rare intervals. Too much open contact with the boys had washed him up in California. He wasn't making *that* mistake in Oklahoma. What excuses Florence made to Mr. Mundy for her frequent absences from home and hearth are unknown; she probably gave none. Bob Dalton got a kick out of cuckolding a jasper.

At Kingfisher, Brothers Littleton and Ben were peacefully cultivating their corn, staving off detectives who kept calling in the guise of book agents, but themselves creating no more commotion than a pair of ground squirrels. Brother Bill, still temperamentally opposed to plow-pushing, gradually extended his operations throughout the Territory.

Wherever he went he made friends with nester-elected sheriffs, who often felt highly flattered to be on good-buddy terms with a brother of the Daltons. But with none of these granger star flashers did Bill make the mistake that he had made by sharing the skillet with Sheriff O'Neil in California.

He trusted no man who wore a badge. If legal papers had to be served in connection with a land deal, he paid the officer the fee required by law and maybe added a little extra. Bill Dalton had learned how to use grafting minor lawmen instead of letting them use him.

Before long, he could start expressing his opinion of the railroads and other monopolies. Obliquely, of course, he was creating public sentiment for his brothers, "persecuted" by the railroads, though he never discussed them. Anyhow, most people had manners enough not to mention Bob and Emmett and Grat before him. But what he said about the "wolves of Wall Street" struck home to the farmers and little ranchers who heard him talk.

Friendly Bill was always complimenting the ladies, always setting up the kids to candy. Foxy Bill was seen and heard all over Oklahoma, joshing with the boys in the barber-shops, denouncing the big interests while studying how to grow big himself. He was doing well with real estate while running a strictly private side business.

In that side business, his gun-slinging siblings were his only clients. He was strengthening their enterprise, now being quietly reorganized as veteran helpers were called back to the job. The Dalton undertaking, of course, maintained its established objective: robbing the trains that chugged back and forth across Oklahoma. For all of Bill's help, however, operations chief Bob Dalton never learned enough about sound business principles to put aside something for reserve capital when the marshals might be pressing them hard.

In fact, Bob often was pointedly annoyed by the advice his older brother proffered. Bill might have the advantage of years, but Bob felt himself the smarter Dalton: he had dodged jail in California while Bill had landed in it. Resentment and rivalry sometimes flared between the two during their in-frequent meetings, with Emmett stepping in to resolve arguments about the way Bob kept the books—or didn't keep any.

Money came hard from the Dalton trade of engine-boarding. It went easy across the gaming tables in the Indian and ranching settlements where road agents always felt safest. A lot of currency or its equivalent found its way into the jeans of Jim Riley's cowpunchers, with whom the desperados staged frequent gambling sprees.

"Swiped cash is fast cash"—the Daltons were the living proof of the pithiest tradition of outlawry. Stories about the gang's having prudently buried treasure all over Oklahoma are even less credible than comparable ones about Jean Lafitte's pirates in Louisiana or Captain Kidd's sea rovers in New Jersey. Buccaneers, of land or water, seldom cached a dollar, and even less often saved one.

Bill Dalton always demanded his cut from a train holdup. Written evidence indicates that he generally got it. Bob Dalton probably spent a lot of money on gewgaws for Florence Quick—they could often be bought from pack peddlers destined to become merchant princes after outlaw customers would be in their graves. Emmett was undoubtedly as free-handed with Julia Johnson. But the biggest drain on the gang's treasury was the disproportionate share of loot that had to be laid out for protection. It was an expenditure that Bill Dalton grudgingly approved of, having no choice in that land of hard-luckers.

Too many people in southwestern Oklahoma knew the Dalton fugitives by sight or reputation, whatever their "road brands"—those various aliases under which they traveled. Tactfully demanding hands were stretched toward them, hands that multiplied and kept asking for more as the rewards offered for the gang mounted.

Men who had hated the Daltons as marshals now cottoned to them as friends. "Tickbirds," the brothers contemptuously called such "friends," because they ticked with information and other services—so long as the money flowed.

The brothers found themselves acting as Oklahoma Robin Hoods simply because it was too dangerous to be otherwise. They had to depend on the tickbirds for temporary hiding places, for misdirections given pursuing posses, for various other things required by men on the dodge.

Tight pockets would have been sheer suicide. Two deputy sheriffs in Guthrie had to be paid and kept drunk at furtive meetings so that any cross-information passed on to their superiors would be flimsy and unincriminating. "Loans" never made good were another way of making the Daltons shell out. Bob "lent" one man $400 to build a new horse stable—because the brothers had a few times lodged their ponies in the old one. Not long afterward, $800 more went to the tickbird's wife to buy a piano for their daughter. Once the girl did bang out "Lead Kindly Light" for the visitors, her performance somehow failing to make the boys feel any more spiritual.

So the Daltons bribed and the upright thundered because they went uncaught. More "Pinks" and railroad bulls swarmed into Oklahoma under more guises. Will Smith himself came from California and went to Ma Dalton's home at Kingfisher posing as a distributor of sample garden seeds. Recognizing him, Littleton politely sent the SP's champion Dalton chaser trudging down the dusty Oklahoma road.

The marshals, often irritated by the presence of so many outsiders, kept hunting and searching in vain. Riches the Daltons never accumulated, but—and this was their most impressive achievement—they built an espionage network never equalled in the records of American banditry.

Their system functioned right within the heart of the enemy camp—at Guthrie, the territorial capital till the civic hustlers of Oklahoma City grabbed the distinction away. Contributing to its efficiency was the know-how gained by the Daltons when they had been of the hunters instead of among the hunted.

Bill Dalton continued doing a top job as intelligence director. Florence Quick kept helping with an incomparable combination of sex and wit. She was the smoothest, shrewdest woman outlaw who ever popped up out of the sagebrush. By comparison, Belle Starr was no more than a sly frontier slut.

Flo was dreaming now of building another love nest with Bob Dalton, whatever heartbreak such a move might entail for Mr. Mundy. The Guthrie marshals' corps suspected that her flexible heart still beat most for Bob—but try and catch 'em together! Then, to make the lawman sublimely embarrassed, Bill, the smartest Dalton, turned up in the capital.

He hung around the Silver Dollar saloon a lot, joshing, drinking and impressing the other customers with that informed tongue of his. Local citizens wondered whether he would hitch up with the Democrats, the Republicans or the emerging Populists, who were urging farmers "to raise less corn and more hell." Backslapping, big-talking Bill didn't seem to be immediately involved in territorial politics, yet the brains of the Dalton combine did nothing to change the general impression of him as a potential vote wrangler.

Soon he was cottoning up to the marshals, who were also outwardly chummy, in the traditional pattern of frontier politeness. They couldn't extradite him to California because that state still hadn't been able to lodge against him any charge that would stick. Undoubtedly, Bill hoped to glean scraps of information from the officers and they, in turn, kept watching him for some slip that would betray his brothers.

Bill, a thoroughgoing legal buff, loved to attend sessions of various courts in the raw young territory. Nesters also enjoyed the trials because they were dramatic breaks in hard, hum-drum living. A good many well-known people showed up at these legal tussles. None was approached more often by men with hoe-callused hands than the brother of the awesome Daltons. And how satisfying it was to drop a certain name around afterward: "Now I ain't a-holdin' by law-breakin', but I reckon the Dalton boys ain't half as bad as them thievin' land grabbers that run the railroads."

Then, with an unctuous clearing of the throat: "I know the brother of them boys—Bill Dalton; he's sure a well-posted feller."

Jovial Mr. Dalton became amply posted indeed on the doings of Oklahoma jurisprudence, territorial and federal. Serving as his voluntary "court reporters" in ten southwestern Oklahoma counties were many of those God-fearing men of the hoe. The way in which the courts functioned was a matter of immense personal interest to the gang.

They needed to know which of their friends were standing trial for horse stealing or cattle rustling . . . what other sympathizers had qualified as jurors in one or another piece of litigation. Trials also exposed tickbirds who came forward as witnesses against Dalton allies, for every conviction might become a trail leading to their principal hideout on Jim Riley's ranch or their secondary ones in the Ouachita Mountains, near the border of Arkansas.

Bill Dalton next added to the string of informers the two "old deputies" at Kingfisher, where the federal court sat periodically. These two guardians of law craved liquor even more than they did cash, and the Dalton front man saw that they got plenty of it—brimming jugs of stomach-scalding Ozark 'shine. Chris Madsen and Heck Thomas suspected that these lawmen had some connection with the outlaws, but tolerated them because the deputies now and then passed on scraps of information to them.

It was a high old time for organized outlawry. The Daltons

were making mock of whatever passed for law and government in raw new country. To make everything worse, more foolhardly plowhands were imitating the Dalton example and taking to a life of crime, on a petty scale. Meantime, Congress had shown no more common sense in a couple of actions reflecting the usual bullheadedness of "statesmen."

It had emasculated Judge Isaac Parker's highly effective court at Fort Smith, and the nooses on George Maledon's gallows dangled without necks to fill them. At the same time, it failed to appropriate adequate funds for the fight against the gangs of criminals that roamed the territory.

The Daltons collected quickly whenever they went rampaging. But the marshals still had to wait six to eight months for their lamentably low pay.

19

DORMANT WINTER, DALLYING SPRING

THE gang remained dormant for several months, except for
some small jobs, which cannot even be traced positively to
them. The men whom Bob had cheated, then fired, were
drifting back too slowly to sustain the morale of the band.
Bill Doolin, who followed sternly the tenet of honesty among
thieves, was reluctant to ride again under a Dalton.

Sensation-mongering newspapers, and a sequence of events
spelling gradual reunion of the brigands, led by Bob Dalton,
were to alter the situation. A rash of train and bank robberies broke out across America. Thus far, the Daltons had
only looked crossways at banks. Yet the screaming journals
—and popular mythology—charged them with every cracking
of a vault, besides every halting of an engine.

Two trains were held up on the same night at St. Charles,
Missouri, and El Paso, Texas, a thousand miles apart. Naturally, the Daltons pulled off both jobs—by the contradictory
accounts of the Wichita *Eagle* and the Galveston *News,* both
of which circulated widely in Oklahoma. At that time, Emmett Dalton was comfortably holed up in the dugout on Jim
Riley's ranch, sometimes giving a hand with the line riding
and being paid standard cowpuncher wages for it. Bob was
getting caught up on his loving with Florence Quick, who was
taking a vacation from faithful Mr. Mundy.

Little is known of that second haven of bliss, which Flo
set up in remote Greer County, Texas. Flo made this new
home of an outlaw pair comfortable, having stuff shipped to
her under an assumed name from the Montgomery Ward
mail-order house in Fort Worth. Some of it may have been
paid for by the unsuspecting Mr. Mundy, who always gave
the girl ready access to his poke.

Bill Powers probably spotted the place for Florence and
Bob. At that time, he was working on a ranch in the general
area and using the alias of "Tom Evans." Powers was a
frequent visitor to the charming menage on the prairies. So
was somebody identified by Ransom Payne only as "Texas
Jack," which was Dick Broadwell's short-handle alias.

True brings low tar and low nicotine to the 100mm smoker.

True 100's.

100's Regular and 100's Menthol:
12 mg. "tar", 0.7 mg. nicotine,
av. per cigarette, by FTC method.

©Lorillard 1975

True Menthol brings low tar and low nicotine to the 100mm smoker.

True Menthol 100's.

100's Regular and 100's Menthol:
12 mg. "tar", 0.7 mg. nicotine,
av. per cigarette, by FTC method.

Warning: The Surgeon General Has Determined
That Cigarette Smoking Is Dangerous to Your Health.

Florence and Bob supposedly spent the winter of 1891 at the Greer County place, though Flo managed to keep her man Mundy on the string. With Bob not minding, she stole enough broncs for resale in Texas to keep victuals on the table. Lending her skilled hands in the wide-loop jobs were Powers and Broadwell.

It was a pleasant winter for Daltons, the most peaceful one they had known in years. Emmett became a now-and-then visitor to the rendezvous, sometimes riding up with Broadwell and Powers.

Bitter Creek Newcomb had the cold months warmed for him by Rose Dunn, who lived near Stillwater, Oklahoma. A prairie Lolita, Rose was also more than friendly with Bill Doolin, although continually snubbing an unattached road agent called Red Buck Weightman. A hive of outlaws, disguised as a town and named Ingalls, had sprung up near the Dunn ranch. There Bitter Creek, Doolin, and Red Buck often went to guzzle and gamble at Old Man Murray's saloon. Most of their time they spent barricaded in the famous Rock Fort, which Bee Dunn had built on his spread as a profitable hostel for freebooters inconvenienced by posses. The "Fort" was but a few miles of easy commutation from Ingalls to the southeast. Dunn had five brothers and cousins who protected their guests by scouting the bushes for lawmen.

Bill Dalton, too, was often around Ingalls, which had been a main jump-off point for the '89 Land Run. Here he could always pick up patches of land that were dirt cheap and make a little on the turnover. He made his headquarters in the combination lodging house and whorehouse operated by Mrs. Mary Pierce, no known relation to Charlie Pierce but a good friend of all bandits who shelled out for her rooms and her girls.

During his land trafficking, Bill Dalton discovered a large, deep cave near the six-shooter hamlet. Quietly he stocked it with guns and ammunition, purchased in roundabout ways. Another link had been added to the Dalton chain of retreats.

Subtly, too, as Bill traveled around Oklahoma, he gave the impression that his brothers had left the country and that their band had dissolved for keeps. He hoped to divert the marshals from their continuing chase, and he wanted to create an atmosphere which would let him bring his wife and children from California.

Brother Bill, unlike old Lewis Dalton, had become a devoted family man. Whether or not he ever visited his son by his luckless first marriage is a matter of conjecture, but he genuinely missed his six children in California and his pretty

wife. Jennie Blivens Dalton was as good a woman as Adeline
Younger Dalton, her mother-in-law, and fared much better
at the hands of her husband.

Of the "bad" Daltons, only Bill had any realistic goals for
his meanness. Bob and Emmett talked incessantly and ro-
mantically about winding up as ranchers in Mexico or Argen-
tina. Bill wanted passionately to give his young-uns educa-
tions and good starts in life. Of course, to accomplish this,
he was ready to rob other Oklahomans with children of their
last acres, take saddle with hoof in some devious horse
trade or, if he could have gotten away with it, steal the dome
of the capitol at Guthrie.

All was well with the Daltons. Very well with Bill, doing
all right for himself in Oklahoma. Well as could be expected
for Emmett and Bob, with prices uncollected on their
brash heads.

More and more feats of banditry had been credited to them
as the icicles began melting on the cockleburrs and ground
squirrels came crawling out of their burrows to soak in the
first warming rays of the spring sun. Daltons were said to have
committed daring holdups from the Rio Grande river to the
Platte, and in states where they would never set foot. The
publicity was helpful: it sent Oklahoma's officers on wild-
goose chases to faraway points.

Spring weather grew warmer and the headlines grew hot-
ter. Certainly Bob Dalton enjoyed seeing his picture in so
many papers, brought back by Florence Quick from Guthrie
every time she made a trip from Greer County to tap
Mr. Mundy and check on the marshals. Emmett equally enjoyed showing ragged clippings to Julia Johnson when she
slipped down a grapevine from her window on his surreptitious visits to her parents' claim on Little Caney River.

Daltons were getting lots of recognition as outlaws, by
golly! More than they ever had been accorded as lawmen.

Yes, spring of that year, 1892, was mighty easy to take.
New season for young bloods full of the wilder juices of life.

Nice months they were. Lazy months . . .

Then Grat rode in.

20

ROBBERY AT RED ROCK

GRAT needed a haircut and a hot meal. As solace for his troubles, he also needed to rob a train.

He had spent the winter holed up in an icy cave of the California hills with a stray mongrel dog and a fellow escapee from Tulare County jail as his companions.[1] His human partner had been one Riley Dean, not to be confused with Riley Martin, another Dalton associate.

Dean had been caught when a combined posse from several counties had risked avalanches to track the fugitives across treacherous ridges and snow-crested canyons, but Grat had managed to get away.

Two thousand miles in one hundred and seven days, Grat had ridden, from California, where a small fortune in reward money lay on his head, to Oklahoma, where his carcass would have also been worth considerable cash. Stolen horses along the way had been his transportation on that long route south and east to home country. Basque shepherds and lone Chinese prospectors had sometimes sheltered him and given him cooked food as a change from raw rabbit meat gotten from deadfalls. Across Arizona, New Mexico, and the sparsely inhabited Texas Panhandle he had journeyed, dodging lawmen who were looking for him along the way.[2]

Grat had been wary when he finally reached Oklahoma, knowing that the marshals would expect him to be heading home. Tickbirds had given him shelter and scraps of information that led him to the gang's headquarters on Riley's ranch. But, remembering an experience in California, he talked to no "friend" too much nor tarried in any shack too long.

While he had been holed up in the Fresno County mountains, his mother had sent a supposed sympathizer a money order which was supposed to be cashed and the sum given to Grat. Instead, his supposed confederate had tipped off the authorities and that had brought a posse to send the fugitive scurrying again.[3]

Bob rushed from Greer County for a reunion with the brother whose "record making" ride had eclipsed that fast

123

one Bill McElhanie and Bob himself had made from California. Emmett cooked mammoth meals to put some fat on Grat's shrunken frame. Ma Dalton embraced her miraculously still-alive son at another of those touching meetings near the colored community of Dover.[4] Then old friends started dropping into the dugout on Riley's ranch to get Grat's first-hand account of the escape that made Oklahoma's outlaw grapevine buzz.

Grat, the hero. Good old Grat. The Dalton boy of the charmed life. And a good man to ride with, however much Bob had fretted you by that short-potting deal. Even Bill Doolin felt so—and Doolin's opinions carried plenty of weight among all of Oklahoma's long riders.

That glow of good will for Grat helped the Dalton gang to reconstitute itself on a potentially effective level. Bob may have promised to stick to fair divvies. Bill Dalton urged him to get the gang's operations rolling again.

The prodigal's return called for a celebration, and clearly Grat was itchingly expecting one. William Marion Dalton showed that he knew how to throw a party—even if other obligations kept him from attending it in person.

June 1, 1892: federal court was in session at Kingfisher, seat of Oklahoma Territory's fifth judicial district. The grand jury had questioned various tickbirds about the present residence of Bob and Emmett Dalton, while trying to verify rumors that Grat was now back in Oklahoma. But no birds had sung, because this was Dalton territory, where a stool-pigeon might get quickly winged.

That night, Marshal Chris Madsen sat in the lobby of a local hotel, discussing the situation with the federal judge and the federal prosecutor of the district. In breezed Bill Dalton, smoking a stogie, looking mighty happy and hailing everybody he saw.

Bill glanced at the big clock over the clerk's desk: nine P.M. Then he ambled over toward the three court officials, sat down with an amiable howdy and began chatting.

Nine-five. Bill's tongue kept running on while his eyes strayed once more toward the clock. Timepieces were important to Daltons, that night.

At that moment, Bob, Emmett and Grat were approaching the little town of Red Rock on the Otoe Indian Reservation, forty miles south of Arkansas City, Kansas. With them rode Bill Doolin, Dick Broadwell, Bitter Creek Newcomb, Charlie Pierce and Bill Powers. Eight men, the corps numbered, the largest mobilization for any job ever attempted by the Daltons.

The night was illuminated by flashes of lightning, sometimes zig-zagging across the tracks of the Santa Fe Railroad that bisected the village. The two or three stores were closed.

Grat's eyes bulged when he saw the rails. He started twitching in his saddle. His hand strayed to his forty-five. Bob reached out and grabbed his brother's wrist.

"Easy, boy," Bob laughed. "There ain't even a boxcar in sight."

The bandits took up different vantage points along the tracks, with Bob keeping a sharp eye on the impatient Grat. Nine-thirty P.M. Back in Kingfisher, Bill Dalton was still gabbing with the men of the court, still doing his furtive clock watching. Here in Red Rock, the boys' fingers brushed gun butts, keyed up and ready, as a regularly scheduled southbound train rounded a bend and chugged into the hamlet.

"Whoopee!" Grat yelled. "There she is! Let's go git her!"

The bandits spurred forward. Then Emmett called cautiously:

"Hold on, boys, there's something funny here. Look at that coach behind the express car. It's dark as hell."

"Maybe we better be gittin' out of here," suggested cautious Bill Doolin.

Bob agreed: "This does look funny." He craned his neck to see better. "That station agent is acting damned queer —as if he's expecting something to happen."

The train had stopped. The agent had gone into the express car. Bandit lookouts could see him conferring with the messenger. The engine kept spitting steam. A few passengers were dozing in the day coaches. Lights shone and flickered and came on again in various cars. But one—the smoking car— remained ominously dark.

Grat unstrapped the Winchester attached to his saddle. "Come on," he said disgustedly: "we're actin' like a bunch of old women."

Bob again restrained the big fellow, grasping the rifle barrel. "Careful, Grat. That deadhead could be as dangerous as a rattlesnake."

Bob's manner was a warning. All caught it except Grat. Bill Powers spoke:

"If I ever git bushwhacked, I don't want it to be from a goddam train, by son-of-a-bitchin' railroad guards."

The train's engineer pulled the throttle. The cars started rolling south as the bandits quickly reined their horses into dense patches of foliage lining the tracks. Afterward they gathered by the right-of-way in glum frustration.

"Gold-bricked again," Bill Doolin fumed, in his harsh voice an implied criticism of Bob Dalton's leadership.

"I think we been hurrahed," commented Bill Powers.

Grat Dalton said nothing but tears of rage and self-pity were rolling down his cheeks. He had been called a train robber in California and he had tried to be one in Oklahoma. He still had only the name, without the authentic fame that should have gone with it.

"Well," Dick Broadwell said resignedly. "Looks like we better be tailin' out."

Bob Dalton raised his hand. "Not yet, pardners." His ears were tuned to a gathering vibration along the tracks. The vibrations grew louder.

"I thought so," Bob murmured. "Here comes the *real* train."

A few minutes later, a second phalanx of coaches, all properly lighted, stopped in Red Rock. Grat Dalton was first man on the engine. Whooping, he sprang from his saddle into the cab to pull a weapon on the surprised engineer.

This train carried not a single officer of the law. A special force, heavily armed, had been posted in the decoy string by railroad officials after they had received word, through some source, that robbery was in the offing. Even on this second train the bandits met unexpected resistance from two courageous express-company employees—messenger E. S. Whittlesey and guard John A. Riehl.

This pair grabbed rifles and began firing to prevent the holdups from boarding the express coach. Sixty volleys were exchanged back and forth between the defenders, shooting through open windows, and the attackers, now dismounted and crouching by the tracks.

After a quarter-of-an-hour battle, the express men gave up the contest. Bob Dalton and two henchmen charged into the car, only to encounter resistance of a passive type from messenger Whittlesey, a man worth the money that the express company paid him.

"Open the safe door, you son of a bitch," Bob ordered.

"Can't," Whittlesey snapped. "Don't know the combination."

Gun threats directed at the messenger failed to produce the code of numbers that would have opened the safe. One of the bandits found a sledge hammer in the coach. He swung it at the safe. The door crashed open. The robbers looted the box. Afterward they ripped open boxes of merchandise, being shipped by express, to help themselves. Some of the swag was feminine finery meant for Bob's mistress,

Flo Quick; Emmett's flame, Julia Johnson; and Bitter Creek's little inamorata, Rose Dunn.

Even the lunchboxes of the trainmen were grabbed by the brigands. The boys must have been hungry after their long ride.

At ten P.M. by the clock in the express coach at Red Rock, the robbery was finished. The jubilant outlaws rode off with their booty into the pitch-black thickets of the Otoe Reservation.[5]

At ten by the clock in the hotel lobby in Kingfisher, Bill Dalton yawned and spoke to his companions.

"*Ten* o'clock, gentlemen. Guess I'll be hitting the hay, but I'll be seeing you for breakfast. Good night."

After he had gone, the judge and the prosecutor looked inquiringly at Marshal Madsen. "Chris," the judge said, "you forgot your manners by not introducing your friend. Who is he?"

Madsen flushed. "He's Bill Dalton, Judge. I didn't figure you'd want to know the brother of Grat and Emmett and Bob—those thieves."

The judge chuckled. "I would have liked to have been introduced to their brother."

Madsen was nettled, but the judge was his superior, whose wish had to be respected. "All right sir," he replied, "I'll see that you meet Mr. Dalton in the morning."

So at breakfast, in the hotel dining room, the marshal introduced Bill Dalton to the judge and the prosecutor. The four sat down at the same table. Chris Madsen and the judge were seated beside each other; Bill and the prosecutor sat opposite them across the board.

Kingfisher's telegraph office was opening as the four began their meal. Madsen was lifting a cup of coffee to his mouth when a messenger ran in with a telegram addressed to him. The marshal read the wire, then handed it to the judge.

"Read it aloud, sir," he said, "so everybody can hear it." He stole a quick glance at Bill Dalton, who looked back at him nonchalantly.

The message was the law's first knowledge of the Red Rock holdup. Signed by the chief detective of the Wells-Fargo Express Company, it said that the Dalton gang had held up the Santa Fe train at ten P.M. the night before.

Ten was the time at which Bill had excused himself for bed, placing such emphasis upon the hour. There was a silence at the table. Unflinchingly, Bill met the gazes of his three fellow breakfasters. He took a sip from his coffee cup, then spoke.

"Well, gentlemen, I can't prove I wasn't at Red Rock *last night*," he said, broadly badgering them, knowing full well that he could prove by these very minions of the law that he was in their company at the time of the holdup. "But I hope to get some of the money if I can ever get in touch with my brothers," he added.

Then he found some reason for leaving, content to enjoy the moment of triumph by leaving the three petrified. But Chris Madsen knew now what he had always suspected: that Bill Dalton was hand in glove with his outlaw brothers.[6]

Fifty thousand dollars was the estimate of the loot made by the Wells-Fargo detective in the wire. Emmett, in his book, declared it to be eleven thousand—thirty-eight hundred of which, he claimed, was buried in "the shifting sand dunes" of the South Canadian River.

That, of course, was poppycock. Desperados are always required to bury money as a part of the plot in any standard outlaw thriller.

"Haunted money, if you like, lying there somewhere," Emmett stated in one of his grandiose fillips. Try to find it!

Madsen's later estimate of the take, based upon a revised express-company accounting, was $1600. Were this figure trustworthy and not a low one put out by Wells-Fargo to reassure frightened customers, the spoils would have amounted to only $200 apiece for each of the eight plunderers.

Four or five thousand dollars, the likeliest total, would have given the bandits less than $900 apiece, with some of the loot having to be doled out to tickbirds to keep them in tune.

In any case, the robbery did a great deal for two Daltons: Bill and Grat.

Long afterward, Chris Madsen uncovered a letter written by Bill from the Silver Dollar Saloon at Guthrie to his wife in California. Quoting from Madsen's manuscript:

"He [Bill] told her about the lucky hold-up at Red Rock, and said for her not to worry about him—that he was with the Federal authorities at Kingfisher the night the robbery was made—and further that the boys had sent him some money."

The money, of course, was Bill's expected cut. In the letter, found too late for Madsen to use as evidence, there was mention of a $130 enclosure to pay a note held by the bank at Visalia and an unstated sum for herself.

Jennie Dalton evidently diverted the cash to bring herself and the children to Oklahoma, though she may have winced at using stolen money for carfare. Two weeks or so after the Red Rock robbery, she and her youngsters arrived to join the head of the family in the territory where the Dalton name had become so notorious.

As for the children's Uncle Grat, he was as proud as any of them would have been over winning a marble game. He was an honest-to-God train robber now. A gen-u-*wyne* experienced coach hopper. Engineers had better watch out.

Yep, old Grat had proved he could do anything his brothers could do. That meant more to him than four aces at poker. Grat Dalton had graduated. Let Will Smith stick that in his corncob and smoke it!

HOOF DUST

THE Red Rock robbery touched off of one of the greatest outlaw hunts in the history of the Southwest. Conductor Harry Wilcox had lost no time in notifying Santa Fe officials of the holdup. After leaving Red Rock he stopped the train at the first town with a telegraph office and sent a message to the railroad's dispatcher at Arkansas City. Deputy Marshal Heck Thomas immediately set out from Guthrie with a posse headed north toward the scene of the robbery. Because of some old grudges, Thomas was particularly anxious to nab Bill Doolin.

Santa Fe special officers from Purcell, Oklahoma, joined the posse that Thomas had led to Red Rock. Curiously, however, the railroad would always decline to make any positive identification of the Daltons as the bandits who had robbed its train. Maybe it would have been bad advertising for the line to admit that its routes were haunted by Daltons.

Up from Guthrie, also, came Logan County Sheriff John W. Hixon, who had once worn a distinguished badge on the savage frontiers of Kansas.[1] Siding him were twenty-five deputies. Hixon, with his flair for melodrama, swore to newsmen that he would "press on until the trail ended or the robbers were overtaken." [2]

Thirteen marshals, led by Deputies Frank Kress and George Orin Severns, based themselves at Purcell to comb the rugged Cimarron Hills, where the outlaws were known to have many friends and volunteer informants. Ransom Payne headed west, leading a posse of sixteen men toward Greer County, someone having gotten wind of the new love bower established there by Flo Quick for her Bob.

Southward a party moved out from Caldwell, Kansas, "fully armed to do good battle." Kansans living on the border of turbulent Oklahoma had become as fearful as their forebears who had been compelled to put up with Missouri as a neighbor. But the Daltons also had friends and tickbirds in the Jayhawker State, including men who did business with

Brother Bill and a certain Coffeyville innkeeper who was always ready to extend them hospitality in stealthy post-midnight visits.

Cherokee police joined in the hunt since the Otoe Reservation bordered that part of their republic called the Cherokee Outlet. Chief Marshal Grimes welcomed help from any quarter, being under heavy fire from the press for having failed so far to catch the Daltons.

Three train robberies they had now committed in Oklahoma. Three times they had gotten away, with their ranks reduced by only one member—Blackface Charley Bryant.

The headlines sizzled. The Territorial officials in Guthrie raved. Strangely, nobody ordered Bill Dalton picked up for questioning or held as a material witness.

Originally the lawmen hoped to round up the bandits in a vast pincer movement covering almost a fourth of Oklahoma. Singly and in pairs, they would find the desperados, or so they hoped, counting on the boys' habit of scattering after a job. If even two or three of them could be brought back dead or alive, the impact upon the gang might be devastating. Certainly, harassed Chief Marshal Grimes could then feel safer in his post.

But Bob Dalton, the ex-marshal, anticipated every move of his former peers. Immediately after the Red Rock holdup, he led the band through big herds of horses and cattle owned by white and Indian ranchers. The hoof tracks of the herds would "kill" the trail of the outlaws by obliterating the prints left by their ponies. A couple of days was spent in this operation.

Then for twenty-four hours the gang split up into four pairs. Circling around within an agreed area, they met the following morning at a spring, forty miles west of Red Rock for a division of the booty. Afterward the eight long riders again dispersed.

Bill Powers and Bill Doolin raced toward the ranch of a shady character named McKinney on the South Canadian River near the Texas Panhandle. The evidence indicates that Powers had once been a hired gunslinger for McKinney. Bob, Grat and Emmett Dalton went to the sizable spread of Lee Moore on the North Canadian, fifteen miles away.

Somewhere in rugged brakes or in lonely canyons camped Charlie Pierce and Dick Broadwell. In some other hideaway under the skies, Bitter Creek Newcomb was spreading his blankets.

Day after day, the baffled posses were riding on the hunt for the most dangerous game. And as they rode, some of them, at least, knew that on the results depended their future and their reputation as lawmen.

John Hixon guessed that the Populists would be running some furious farmer against him for sheriff at Guthrie. Various deputy marshals knew they would be reduced to the hated hoe if Bill Grimes lost out as their chief. Ransom Payne hoped to get the job through his Kansas political connections if the ax descended on Grimes, his friend. Railroad officers hoped for promotion if they could bag an authentic bandit for a change instead of poor itinerants beating their way to jobs in the Kansas and Nebraska wheat fields. Indian policemen looked for coups that would land them appointments in the law-enforcement bodies of the palefaces.

Of the more than one hundred lawmen who were after the eight outlaws, Sheriff Hixon was the first to give up the chase. Guthrie, tough as Tombstone, might get even worse if he stayed away too long. Sixty miles west of Red Rock, he called off the hunt and brought his twoscore of deputies back home. On June 4, just three days after the robbery, his party, looking rather hangdog, returned to the capital.

By that time, the bandits were reported as having been seen at Fort Supply, an old army post where Indians had formerly come for the rations. A posse set out for the nester community that had grown up around the antiquated fort, led by an elderly constable bucking for sheriff.

The hopeful manhunters' ponies stirred up bushels of hoof dust. Annoyed prairie dogs squatted by their rows of burrows "barking" angrily at so many horsemen upsetting their peace. Lone riders who had never ridden with the Daltons sighted the posse at distances and made tracks for Texas or Colorado.

Now the pursuers began picking up "clues" that brought only more sweat and fatigue instead of reward and glory. Tightmouthed citizens began opening lips to report that this or that member of the gang had been seen here or there. Sagging spirits lifted when nesters or cowboys gave out with such leads that seemed to be so promising. Then hopes were dashed when the tips led only to some innocent emigrant "prospecting" for land or, more often, to nowhere.

By now the possemen should have realized the power of the Dalton grapevine—should have spotted a tickbird when they saw one. They didn't. Dalton sympathizers were having fun, hurrahing the harassed upholders of authority.

Officers would light down before some nester shack or some cowboy camp to make inquiries, to be received with buttered courtesy. They would be plied with solicitous in-

quiries: would they like a bit of grub or a drink of fresh
water from well or canteen? You never saw such cooperative
folks, such good citizens, so respectful of the badge, till the
badge flashers had ridden on.

Then all who had witnessed the scene would erupt into
cyclones of laughter. "The way them geese are flyin' ain't
the way I saw the Dalton boys flyin' the other day," somebody would remark.

"Damn right," would come an agreeable rejoinder. "The
Daltons ain't done nothin' but rob a train or two. I ain't
seein' myself sidin' no railroad."

Then would follow denunciations of the railroads, with
all big interests thrown in for good measure. A wagon freight-
er would express fear for his livelihood if the Iron Horse
extended its range to this patch of Oklahoma:

"Nobody will need me for haulin' if the railroad comes
through. Why, they kin run twenty locomotives on a smid-
geon less than it takes me to feed my twenty horses. You
oughter see my hay bill!"

This curious psychological warfare began having its ef-
fects upon the lawmen. Surrounded by people who despised
them, they found it hard to take such spite even when it
wasn't expressed openly.

More and more of the manhunters began finding good
excuses for giving up the chase and going home. Two federal posses, deputies of worried Bill Grimes, hung on a little
longer. A band of six men commanded by Marshal John
Swayne pounded the cow trails and pig runs of the Panhandle. Another unit of thirteen, headed by Marshals Kress
and Severns, stuck to the job.

Swayne's outfit came within ten minutes of jumping Bill
Doolin and Bill Powers at McKinney's ranch. The two
showed up, in quest of fresh horses, immediately after
Swayne, something of a frontier detective, had checked
every slab of bacon and sack of flour in the ranch commis-
sary. Short supplies would have indicated that McKinney had
been boarding visitors.

"Git goin', fellers," McKinney said tersely when the two
Bills appeared. "The marshals are thick as fleas and just
left the place."

A mile away, the possemen were scouting the brush along
a creek that ran through McKinney's property. Doolin and
Powers, justly alarmed, claimed the fresh mounts from their
old chum, then broke all records getting to Lee Moore's
ranch. There they warned the three Daltons that the marshals
had struck a hot trail.

Somewhere some tickbird had sung wrong, or maybe some Indian, not understanding English well, had made an unwitting betrayal. No time to investigate. All five desperados said hasty good-bys to Moore and hit the road.

They headed for the Cimarron Hills, favorite hiding area for freebooters on the dodge from Texas and Kansas. There they were spotted by the Kress-Severns posse jaunting across the Cherokee Strip, of which these mountains were the backbone.

Pressed by the officers, the bandits dodged into the wild country of the combined Cheyenne-Arapahoe reservation. There were mutual sightings between hunters and hunted, but no skirmishes. The quintet played this sort of tag with the posse for a day or so, then circled back into the Cimarrons.

Tired horses finally brought an end to the chase. The mounts of the marshals were becoming exhausted even before the desperados stole a bunch of fresh young ponies. That was the payoff. The marshals found the horses the gang had abandoned and loaded them on the stock cars of a train bound for Guthrie.

Sadly Kress and Severns boarded the passenger coaches with their deputies. On the same train they met Swayne's unit, which had the same ill luck to report.

Nineteen crestfallen lawmen got off the cars in Guthrie on June 16, 1892, to face a storm of criticism. Marshal Grimes now found it a task to walk down the street, such was the buzz of tongues. On June 17, 1892, the Stillwater *Gazette* published the ignominious postscript to the futile prowl:

All of the pursuing party have now returned and the chase of the bandits has been entirely abandoned.

Where would the Daltons strike next? Miss Florence Quick knew the answer, but she wasn't telling.

THE GOOSE THAT FLEW

LOYAL woman that she was, Flo Quick was proud of her man for making the marshals look sick. Bob Dalton had proven himself to be a superb captain of bandits—far more efficient at breaking the law than he'd ever been at upholding it. His old colleagues among the marshals were ruefully saying so.

With slick strategy, Bob had made the trained hounds of the law run cold trails in hot country. Flo Quick realized that he had added to that legend of invulnerability that was proving almost as great a protection as the flocks of tickbirds. His mind always seemed a jump ahead of the lawmen's. His followers' broncs were always swifter than the mounts of the badge wearers.

All this was to the good, as one part of Florence's feminine intelligence was quick to see. But the lawmen had scored one triumph during the hunt, a coup that had been effective even, if as usual, Marshal Ransom Payne was cast as the comic relief in the Dalton drama. Payne had led his posse to the love nest in Greer County—to find that the birds had flown before he got there.

Cooking utensils were hanging in orderly rows from nails on the kitchen wall. The beds were neatly made, though dust was beginning to streak the brightly colored counterpanes. Flo's wardrobe, including plenty of silky Montgomery Ward negligees, was gone with its owner and her paramour. Payne was depressed as he searched the premises.

A week or so before the Red Rock robbery, Flo and Bob had cautiously left the house, with the intention of returning after the job. The gullible Payne always believed that the woman involved was actually Daisy Bryant and a sister of Blackface Charley. "Mistress Daisy was . . . too much even for Ransom Payne's experienced and vigilant foresight," he confessed, through his hack writer, in that purplish testament, *Eyewitness*. If Marshal Payne had been as keen as he rated himself, he would have found Florence, alias

"Daisy," often known as "Tom King," right under the noses
of the marshals in Guthrie.

Shortly before Red Rock, she had stolen back to Guthrie
and to another of her intermittent domestic sessions with Mr.
Mundy. This move, of course, was to give her an alibi
comparable to Bill Dalton's when his brothers and their sad-
dlemates would pull the haul. Then, during the hectic chase
that ensued, Florence began doing some straight thinking—
with the woman side of her mind uppermost.

Being a female, she wanted security and expected her man
to furnish that security. Along with the deviant rest of her
went that compulsive urge of most women, good or bad,
for maternity. She had pitched in to help Bob with his
"career," hoping it would lead to her equivalent of the traditional cottage-with-vines: the *hacienda* in Old Mexico. But
all of Bob's earnest efforts had brought in only fame—and
no fortune.

Red Rock had gone off with a bang. But the grapevine
soon brought Florence word that Bob's pocketbook wouldn't
be much inflated by his share of another slim take. Another
report that came to her ears also disturbed her no end.

According to the Wells Fargo Express Company, the
bandits had not been able to open the "through" safe, destined for some point in Texas. If true, their piddling return,
after all the hullabaloo, had been the $1600 in the measly
local box they had smashed.

Flo kept mulling the whole thing over as she hung around
the Guthrie telegraph office to get the latest coverage on the
hunt for the Dalton gang, she being on pleasant terms with
the telegraphers, as she was with Guthrie's handful of news-
papermen. Bob would soon be broke again despite all the
history he was making. And the lady, love him as she did,
was getting a bit tired of being always his banker.

Unexpectedly, too, Mr. Mundy was showing resentment
at being continually tapped for funds by his expensive
"wife." Florence's demands were eating up all the profits
from the butcher shop that was his livelihood. In conse-
quence, a thousand dollars that Bob urgently needed wasn't
forthcoming when she had tried to pry it out of Mundy just
before the Red Rock job. Florence's own purse was short at
that time, because bronc-snatching was getting harder, with
Oklahoma continuing to sprout settlements where only cot-
tonwood and wild roses had grown.

The liaison with Mundy was nearing its end. Flo wouldn't
miss the man but she certain sure would miss his cash.
Train robbing was something in which Bob would never be

well paid. Horse stealing clearly would follow an inevitable course of diminishing returns.

Then what was the answer?

She made up her mind after word came that Payne and his outfit had located the lovecote in Greer County. Twice now, she had had a household blasted from under her. No use trying to start another, a country where lawmen of one kind or another were always on the move.

But Old Mexico! The Mexican border stretching from Texas to California, in particular. There, more than one alumnus of outlawry kept thriving so long as he left untouched the livestock of his Mexican neighbors and stole only from the ranchers of his native country.

What a home she would build for Bob and herself, across the Rio Grande! But you had to have some money to make a new start, even in the bankrupt republic of Mexico. And Bob was making hardly enough from buccaneering to pay off the tickbirds.

While the post-Red Rock chase was at its hottest, Florence quietly notified Guthrie City Marshal Ed Kelley that she would have Bob Dalton at her house on a certain date. Her payment for betraying him would be a share of the handsome reward hanging over his head.

Kelley was astonished. General gossip in the Territorial capital rated Florence as Bob's staunch sweetheart. And why should the outlaw endanger himself by slipping back into a town that was geared for his extermination?

Kelley finally decided that Flo had gotten jealous of Bob about some other woman, and that the outlaw was risking death to square matters with her. All men were fools about women. And more than one bad actor had been sold out by his girl friend.

Kelley decided to go along with her on the betrayal scheme. Flo, however, refused to go further unless the Santa Fe's general agent in Guthrie wrote a check made out to her, to be handed over as soon as Bob Dalton was delivered dead or alive.

The city officer got in touch with the Santa Fe men, who agreed to back the play, but with one condition: Marshal Chris Madsen, then out of the city on duties connected with the pursuit, would have to make a positive identification of the character as Bob Dalton.

This stipulation Kelley kept to himself when he consulted again with Flo. The city marshal was not personally acquainted with Bob.

At the appointed time, Kelley arrived, with three or four

of his local policemen, at the home that the six-gun gal shared with Guthrie's foolish butcher. Mundy was absent when the officers stepped on the porch, and Flo was inside making love to a gentleman who was appropriately happy.

At a command from Kelley, the officers outside checked their guns. Bob Dalton was a mighty bad man and this looked like a mighty big showdown. Flo's guest must have heard the click of pistol triggers being cocked. The marshals heard an anguished shout:

"Don't shoot! Don't shoot! I'll surrender."

And the man inside did surrender, meek as a lamb, when the officers rushed in with forty-fives drawn. Marshal Kelley was puzzled: Bob Dalton letting himself get caught without cocking a trigger! Why, the man was shaking like a mangy chicken thief captured by a rural constable.

"This is Mr. Dalton," Flo Quick declared in a hard voice. "He's your man."

The prisoner tried to say something but couldn't. He just stood there, trembling, tears rolling down his cheeks. Kelley's squad looked on dumbfounded. Marshal Kelley clamped handcuffs on the fellow.

Kelley and his force escorted the man to the Logan County jail, where Sheriff Hixon ordered him placed under a strong guard. Madsen was still traveling, but keeping in touch by telegram with Chief Marshal Grimes at Guthrie. At midnight, following the arrest, the Dane was aroused by a wire delivered at the hotel in Winfield, Kansas, where he lay sleeping.

"Bob Dalton in county jail," was the substance of the message. "Reward payment hanging on your identification."

Florence Quick had demanded the promised check, but the Santa Fe agent had found some way of stalling her. Madsen hurriedly dressed, left the hotel and took the first train for Guthrie, arriving there early in the morning. An excited local policeman conducted him to the jail.

"We got him!" the officer boasted. "Got Bob Dalton! Turned in by his own woman, too."

Chris Madsen made no comment. At the jail, he asked Sheriff Hixon to have the prisoner brought before him.

Cringing and sobbing, the captive faced the federal man. One quick glance was enough for Madsen. He turned to the city and county officers gathered with him for the "identification."

"You boys sure let yourselves be hurrahed by Dalton's woman," he said drily. "Just take a look. This fellow's at least six inches taller than Bob. He's stout and gawky where

Bob is slim and as slick as a cat in his moves." He shook his head. "Nope, you picked up the wrong man."

The prisoner's tears stopped. "You're right, Marshal. I ain't Bob Dalton. I'm just a poor boy from Kansas. And I'd be right obliged if you'd wire my dad to come and git me out of this jailhouse."

Madsen, trying not to laugh, asked kindly, "How long you been here in Guthrie, son? What were you hunting—a card game, a woman, or both?"

The yokel nodded woefully. Then he wiped his eyes with his bandanna and spilled his sad story. A few days before, he had come to Guthrie, where he had met Florence Quick in one of the local booze joints. She had switched the conversation to the raging search for the Daltons, then asked him if he'd like to help trap Bob for a share of the reward. That offered sum, she said, was a thousand dollars; in reality, it was much more.

He was to get half of the thousand if he would impersonate Bob Dalton. "No risk, dearie," she'd assured him. "They'll have to let you go when they find you're *not* Bob Dalton. Meantime, I'll have collected that thousand and you'll get half—*five hundred dollars.*"

Five hundred dollars. The yokel's eyes had bulged. He'd never seen more than fifty in one heap in his whole life.

He had almost backed out when Flo had told him that he'd have to make some token show of resistance for the officers who would come for him: gunning wasn't his style. Yet the dunce had even agreed to this when Flo had promised him her choicest favor: herself. But he had faltered on nerve when the showdown came.

Madsen and the other officers listened to the tale, some soberly, some with eyes twinkling. After it had been spun, he remarked to the youth:

"Boy, you had a close shave. That woman would have a man killed for a thousand dollars—or less. Any man except Bob Dalton. And you'd have been a dead duck if you'd even looked like you wanted to pull a gun on Marshal Kelley."

He spoke to Sheriff Hixon. "Release this man, John. You won't be seeing him around again."

The Kansan bolted through the jail door, and ran like an antelope when the sheriff followed Madsen's advice.

Flo felt quite put out as the expected reward faded away with her pawn. Old Mexico seemed a long way off—like Bob, dodging those posses in the Panhandle.

OMINOUS HOLDUP

FLORENCE QUICK was bitter after her money-raising scheme fell through, but at their next tryst she and Bob passed it off as a huge joke upon themselves as well as upon the poor Kansas plowhand. Having laughed it off, they reviewed plans for another descent upon a railroad.

A settlement in the Cherokee Nation, not far from the Missouri boundary, was to be the place. Pryor Creek, it was called, named for the stream on whose banks it sat. The line was again to the Missouri, Kansas and Texas. The time was to be in July, the month the Indians called the "outlaw moon."

Flo had chosen the place before meeting the yokel and pulling that cynical trick on him. The ground was familiar to the Daltons. Vinita, where they had partly grown up, lay just thirty miles away. But at comparably and unpleasantly close distances were Claremore, where Bob had shot the Cochran boy; and Tahlequah, the Cherokee capital, from which Grat had once ridden out as a tribal policeman.

It was, in brief, country where everybody knew the Daltons. Cherokee police chief Charles Le Flore, a seasoned officer, was particularly anxious to get Grat for turning renegade.[1] Those mixed-blood aristocrats, the Rogerses, still wanted to collect in blood for their horses, driven off to Kansas. And *their* kinsmen, the wealthy Adairs, were itching to help and ready to contribute powder or rope for such a commendable undertaking.

By now, however, the Daltons were bolder. The boys strutted. They bragged so much that Bill Doolin got plain sick of it. All around Oklahoma, Emmett was boasting to second-string outlaws that they'd actually gotten $11,000 from the Red Rock robbery.

"Yep," Emmett would tell visitors to the dugout on Riley's ranch, "we sure cleaned up. Jesse James never did no better."

The boy, who had once ridden Jesse's horse, was now obsessed with the idea of outdoing Jesse. His harmonica was forever wheezing out that doleful *Ballad of Jesse James*.

Sometimes he would put the instrument back in his pocket and sing the song in his brash, big voice. That ominous refrain never made him feel morbid:

> *"And the dirty little coward*
> *Who shot Mr. Howard;*
> *He laid poor Jesse in his grave."*

Lean, hungry second-stringers began riding to the dugout, seeking to throw in with the Dalton gang. Emmett's boastfulness had excited their greed and drawn them like fruit flies to overripe grapes. Bob fed all the applicants, then sent them away with handshakes, announcing regretfully that he had no vacancies.

Not once did it occur to Bob or Emmett that one or another of the disappointed jobseekers might do something to undermine the band. No Dalton yet had been betrayed by a fellow professional or even by one of the ambitious semi-pros who alternated between crime and cowpunching.

A little while later, some tickbird reported to Bob that the Cherokee police were getting mighty active and taking on more men at Tahlequah. Bob just yawned. He figured he could handle *any* Indian posse.

The risks were rising but the Daltons, at this stage, didn't give a whoop. Besides, for all of Emmett's windies, the bunch was dead broke. Penury combined with recklessness to cancel out caution. Had Florence Quick been successful with that reward-money ruse, the Pryor Creek job might never have been pulled. As things were, however, Bob agreed with Florence that Pryor looked like a good prospect. After the M K & T had coughed up there, Bob would short-pot the non-family members of the gang for every nickel possible. Then Flo, Bob, Emmett, and Grat would streak out to Old Mexico.

Julia Johnson would come along too, if Emmett could persuade her. Right then, the loud-mouthed one was deeply disturbed over reports about Julia's having been seen with other boyfriends in her community on Little Caney River. Well, Mexico was full of girls. Florence and Bob would see to it that Emmett and Grat didn't sleep in unwarmed beds.

Bill Dalton preferred to stay in Oklahoma, having just gotten his wife and children settled in their new home here. Political ambitions were again stirring within the gang's outside man. He was often seen hobnobbing with members of the Farmers' Alliance, and he was trying to cultivate the friendship of a Kingfisher politician, James Yancey Callahan, who, in 1896, would be elected territorial delegate to Congress by a coalition of anti-monopoly groups. On the Democratic side, Bill was cottoning up to J. K. Lane, militant preacher and member of the Territorial senate, later a representative in the Texas legislature.[2]

While the bandits dreamed and schemed, Flo Quick went to Woodward, far from the scene of the intended robbery, in western Oklahoma. There she put up with friends or relatives and posed as a modest, conventional young woman, using one of her names that had not been connected with outlawry. Bob visited her at least once, incognito, anybody who noticed him seeing just another cowpuncher sparking a girl.[3]

They talked at length about that *hacienda* they were going to set up in Old Mexico. Florence, it seemed, was beginning to get worried about Bob's safety. Plying the bandit's trade in Oklahoma was courting a bullet in the guts. Those American cattle on the Mexican border would be easy pickings.

After their session in the prairie town, Bob went back to Riley's ranch, not knowing that Chris Madsen now had it spotted as the gang's central hideout. Some informer had sung to the marshal, maybe one of a new batch of nesters in the Gloss Mountains, irked because Jim Riley's gunslingers kept them from cutting timber on the government-owned public domain that he leased from the Interior Department for a few cents an acre.[4]

Florence left Woodward for Silver City, where she and Bob had first shared the joys of concupiscence. Her purpose in that New Mexico border town was to look around for land across the Rio Grande. Whatever tracts Miss Quick inspected, no deeds were drawn up before any Mexican notary. She had no money to put down. Not even to such a pretty American *muchacha* would the courtly Aztec landowners extend credit, whatever unusual consideration may have been offered as a binder. Dejected, the would-be home girl returned to Woodward, where she waited for Bob to bring in the wherewithal.

On July 13, 1892, Bob and seven associates camped in a dense brake of the Neosho River halfway between Pryor Creek and Adair. His partners were Grat, Emmett, Bill Powers, Dick Broadwell, Charlie Pierce, Bitter Creek Newcomb and Bill Doolin—the same skilled crew of helpers that had functioned at Red Rock. Once on the chosen ground, however, the mood of the bandits became a bit tense. Grat jumped whenever the hoofs of a calf crackled in the brush or curlews, looking for bugs, rattled heaps of dead leaves strewn along the banks of the Neosho.

Bob was also concerned because of an unexpected development. As a marshal, he had known Pryor Creek as just another half-breed settlement, centering around a depot and a tiny post office. But the recent opening of the joint Cheyenne-Arapahoe reservation had brought more legions of nesters to stir things up in formerly sleepy hamlets. Within three months, Pryor Creek had swelled to 1500 people. Other crossroads places were also burgeoning into thriving towns, a process which spelled trouble for long riders anywhere in the West. It was something to ponder, yet the boys were there not to study history but to rob a train.

On the morning of July 15, the scheduled date for the robbery, a nester walked into the outlaw camp and halted suddenly when he saw the guns of the eight strangers.

"Campin', gents?" the farmer asked.

The bandits glanced at each other. Grat would have drawn a gun and killed the inquisitive man if Bob hadn't been around.

"Just passing through, friend," Bob finally replied.

The nester explained that he was looking for some strayed hogs. He left, looking puzzled, glancing back once or twice toward the campers.

Grat flicked a mosquito from his nose. "Bad-luck sign," he said gloomily. "Like a black cat crossin' our path."

Bob and Emmett laughed at such superstition, but it had its effect on Bill Doolin, raised on signs and omens in the hills of Arkansas. There was some argument. Doolin and Grat were ready to call the game a draw and beat out. Emmett strongly objected—this was one more chance to playact at being Jesse James. Bob, spurred by Florence Quick's demands that he bring in some money for a change, agreed with his younger brother.

All eight of them realized that the nester might hurry to Pryor Creek and tell the Katy station agent of the suspicious "campers" in that grove of the Neosho. With the whole section alerted for the Daltons, hell could then pop. As a matter of fact, the station agent was notified.

"We'll outfox 'em if that fellow was a snooper," Bob Dalton finally decided. "We'll let the lawdogs bark in Pryor Creek" —he winked—"but we'll be robbing the train in Adair."

The gang broke camp and headed down the Neosho toward Adair, a town competing with Pryor Creek as prospective county seat, and of about the same population.[5]

Till nine P.M., the bandits lingered on the outskirts of the little town. Then, led by Bob, the gang charged into the community, dismounted at the depot and thrust Winchesters into the face of the local Katy agent.

They made him hand over all his cash receipts and appropriated everything of value in sight. Holding up a station was a new wrinkle in railroad robbery. No passengers were waiting to board the train on this run between Kansas City, Missouri, and Denison, Texas, so the bandits made themselves comfortable on the benches in the waiting room pending the arrival of Passenger Train Number Two, due at 9:42 P.M.

The train was on time. Marching the station agent ahead of them, the boys hurried from the depot as the engine slowed for a stop. Bitter Creek Newcomb drew a rifle on a crowd of startled loungers idling around the platform, bunched them together, and ordered the agent to join the group.

Grat and Emmett climbed into the engine cab to cover Engineer Glen Ewing and the fireman. At that moment, four men dashed from the smoking car into a coal shed beside the track. The Daltons paid little attention to them. Scared passengers could be expected to run like rabbits into some convenient hole.

A few men, later identified as special deputy marshals, then appeared on the smoker platform, yelling and flourishing weapons. Bob and two other bandits raised their guns threateningly. The bravos of the law scurried back inside the coach.

Bob, Broadwell and Powers were meantime trying to gain entrance to the express car, but Messenger George P. Williams had locked himself inside at Pryor Creek and refused to open the door. Grat and Emmett forced the engineer and fireman from the cab to the side of the tracks opposite the depot. The engineer looked at his captors and said: "We expected you fellers at Pryor Creek."

Grat gave him a prod with his gun barrel and growled, "We didn't wanta disappoint you—so here we are."

Messenger Williams was still declining to open the express coach. Bob Dalton was threatening to blow up the car with dynamite.

A volley of lead burst from the unlighted coal shed. Bullets spewed against the engine, around Grat, Emmett, and the two trainmen, standing in sharp silhouette from the glare of the engine firebox. Three men who had dashed into the shed were no scared passengers but three of Oklahoma's top officers:

United States Deputy Marshal Sid Johnson, of the federal court in Wichita, Kansas; Captain J. J. Kinney, chief of detectives of the M K & T's special force for the Cherokee Division; and Captain Charles Le Flore, head of the Cherokee National Police. A fourth man, too, had managed to reach the coal shed—a railroad guard named Ward.

In a brief but furious battle, the Dalton luck held. Their rifle fire seriously wounded Marshal Johnson. Kinney and Ward suffered minor flesh wounds and Le Flore had an arm "burned" by a bullet. The worst casualties were those from shots that went wild.

The town's two physicians—Doctors Youngblood and W. L. Goff—were sitting in a drugstore when bullets sprayed through the window. Both were badly hit. Goff died a few hours afterward. Youngblood was many weeks recovering.

When the firing from the coal shed ceased, Grat and Emmett ordered the engineer and fireman to move to the other side of the track. There the bandits, holding guns on the trainmen, joined Bob, Broadwell and Powers, who were still trying to bully the messenger into opening the express-car door. Newcomb kept riding herd on the loungers. Doolin and Pierce were standing track guard, the assorted lawmen inside the cars apparently hiding with the passengers behind the seats and forgetting all about the fight.

Again Bob Dalton demanded that Messenger Williams cooperate. Again he threatened to dynamite the car. Spiking the order, another of the bandits fired three or four shots into the coach. The volley just missed Williams's head, whereupon the messenger changed his mind and unlocked the door.

The outlaws made a quick finish to the job, once they had gained admission. They forced Williams to open the safe, even though he protested that he didn't know the combination. By now, this was an old story to them. After looting the box, they bound him and shoved him into a corner of the coach. Then all eight mounted horses and rode furiously toward the rugged Dog Creek Hills.[6]

Seventeen thousand dollars was the amount of the haul, as estimated by Emmett, in his book, *When the Daltons Rode*. If Emmett's figure was correct, the individual share of the bandits would have been more than $2,000 apiece—the handsomest money they would have earned yet from tapping express cars.

Five or six thousand seems to have been the most plausible total—which would have meant only $800 or $900 per capita for America's doughtiest outlaws. Almost any storekeeper in Oklahoma could net more over a three-month period, without having guns blazing at him.

It was the last train robbery for the Dalton gang. They should have made the most of it. Something had gone wrong at Adair. Somewhere the grapevine had snapped.

Even Grat Dalton had sense enough to see that.

THE DOWNGRADE BEGINS

METHODICALLY, efficiently, Deputy Marshal Christian Madsen had rearranged the cluttered records of his superior's office in Guthrie. He had separated reward posters and other material about the Dalton Gang from data on other wild bunches raising hell in Oklahoma Territory. Chief Marshal Grimes had not been a very good public housekeeper, though he was doing his best to be a good public servant.

Chris, tidy like most Scandinavians, had tackled that jumble of records, disturbed by the confusion that had helped prolong the careers of the six-shooter gentry. He had asked rural sheriffs for full reports on the rough tablet paper they had to use because most counties were too poor to pay a printer for formal stationery. Field deputies were also required to send him ample accounts of operations.

Bob and Emmett Dalton would have laughed at such precision and rated the forty-one-year-old Madsen as a fussy old codger. But Madsen was the forerunner of the modern, scientifically trained law enforcer. He was also an officer with genuine human sympathies. One reason for his not being harder on Bill Dalton was consideration for Bill's wife and children, trying to make a new start in Oklahoma.

Yet Bill's crowing behavior at the time of the Red Rock affair had made Madsen's shrewd mind tighten like a vise. Bill, he deduced, was up to his neck in all the doings of his brothers. When the demagogue overplayed a smooth hand, Madsen set his talent for efficient procedure to the crippling of the Dalton Gang.

His first step was to start pruning the Dalton grapevine. He had staff deputies, ones who were not too well known, wander on their lonesome across sections which the Daltons frequented, posing as drifting landseekers who had lost out in the various runs or cowboys whose jobs had been made forfeit by the invasion of the plow.

These men were obviously long-time residents of the area. They spoke in the drawl of Oklahoma or the states that bordered it. Oklahoma was full of drifters, and Madsen's undercover men seemed to be just that much more flotsam on the great tide of hungry, restless itinerants.

Naturally there was talk about the Daltons wherever Madsen's rovers stopped to camp with somebody else on the move. You heard more conversation about them, in intimate chat around supper fires, than you did about such matters as cotton prices and the free coinage of silver, so troubling settled folk. Sometimes these informal detectives, pretending to be admirers of the Daltons, would ask adroit questions. Inevitably they would hear the names of others who had boasted about entertaining the outlaws or, even, receiving gifts from the gang.[1]

Madsen's men had instructions to report back for evaluation everything they heard. Soon, Chris had another bulging folder in his carefully kept files: lists bearing the names of those who sucked from the Dalton grapevine, who kept them informed of court proceedings and the movement of known lawmen.

It was an intricate, delicate process for a man who had been a badge wearer only eighteen months, but Madsen managed. Soon, accumulated data indicated that the main hideout of the Daltons was on Jim Riley's ranch. Since the place was such a natural citadel, it was impractical, for the time being, to send a posse for a mass attack. Ways were found to have the place watched for the comings and goings of sojourners. Madsen and his men were slowly surrounding the Daltons.

Bill, the gang's traveling vice-president, must have guessed that something was in the wind, particularly when so many formerly cooperative tickbirds started getting nervous and obviously scared when he dropped by. Too many county and federal grand juries had been calling in sundry citizens to inquire about their friendships with the outlaws for Bill to be unaware of it.

Meantime, considerable whispered criticism had started about Bill Dalton, whose popularity was beginning to slip. Talk had it that Bill was hiring gunslingers to help in his land dealings. If a homesteader didn't want to sell his claim for whatever Bill chose to pay, he was likely to be visited next day by a stranger, hard-eyed and be-pistoled, who suggested that a move would be in the interest of his family. Those who let themselves be buffaloed made the hustling realtor their indirect heir. All he had to do after their departure was to appropriate the claim by paying any back taxes on it or simply by making one of the pistol sharks his "tenant."[2]

Bill's name, too, was becoming synonymous with outlawry to many respectable Oklahomans who had reserved judgment when he had first come home. Emmett and Bob were losing favor among the independent road agents, with whom they had once maintained cordial personal relations, Emmett for his exaggerated brag about the Dalton pickings, Bob for refusing to hand out occasional employment that most of them were itching to get. One of these was ultimately responsible for the harassment inflicted on the gang at Adair.

During those weeks of the outlaw moon, the marshals picked up an old grizzly of whining tongue and greedy paws. Bootlegging was the charge this time, but Oklahoma lawmen knew the suspect as being also a wide-looper and a hot-iron artist. Prospects looked bleak for the veteran of the back trails, what with a federal indictment for peddling whisky to Indians hanging over his head. The marshals promised him they would run him down and puncture his booze-soaked hide if he jumped bond.

So the bootlegger came to Madsen's office in Guthrie, hoping to exchange information for leniency and, maybe, a little cash. In a woeful tone, he told this marshal about having been turned down by Bob Dalton when he'd wanted to throw in with the gang. Bob had curtly told the applicant that "the band was already too large."

The man's professional pride had been hurt, his expectations dashed. Hadn't he heard Emmett brag about all that loot the boys were scooping up from express coaches? And Bob had acted like a ranch foreman turning down a job-hunting saddle tramp!

Wounded, the sensitive fellow had brooded over the whole thing for weeks. He kept remembering talk about Pryor Creek, overheard while he'd been enjoying the rough hospitality of the Daltons, and knew that they were planning to stop the train there in mid-July. Around that time he had decided to play stool pigeon.

Madsen was suspicious of his informant, believing that he might be concocting the story about the Daltons to court mercy for himself. "We were so used to those tips that I paid little attention to his story," so the marshal recorded, "but did send a telegram to the head of the railroad police, Mr. J. J. Kinney, and he organized a posse of thirteen men, who were placed in a special car." [3]

Kinney, in turn, had notified Marshal Johnson and Cherokee Police Chief Le Flore. The three lawmen had then started assembling forces to give the Dalton gang a fight for the money at Pryor Creek. Johnson appointed men as special deputies in Muskogee. Le Flore mobilized what he thought to be a crack squad of his force.

Kinney chose a baker's dozen of railway officers, who knew that they might have to swap shots with Daltons when he had signed them on. He had planned a mop-up operation on the gang because the M K & T central headquarters people were bearing down mighty hard on him as a result of Red Rock. Forty or fifty men must have been in that combined force. The train robbers could not be expected to number more than eight. Detective Kinney just naturally hoped to leave their corpses strewn along the tracks.

The joint company of bandit hunters had been quickly mobilized after the receipt of the telegram from the station agent at Pryor Creek, which followed the visit to the Dalton camp of the man who was very likely an undercover operative for the railroad. All the lawdogs had been loaded into that special car at Muskogee.

All along the way to Pryor Creek, these heavily armed passengers had bragged about what they would do to the Daltons, once they encountered those erring young men. They dreamed great dreams of what they would do with the reward money that had been posted for Bob and his bandits. Marshal Johnson, who hated brag, started getting disgusted and a bit dubious.

"You boys better start puttin' ammunition into your guns instead of your mouths," he warned. "There'll be plenty of shooting when the time comes, and with rifles."

The boasts were becoming less loud by the time that the train reached Pryor Creek. Johnson and Kinney and Le Flore noticed that some of the loudest were looking a little pale around the gills, and seemed mighty relieved when the outlaws failed to show in the town. No Daltons, but the railroad would pay them something for their time, and they'd had a good joy ride.

Their faces showed consternation when Detective Kinney announced that they would ride on to the next town. He guessed that the Daltons had pulled a ruse. The intuition of a born lawman had forced the bandits, cocky after three unchallenged train boardings, into the fight that so injured their prestige.

At Pryor Creek, so Kinney later told Chris Madsen, the sorry "defenders" had become boastful, and prided themselves on driving the Daltons away without firing a shot.

"Not so when they reached Adair," Madsen wrote in his journal. "Here some of the posse threw their guns away."

But Madsen, after conferring with Kinney, placed greater

pressures on the Dalton grapevine to amputate more of its tendrils. He asked county sheriffs to keep him informed regularly on the doings of tickbirds and to keep them harassed by constant investigation.

Already now the gang had been pushed out of its jolly hovel on Jim Riley's threatened barony. Homestead claims, which several of the bandits had staked out before turning train robber, would be forfeited to the government and Mr. Riley would also be losing the grass that he had kept by having his gunslinging friends file on the land.

The Adair battle was the first mile of the downgrade for the band. It was also "the first time the Daltons had met any real obstacle," said Chris Madsen. Emmett confirmed the marshal's observation when he had his ghost writer, Jack Jungmeyer, record:

"This was the first time that we had encountered anything that amounted to real resistance."

From now on the Daltons would be swallowing overdoses of "resistance." The outlaws lay low after Adair, scattered, reunited in temporary shelters till they holed up somewhere along the Verdigris River.

Almost three months had passed after the Adair holdup, when around October 1, 1892, Marshal Madsen in Guthrie received a letter from his federal counterpart at Fort Smith, Arkansas.

The Daltons, it said, were organizing for a raid on the banks, either at Van Buren, Arkansas, or at Coffeyville, Kansas.

ANOTHER PIGEON COOS

ONCE again, the informant was a man on the wrong side of the bars. Madsen did not reveal his name in his interesting journal. Even until his death in January, 1944, there were still living senile brush poppers ready to slay anybody who had peached on Daltons. One such was Riley Martin, who died at a nostalgic ninety, in the Texas cedar brakes, in 1960.[1]

"Bob Dalton hunted me when he was a lawman and protected me when he was a law dodger. I'd still kill any sidewinder who ever harmed him." So, Martin, who had learned engine boarding from Harry Longabaugh, alias "The Sundance Kid," told this writer back in 1945. That Riley had not ridden with the Daltons might have been due partly to the hiring policies of the gang, but more because of the objections of his Indian wife.

The anonymous outlaw who chirped was a prisoner in the federal dungeon at Fort Smith. Madsen's document says that Chief Marshal Jacob L. Yoes had "done favors" for him. Yoes, a respectable burgher, was also president of the Clinton County Bank in Van Buren, Arksansas. What those "favors" were remains unknown—no doubt various leniencies accorded for information given on this or that practitioner of banditry.

Madsen wrote that the prisoner "had been either with the Daltons and learned their plans from them or had obtained the plans from some who were able to know in advance what they were to do." Chris, who went in for plain, unadorned prose, was not often so prolix. Probably he was deliberately protecting the identity of some living person. Emmett Dalton was still very much alive when Madsen started his terse autobiography, later secured by Homer Croy through Chris's son, Reno Madsen, of Fort Worth.

Madsen speculated that "The Daltons may have refused to have him [the informer] in with them or he might have figured on getting some reward for his information. But whatever his reasons had been, the information was correct."

Completely correct. The letter that the informer wrote was

an informal kind of warrant for America's leading bandits.
Madsen was outraged when he received the letter.

The brothers had "old friends and old playmates in the
town," Madsen wrote disgustedly. "They had done business
with the banks and merchants and associated with the people,
sociably. Now they were bent on robbing and possibly killing
their old acquaintances without any reason, except to make
more money to continue in their revelry."

That the Daltons had many reasons for staging a grand raid
in Coffeyville became evident later. Madsen evaluated the
letter in some grave sessions with Bill Grimes and with
Heck Thomas, who had been pursuing the Daltons since
Adair. Would the brothers actually invade Coffeyville to try
the hazardous stunt of robbing a pair of banks in a community where everybody, from the mayor down to the
town halfwit, knew them? Or would they be content with
breaking one bank in Van Buren—a bank run by a marshal?

Van Buren was the county seat of Clinton County. A pleasant village subsisting on three or four local industries, it lay
on the Arkansas River, just nine miles, by an excellent road,
from Fort Smith. The short distance from Parker's seat of justice made it possible for Marshal Yoes to function both as lawman and banker. It was a churchy sort of a place, its calm
broken only occasionally by small-fry badmen who drifted
across the river from Oklahoma.

Marshal Yoes had been a friend of all the Daltons in the
days when they had been riding for the law. He had
mourned the death of Frank Dalton, killed in the fight with
the whisky runners, and he had tried to be patient with Grat
even after a monumental drunk that the big fellow had in-
dulged in at Frank Barland's saloon in Fort Smith.

But nowadays, Chris Madsen realized, the Dalton boys
didn't like to be reminded of any obligations, friendly or
otherwise, to marshals. Now they were bent on discrediting
their ex-brethren of the badge wherever they could. And
what neater way of buffaloing a lawman than to rob his
bank?

What a fool the head marshal would look like if they visited the bank at Van Buren and made off with the cash of
Clinton County's farmers and businessmen! All over Arkansas and Oklahoma, citizens would be asking that if Jacob
Yoes couldn't protect his own bank against the Daltons, how
could he guard others?

Riley Martin told this author, one sundown in a cedar
brake, that Bill Dalton favored Van Buren as the next the-

ater of banditry. The spot appealed both to his caution and
to his perverse sense of humor.

Robbing two banks anywhere at once was something that
not even the Youngers or the Jameses had tried in their hey-
day.[2] Robbing two at Coffeyville, with Daltons being so identifiable, might be sheer suicide. Bill Dalton was worried, too,
for his own business dealings in the Coffeyville-Bartlesville
area if his brothers came ripping into that Kansas center. He
had been worried enough about their hiding out at various
retreats in the section since the Adair holdup.

Other considerations, too, must have influenced Bill. Kansas was sure to swing to the Populists in the November, 1892,
general election, a few weeks hence. William A. Peffer,
founder of the Coffeyville *Journal*, was already sitting in
Washington as a Populist senator from Kansas. Bill Dalton
wanted to court his favor and get his backing for Bill's own
political ambitions in Oklahoma. Unfortunately, the Senator
was continually advocating the extermination of Bob, Emmett
and Grat, along with that of such other major nuisances as
the big industrial trusts and the swindling rings of wheat
speculators.

But Van Buren was a state and a territory away, over in
Arkansas. Publicly, Bill Dalton could disclaim responsibility
for whatever capers his brothers cut there, even if to close
cronies he could still make sly jokes about his brothers
tilting a bank run by a marshal. Some prospective Oklahoma politicial supporters might just naturally eat it up.

At first the marshals in Guthrie also believed that Van
Buren would be the next target for a Dalton haul. Disguised
federal lawmen were sent to the Arkansas town to pose as
men looking for work at the town's flour mills and broom
factory. The sheriff of Crawford County augmented his
force of deputies. So did the chief of Van Buren's tiny
police corps. Plans were being made to give the Daltons a
big party, if, and when, they showed up.

Coffeyville? "Naw, they wouldn't be that damned big
fools," one marshal declared in a conference at Guthrie.
Heck Thomas concurred after his pursuit had caused the
gang to clear out from the Verdigris belt. He had sent undercover men to hire out as cowboys at different ranches in
the area and keep watch for the outlaws. Some weeks had
passed since these operatives had spotted any of the members of the band.

Then came news that caused officers to become as alert
and taut as bird dogs poised for a covey.

A few days before Yoes had written Madsen, Bob Dalton

paid a stealthy, midnight visit to Coffeyville. He banged on
the door of Frank Benson, an employee of a drugstore conducted by George Slosson & Company, near the local post
office on Walnut Street. Clad only in his nightshirt, the
astonished Benson answered the knock and instantly recognized his caller.

Mr. Robert Dalton, of *the* Daltons. Bob was packing a pair
of pearl-handled pistols, one in his belt and one in his hand,
pointing toward an old neighbor. He had an urgent reason
for his visit, though he didn't go into all the particulars.

He wanted a gallon of whisky. With the Populists having
voted out liquor when they elected Peffer, the contaminating
stuff could only be sold as medicine by drugstores.

Mr. Benson protested that his virtuous firm didn't deal in
firewater at all. Mr. Dalton nevertheless insisted that this
sterling citizen dress, open up the drugstore, and give him
the hooch. There was some debate, with the druggist standing his ground. Finally he got rid of Bob, telling him that
another pharmacy, Rammel Brothers, sold whisky.

The Rammel establishment was on Union Street, across the
square from the competing Slosson Store. By coincidence, it
was also right next door to one of Coffeyville's two banks—
the First National.

Benson was too shaken by the incident to make any loud
noise about Bob Dalton's visit, but he did confide in one or
two friends at a time. Word got back to the marshals,
through somebody or other, that Bob had been in Coffeyville.

Had he come to rustle booze for Grat? Or had this errand been an excuse for Bob to brush up on the town,
familiarizing himself with old landmarks, estimating distances between banks, making a layout for an intended job
in his canny mind?

The lawmen in Guthrie and Fort Smith could only guess.
But obviously, the Daltons were nowhere around Van Buren.
Much relieved, Marshal Yoes quietly shipped some rifles to
Coffeyville. Emmett would afterward remember that "it
looked like everybody in Coffeyville was carrying a gun."

COFFEYVILLE PREPARES

RUMORS swept Coffeyville to the effect that the Daltons were coming to rob the banks. All but a frightened few of the town's citizens were getting set for the kill, making preparations to manhandle the West's worst desperados.[1]

Their plan to hold up two banks at once in the town where, as kids, they had played marbles and mumbley-peg was, in retrospect, pretty silly. Bill Doolin, who saw it that way even then, attempted to talk Bob out of the whole thing.[2] Discussion seethed into another quarrel about Bob's continued short-potting. Seconding Doolin were two close members of the gang, plus a third one who, until then, had not openly participated in its councils.

Bitter Creek Newcomb, once Bob's shadow, was now mad as a hydrophobic fox because all his hard work wasn't bringing in enough money to buy play-pretties for Rose Dunn. Charlie Pierce was nursing hurt feelings because his old pupil and saddlemate, Emmett, had helped cheat him. To the astonishment of everybody, they got the support of Bill Dalton.

Bill had hoped that kid brother Emmett would stay hidden out at a friendly ranch, twenty miles from Tulsa, until he had gotten over his stripling's yen to imitate Jesse James. But it was Emmett, by best accounts, who had written Bob, under some assumed name, suggesting this insane venture.

The boys would be straying from their specialty—train robbing. Whatever they did to get back at his hated enemy —the railroads—had his approval. But the idea of bank-busting made him uneasy: it could affect his private pocketbook. He might not like banks as a matter of principle, but he did have to do business with them in his land dealings, and any assault upon them by his brothers might jeopardize his credit. As he thought it over, he was sorry he had ever encouraged the boys to consider tapping the bank at Van Buren. He should have encouraged them to stick to their field of proven competence—engine-boarding.

Coldly, calculatingly, Bill Dalton realized that his brothers might not return alive from Coffeyville. Even if they did, after successfully robbing the local banks, they would be of no further use to him. He would not go out on a limb for them again, as he had for Grat and Bob in California.

Yet outlawry, properly planned and carefully executed, might yield ample returns. Bob and Emmett and Grat had thus far made a lot of noise but come off with little profit. Bill Doolin was head and shoulders above them in discretion and solid horse sense. He was a natural chieftain, a man who regarded his job as serious work instead of hilarious sport. Moreover, Doolin knew how to command the lasting loyalty of associates. Brother Bob outraged loyalty.

So, when the showdown came, Bill Dalton threw in with Bill Doolin. Camped in the Verdigris bottoms were Bob, looking a bit strained over so much fussing, but still jolly and debonair; Emmett, gabbing incessantly about Jesse James; Grat, who would sober up just in time for the coming foray; Bill Powers, anxious to share gold as well as glory; and faithful Dick Broadwell.

Bitter Creek Newcomb and Charlie Pierce had ridden off somewhere together after a series of bitter arguments in another temporary rest spot of the gang. Bill Doolin and Bill Dalton were conducting earnest discussions on a corner of Fitzgerald's ranch at Cowboy Flat, fifteen miles southeast of Guthrie. Camped with them was a tickbird, probably a cowpuncher for the Fitzgerald outfit. There they meant to wait till they heard how things went at Coffeyville. The two Bills' budding friendship seemed to be a promising one, and their talks were hopeful.

Florence Quick, loving inspiration of Bob, was missing around Guthrie. Mr. Mundy had finally decided that she wasn't his kind of a girl and had disposed of her, along with the butcher shop. Possibly, she had gone to visit her mother and her father, Dan Quick, a stock raiser in another part of Oklahoma.

Other figures flitted in and out of the Dalton warm-up for Coffeyville. One was a half-lame alumnus of the stagecoach-robbing days called Buckskin Ike. He was wandering around New York up until a few years ago, having been run out of old Tascosa, Texas, by Sheriff Jim East, but continuing to claim that he had almost been taken on by Bob Dalton to help hurrah Coffeyville. He probably did know the Daltons, but that was as far as it went.

There was also an Indiana-born saddle tramp named George Padgett, of whom a little more later.

Another one was that posturing bushwhacker, J. Frank

Dalton, who in his dotage would claim to be Jesse James reincarnated. Strong facial resemblances and similarity of yarns indicate that he may have been Kit Dalton, second cousin of the notorious brothers. At first J. Frank claimed to have been their "uncle" but his stories of their misdeeds do not accord with known facts. While posing as old Jesse, he was identified by a California kinswoman as a member of the family.

Lastly, there was the flaming Texan, Riley Martin, hater of sheriffs and sheep, who always claimed that he tried to discourage Bob, Emmett and Grat from tackling two banks when they came to his shack in the Creek Nation asking him to join up. Riley was no braggart; it took years for this author to get more than fragments of information from him. He knew much that he never told anybody.

These namesakes and casual acquaintances would keep turning up to claim some share in the Dalton saga. Some would pretend relationship with the brothers, to seek acting contracts in one or another medium of drama. Some would say that they had ridden with them as marshals and tried to keep them from renouncing the badge.

In Coffeyville, as well as in the Dalton camp, history was being forged. Coffeyville's businessmen, however, were not out to make history but to punish those who desecrated the sanctity of commerce. Outlawry was bad for trade: it kept emigrants from towns and customers from stores.

Coffeyville was booming. It now had 3,500 people, after Kansas's first natural gas had been tapped in its environs. Residents were often finding filmy residues in the water they drew from their wells. Oil, it was, and soon the area would become one of the West's outstanding producers of that liquescent wealth.

Coffeyville now had six doctors, even if unlighted streets required that they carry "lanterns and pistols when making night calls." Caravans of covered wagons transporting homesteaders still rolled down the dusty, unpaved streets. Liquor was still obtainable if you had the price, in spite of the dry laws.

But who was thinking about drys and wets with Grat Dalton and his brothers planning a visit to their home town? Not livery-stable proprietor John Joseph Kloehr, president of a local gun club, champion trapshooter of Kansas. Not Henry Isham, the hardware man, nor his two clerks, Lewis Dietz and Arthur Reynolds, who loved to shoot firearms as well as sell them. Not Charlie Gump, the drayman. Not Lucius Baldwin, a young employee of Read Brothers general store.

Not the bristling old grayheads who had helped hang claim jumpers in the famous, vigilante-type "Bunkers Courts" established after the old Indian trader, Colonel James A. Coffey, had founded the town back in 1868. Coffeyville had watched the Daltons grow up to turn into Bunkers. Now it meant to finish them with a quick trial in the court of old Judge Colt.

There was much unloving recollection of the boys and their trifling father at Kloehr's livery stable, Smith's barbershop and wherever else males gathered. Storekeeper Alex McKenna thought of the Daltons as a bunch of deadbeats; possibly Lewis Dalton had died owing him money. J. H. Wilcox, the cattle dealer, allowed that Daltons had rustled more stock than they had ever brought back while serving as marshals. Cyrus Lee, the iceman, swore grimly that it would take a lot of his merchandise to cool off the brothers after they had gotten where Coffeyville was going to send them.

Bill Dalton, too, came in for his share of criticism. Word had gotten back to Coffeyville about his peculiar methods of clinching land deals—with hired guns instead of a checkbook. One yarn about the gang claims that he tried to borrow operating capital from both of the banks—the First National and the Condon—then sent his brothers to get the money, in the Dalton manner, after he had been refused.

What dissipated the last ounce of sympathy for the brothers in Coffeyville had been the shooting, if accidental, of those two doctors at Adair. Charley Montgomery, whom Bob had killed near the waiting Kansas town, wasn't anybody to mourn. It was a pity, some thought, that Charley hadn't plugged Bob in a double slaying that would have rid good folks of both.

But even a rough frontier society had to recognize certain classes of noncombatants if it was to survive and progress. Teachers, preachers and physicians fell within that classification. So the Daltons didn't like railroads; who did? But two indispensable citizens at Adair had been innocent victims of the wrath that the brothers and their cohorts had felt against the carriers.

Through seventy-two tense hours, Coffeyville planned for the Daltons the biggest reception that the town had ever planned for anybody, including visiting notables.

Some of the arms sent by Marshal Yoes from Fort Smith were undoubtedly stacked in the hardware store of Isham Brothers & Mansour, which was next door to the First National Bank on Union Street and directly opposite, on the other side of the square or "Plaza," from the C. M. Condon & Co. private bank. The hardware store was, at that time, "a large one-story brick building—with heavy plate-glass windows and doors" intended for extra protection against random gunmen.

The store had two entrances from Union Street. Its presence served as a protection to the First National Bank, since anybody who approached that institution would have to pass it. And, like all Western hardware dealers, the owners were only too glad to "lend" guns and ammunition in a hurry to citizens to use against bandits.

Equally accommodating was the hardware firm of A. P. Boswell & Company, operating from a big two-story brick building ten doors north of its competitor, and with the same vested interest in exterminating outlaws. The Boswells, gentlemen of substance, didn't care much for the wolf breed. And one clan of that breed Coffeyville was just naturally meaning to exterminate.

Yes, Coffeyville was arming. So were the Daltons.

27

THE DALTONS LOAD

THE Daltons meant to be decked out from 'head to foot for their Coffeyville homecoming. More Americans knew about them than about any other of its former residents, except Billy the Kid. You couldn't expect them to come back looking like saddle tramps who hadn't made their marks in the world.

So it would be new clothes for Coffeyville. The boys aimed to look sharper than the local dudes squiring their girls to Saturday-night socials, nattier than Lucius Baldwin, who sang in the Methodist Church choir, his warbling enchanting the ladies.

Well-cut pants and fine broadcloth shirts, the Daltons selected—while making an after-hours visit to one of the two general stores at Gray Horse in the Osage Nation. They left the money on the counter for the proprietor to pick up the next morning. Bob had keys to both stores, given him by merchant friends of his, ever since he had been the Nation's police chief.[1] It was an arrangement which served the boys well when circumstances made daytime shopping difficult. No Dalton ever pulled a gun on a country storekeeper in Oklahoma, or ever failed to pay spot cash for purchases.

New horses were next on the list. Naturally they didn't want to come home riding plugs. Procuring broncs was Florence Quick's standing assignment and she rustled five ponies that were tops in speed and tractable besides. They were probably the best horses that Daltons had boarded since the Jesse James mare.

New saddles, too, the boys wanted for the great double haul at Coffeyville. Nothing like those flattened Texas hulls that the town had laughed at when the Daltons were little more than stirrup vagabonds. The Daltons had class now, being the top desperados of these United States. They needed fine Mexican saddles, and gaudy silk tassels dangling from the bridles, and hand-carvings on tree and hind bow that Mexes went in for. Side bars of burnished wood-and-leather. Stirrups chiseled from plated silver. So the boys got five

161

impressive Mexican saddles somewhere. Maybe they were slightly used ones, bought cheaply from cowhands who once had splurged and now were broke.

New guns, too, were needed for the big homecoming; new guns, above everything. Killing tools as fine and deadly as anything the lawmen of Montgomery County could get in Coffeyville or any iron-butted marshal could buy from the mail-order houses in Kansas City.[2]

Bob Dalton bought ten new Colt forty-fives, each as pretty as a diamondback rattlesnake waiting and ready to strike. They were probably purchased at hardware stores in Tulsa; between robberies, the bandits often went to this booming prairie town for watchful relaxation in its saloons and whorehouses.

Each of the outlaws owned a high-powered Winchester of the very latest model, with performance that could be relied on to the last trailing wisp of smoke. Bob owned a brace of them, kept in superb condition. Emmett was also equipped with two, which he kept carefully oiled and cleaned.

From the stockpile of pistols, acquired by Bob, each man chose the weapon that best suited his personality and trigger finger. Bob himself selected a .45-caliber Bisley model that had come with the rest of the Colts. It was a good gun, less ornate than the well-used "blue Steel" Smith & Wesson, .38 caliber, which was its companion belt piece.

Each bandit carried, as standard equipment, a hundred rounds of ammunition. Cartridges of any specification could be bought at almost any general store in this country of the gun.

A persistent legend says that the Daltons left their old guns, including Emmett's .44-40 Colt, at their mother's farm in Kingfisher County. It is to be doubted: Adeline's boys were always careful not to expose their mother to trouble, one of the few things that could be said in their favor. Used weapons were always negotiable in the West; the Daltons either sold their discarded hog irons or got trade-in allowances when they bought new guns.

It was late September, 1892: hunting moon, as the Indians called it, and the reduced gang was eager to get back into business. Train-robbing had paid off poorly in cash. But take banks: they were the places where you found the real money! When you wanted anything, from a slut to a dollar, you had to go to the place where it was kept. Then, if you were a Dalton, you took it.

Coffeyville, with its two banks, was a big undertaking for

that handful of outlaws. Generally four men were a minimum needed to tap just one bank. Now, five ambitious lads were supposed to take two, and they had no previous experience in bank-robbing as such.

But the job didn't seem so scary when you gabbed it over. The Daltons knew every trail leading in every direction from Coffeyville. That shouldn't make the escape too hard. Besides, look what Bob and Emmett already had gotten away with in that community of jaspers. Killing Charley Montgomery and leaving his corpse for old man Lang to bury at government expense. Later, when prices had accumulated on their heads, making post-midnight visits to a hotel called the Farmer's Rest, where the frightened—or, maybe, friendly—proprietor always scraped them up a meal. More recently, there was Bob's jaunt into the town, when he'd rousted Frank Benson from bed and demanded that gallon of whisky.

Dick Broadwell and Bill Powers, who had never been there, felt that Coffeyville, must be as tame as an old ladies' sewing circle. They laughed uproariously at Dalton recollections of the swaddling city on the Verdigris River.

Grat remembered happily that he'd been able to whip every boy in Coffeyville when the family lived there. Emmett knew Tom Ayres, the cashier of the First National Bank. He'd be no problem, declared the youngest Dalton. Everybody knew that bankers were cowards.

Coffeyville's two banks hired no guards. The local lawmen had had plenty of chances to jump Daltons over the years and had never risked tangling with the home-town bad boys. They'd run like rabbits when triggers were pulled.

Bob and Emmett believed all this out of supreme confidence in their own invincibility. Grat believed it because he didn't have any better sense. Broadwell and Powers swallowed it because the Daltons, as almost-native sons, ought to know what they were talking about.

The calendar said October 1, 1892. The double robbery was set for October 5. New weapons were tested for the last time for range and accuracy. New horses had final tryouts in impromptu races. Post-robbery plans seemed to be in foolproof order. After the haul, the Daltons would tear out of Coffeyville on their speedy mounts and double back across the Oklahoma line into the remote hills of the Cherokee Strip. There a Negro teamster, with a covered wagon, would be waiting for them. Broadwell and Powers could take their share of the loot and go where they pleased—to hell, for all Bob Dalton cared.

In the Cherokee Nation, the brothers would be joined by

the Misses Florence Quick and Julia Johnson. The Negro, an ex-cowpuncher, would transport the party, disguised as emigrants, west across No Man's Land into the even more isolated mountains of New Mexico. From there the two affectionate couples and Grat, the stag, would make their way to Old Mexico. Oh, it was a sweet prospect.

Julia Johnson, a bit dubious about the whole thing, had made only a halfway agreement to such a bizarre elopement with Emmett, but Flo Quick was downright delighted. There'd be no more rolling of yokels for her. No more desperate subterfuges to get money for Bob; he'd be bringing plenty out of Coffeyville. She was dreaming again of comfies and counterpanes, of pattering little feet—with only Bob Dalton pulling her to him at night in some beautiful *casa* beyond the Rio Grande.

Bob's gun girl might have been less enthusiastic about all their prospects if she had known what Chris Madsen had done to assure the Daltons a rousing reception in their home town. Even the marshals felt that the band would stage a successful coup at Coffeyville, and then make a quick break back to Oklahoma, but they were not counting on anything as audacious as the robbery of two banks by daylight.

Since Coffeyville lawmen wanted to stage their own showdown with the plunderers, Madsen dispatched none of his own men to the town. He did, however, detail deputies to intercept the gang on its expected return from the Kansas community. By the record of his journal:

"Some of our best men were detailed to be ready to go at once to such places as might be designated, should the holdup occur and the outlaws succeed in getting away. It was our intention to try to get ahead of them, and waylay them before they could get to their fresh relay of horses."

Florence Quick would, of course, have provided the relay. Madsen, as good a field man as an office expediter, was eager to redeem the reputation of Oklahoma's marshals by bagging its toughest assemblage of outlaws. He had to forego the prospective honor because of his clerical efficiency and his skill as a director of operations. He wrote rather wistfully:

"I was anxious to take a hand in the capture—but I had to remain in the office, in order to keep in touch with the banks and the deputies in the field."

It was October 2, 1892. Bob and Emmett had said what they supposed were only temporary good-bys to their almost-everloving girls. The Negro driver had brought the wagon to the Cherokee Strip, as planned.

The Daltons had no inkling of what Chris Madsen had been up to in Guthrie; otherwise they might have deferred their initial try at this new craft of bank robbing. As it was, they were moving cautiously along the old Whiskey Trail, which led along the Verdigris River into Coffeyville.

This dimming road was a familiar route to the Daltons. Along it, Frank had chased booze peddlers, to wind up buried in a Coffeyville cemetery. The boys' father likewise lay in his grave at Dearing, not far away. In fact, the family owned a cemetery lot in Coffeyville itself.

By the third of October excitement was mounting among the five outlaws. They kept their eyes peeled for marshals along the almost abandoned road, but they saw no signs of badge wearers. Things looked rosy, although an argument did arise between Bob and Emmett over the disposition of their forces at Coffeyville.

Bob had decided that he and Emmett would take care of the First National Bank, and that Grat would be in command of operations at the Condon, with Dick Broadwell and Bill Powers under him. Thinking Grat far too reckless for such an assignment, Emmett suggested that *he* ought to be in charge of things at the Condon Bank, with Broadwell or Powers assigned to help Bob at the First National.

Bob was obstinate. "No, Emmett," he replied; "no more shuffling of the deck. I want you with me at the First National. Then I won't have to be worrying about what's going on behind me when I get into action."

It sounded callous, but if any brother went down at Coffeyville, he preferred it to be Grat, the expendable, not Emmet, his trusted favorite.

Emmett was still worried but he buttoned his lip. He knew Charlie Ball, the cashier at the Condon Bank, and that Ball "was a cool headed fellow in a pinch."

The fourth of October saw early camp for the bandits, what with a big day ahead. They crossed the Kansas line to reach the farm of P. L. Davis, on Onion Creek, three miles from Coffeyville. Davis had known the Daltons most of their lives, but no evidence exists that he was aware they were on his property this day.

At three P.M., the boys reined in to rest, to make a final review of plans, and to feed their horses. By order of Bob Dalton, Dick Broadwell dismounted and cut Davis's barbed-wire fence with a pair of nippers.

They rode across the farmer's freshly plowed field to a patch of dense timber on the banks of the creek. Each pony was tied to a separate tree; the outlaws walked around for a while to stretch their legs, saddle-stiff from so much riding. Two of them were ordered by Bob to mount and ride toward the cornpatch of Mrs. J. F. Savage, on an adjoining farm.

The foraging party came back with plenty of feed for their ponies. Talk was low and subdued as a supper of freshly baked biscuits and hard-boiled eggs was eaten. Molding fragments of the meal were found on the site a few days later. They may have gotten the food from some sympathizer in the neighborhood: Daltons still had a few close-mouthed friends among Montgomery County farmers.

An apocryphal story has the road agents spending the night in an Oklahoma farmhouse, south of Coffeyville, and engaging in target practice by shooting at rafters in the barn. Other tales comparable to it are to be found in a collection of folklore about the gang, preserved in the city's Dalton Defenders Museum.

Midnight came, ushering in the fifth of October, the appointed day. The five were still awake, unable to stretch out on blankets because of their tense eagerness. At one A.M., they were still conversing, going over plans again and again.

Bob had drawn a rough map of Coffeyville with a sharp stick in the damp soil. The "chart" showed where each squad would enter its target bank, where it would make its exit after the haul, and where the two parties would converge for a quick flight. Bob, Emmett and Grat already knew every street and alley of the town; the crude plat would be memorized by Powers and Broadwell. Bob hoped that the raid would take no more than fifteen minutes.

Disguises that the Daltons would wear were fetched out and tried on. The boys wanted Coffeyville to know who it was that sacked its banks—but not too soon. Powers and Broadwell could get by with ordinary bandanna-masks, since nobody was likely to make any spot recognitions of them.

At two A.M., the outlaws divested themselves of articles that would easily identify them or incriminate families or friends. Letters, tin-types, stray business cards of merchants were thrown into the fire.

Finally they turned in, with each taking a stand at sentry duty. Emmett drew the dogwatch, from four A.M., to daylight.

Grat took a final nip on a jug. The muffled fire cast faint gleams on gun metal. The lights of Coffeyville flickered in the distance.

28

HOMECOMING

THEY rode toward Coffeyville a couple of hours after milking time, three of them local boys, two of them strangers. In the past, the three had known many kindnesses from the people of Coffeyville, kindnesses they would have found it hard to repay with all the money in the town's two banks.

Now they weren't wearing Coffeyville's hand-me-downs, thank you. They weren't waiting for the church ladies to bring basketfuls of cast-offs to clothe ragged Daltons. Or envying their playmates, now grown men, for their bright new squirrel guns or shiny tassels dangling from the bridles of their ponies.

No sirree, neighbor! Daltons had style now. Class. Daltons had gone up in the world, like Coffeyville—though advancement had been in different directions. Daltons didn't want a damn thing from the old home town.

Nothing, that was, except its money. And revenge for charity offered—and accepted.

"We're going to square accounts with Coffeyville," Bob had promised when they rode out of their camp that morning.

They meant to arrive in the town square at about the time the banks opened, before businessmen started making withdrawals for the day's trade. The less cash left in those vaults, the less for the Daltons.

The freebooters rode slowly across Davis's field to reach the county road that led to the town. The three brothers wore false whiskers which made them look more formidable than usual. Bob's face was hidden by a heavy black mustache and goatee. Emmett was sporting a big brush of whiskers and feeling as important as Jesse James, who had worn real ones. Grat had donned whiskers that gave him "the look of an ancient pirate," but which didn't conceal the dried dribble of tobacco juice on his chin. Broadwell and Powers were without disguises, Bob having assured them that nobody in Coffeyville would recognize them.

Bob may have been careless, or even cynical, about the

two non-family members of the gang. Their pictures must
have been on reward posters filed in the sheriff's office.
Broadwell was from Hutchinson, Kansas; some visitor to Coffeyville might easily recognize him in this other Kansas
town.

They rode at a snail's pace, deliberately holding in their
horses. Emmett was having trouble with his charger, Red
Buck. The town was only two miles away; it would be best
to dally along, lest they arrive before even the stores
opened. Early loiterers might attract unwanted attention,
too much interest from early-bird citizens greeting the balmy
morning.

Besides, a slow trip would give them time for final par-
leying, a careful recapitulation of the daring plan. It would
also enable them to take stock of anyone they saw along the
road. Somehow, perhaps through whoever had sent them
supper, Bob had learned that Coffeyville had been stirred up
for a while, expecting a Dalton visit, but that the excitement had simmered down.

The first person to glimpse them was a little girl, the
daughter of Mr. and Mrs. James Brown. She was on horseback, too, bound for Coffeyville on some errand for her parents. She saw the five when they emerged single-file from the
Davis field, and crossed a dry section of Onion Creek to its
north bank. They continued along north, the girl following
them curiously till she turned her pony at a crossroad leading east into town.

Apparently the five were not aware of the child behind
them, or paid no attention to her if they were. She of course
did not realize that she had spotted the Dalton gang. She
just had a natural inquisitiveness about strangers.

After she had abandoned her childish scout, the five
found themselves on a stretch of road seldom used by anyone except the farmers who lived along it. There they were
seen by William Gilbert, getting an early start in his fields.

Farmer Gilbert, a plain, honest fellow, took them for lawmen. Posses from Indian Territory frequently were seen in
Montgomery County. Snatches of talk he heard from the
group strengthened his impression. He noticed that they
were wearing broad-brimmed black slouch hats, tilted forward. Later he would say that "no arms were visible" on the
men. Probably, too interested in his own tasks, he did not
look closely enough at them.

Now the Daltons had been seen, with no sign of their
having been recognized. That was heartening. They buttoned
their jackets more closely as they jogged along, swapping

comments about what they would do with the Coffeyville loot.

Along the way they passed the farm where the three Daltons had lived as children, that "big light green house" with the "red weathered barn" that Emmett would, in later years, sentimentalize about. Right then, none of the three had any inclination to rhapsodize on Home Sweet Home.

Home, hell. Here the church hens had come with the charity baskets, with Ma Dalton forcing her brats to pretend gratitude, under threat of the strap. The shack where supper as a rule had been cornbread and clabber. The fields that had been rated the sorriest in Montgomery County.

Bob Dalton flipped his reins impatiently. Grat and Emmett were not overcome by nostalgia, either.

The five reached a junction of two land-section lines, next to a dairy and cheese factory. They were on the outskirts of the town itself. The sun was higher. Bob looked at his watch and gave a terse command.

The gang headed east down a road that became Eighth Street inside the town limits. They spurred their mounts to a brisk trot along the dry, loose-surfaced road. Clouds of dust rose, sifting onto their faces. Half a mile west of the town line they passed two more local citizens.

R. H. Hollingsworth and his wife were bound west, away from Coffeyville, in a carriage pulled by two horses. Contrary to Gilbert's impression, the Hollingsworths later remembered those swift riders as being heavily armed.

A hundred yards farther on the outlaws met John M. and J. F. Seldomridge, also traveling west in a vehicle. The Seldomridges felt that the five men riding toward town were bad actors. The beards worn by three of them were, they believed, false. Being prudent men, they continued on their way instead of turning back in an attempt to warn the town.

The five reached the city limits. At the corner where the Episcopal church stood they turned from Eighth into Maple. Bob, Emmett, and Grat were riding abreast in the lead, Broadwell and Powers trailing. A few townspeople noticed them but thought they either were cowpunchers or a posse of federal officers. Apparently no one recognized a familiar Dalton face beneath those silly whiskers.

On Maple Street, the five passed the local office of the Long-Bell Lumber Company. Here they rode down an alley leading toward the public square. A number of people were in the alley. Three or four teams of horses were hitched at the back entrance of Davis's blacksmith shop, which fronted on Walnut Street. An oil tank, drawn by two horses, later

would be halted and left near the delivery stable of Mc-
Kenna & Adamson's general store.

The men dismounted and hitched their horses to the back
fence of a lot owned by Police Judge Charles Munn. The
banks were a few hundred yards away. Bob had figured the
alley would be a good escape route to use after the comple-
tion of the double haul.

Unrecognized, the Daltons and their two confederates
walked toward the square, the brothers in the lead, the others following, all five bunched closely together. A stonecut-
ter who was a stranger in town had seen them dismount;
noticing they were armed, he followed them for a few steps;
then turned back. He must have decided that whatever was
a-brewing he would be better off out of it.

People were moving about the square, some afoot, some
in buggies. The five entered the square at a dogtrot, their
Winchesters under their arms.

Storekeeper Alex McKenna was standing in front of his
shop. His sharp gaze quickly penetrated the brothers' stock-
company disguises.

"The Daltons!" he shouted; "there go the Daltons!"

From his ice wagon, Cyrus Lee also saw the real men
behind the phony whiskers. "The Daltons are robbing the
bank!" he yelled excitedly as Bob and Emmett entered the
door of the First National.

"The Daltons!"

The cry reverberated up and down the square as Grat,
Powers, and Broadwell entered the Condon & Company
bank on the opposite side of the street.

Men began to run toward the hardware stores. Within a
couple of minutes, merchants were passing out guns.

The Daltons had come home, and a warm reception was in
the making for them.

29

THE DEFENDERS

THREE respectable citizens of Coffeyville were the earliest customers of the First National Bank on that morning of October 5, 1892. The three, all men of substance, were Abe W. Knotts, J. B. Brewster, and C. L. Hollingsworth. The next two patrons were a pair of former residents, Robert and Emmett Dalton.

Knotts, Brewster and Hollingsworth were standing in the broad front room of the bank. Behind his counter, Cashier Thomas G. Ayres was handling a transaction with Brewster while Knotts and Hollingsworth waited to be served. Teller W. H. Shepard was sitting at his desk near the vault, which contained an estimated $18,000.

It was about nine-thirty when Bob and Emmett barged in and slammed the doors after them. No finesse here; they didn't see any necessity of handling the home folks with kid gloves.

"Hands up!" Bob shouted. "You customers stand right where you are."

He leveled his Winchester at the cashier. "Hand over all the money in the bank, Tom," he barked.

Emmett's rifle was trained on Shepard and he was cursing a blue streak to enhance the effect of the guns on the five startled men. Then he caught sight of citizen Jim Boothby and a young boy named Jack Long, peeping through the window after hearing from one Jesse Morgan that the Daltons were robbing the bank.[1]

"Get in here, you son of a bitch!" Emmett yelled at Boothby. Scared, the man obeyed, stepping inside the bank. Emmett rapped his gun barrel against the window.

"Get away from here, son, before you get hurt," he ordered the boy.

Young Jack Long then walked next door to Rammel Brothers drugstore, where he saw expert marksman George Cubine holding a Winchester. Other men were running out of the hardware stores, shouting and flourishing rifles and shotguns.

Inside the bank, Tom Ayres was stalling for time, deliberately dumping small lots of gold and currency into an empty grain sack held by Bob. The hubbub of voices outside made him believe that help was coming. Bob wanted faster action; leaving Emmett in charge of operations here, he hurried through the hallway to a private office in the back. Beyond this room lay a door with a thick iron grating, held by a spring lock, that led to an alley which the gang had selected as its escape route.

At his desk in the office sat the bank's bookkeeper, Bert S. Ayres, son of the cashier. Swinging his gun, Bob ordered Ayres to "go up front" and help Tom Ayres hand out the money. The bookkeeper obeyed reluctantly when Bob, cursing, threatened to shoot him if he didn't move faster.

Within a few minutes all cash that had been in sight was in the grain sack. Bob ordered Bert Ayres to deliver the money in the locked vault.

"I can't," the bookkeeper answered. "I don't know the combination."

Bob then commanded the cashier: "Tom, you go and get it." Tom Ayres opened the vault and brought out some more stacks of currency. Bob dumped the rolls of bills into the bag and asked suspiciously, "Is that all?"

Ayres, still playing a delaying game, answered, "There's some gold in the vault; do you want that too?"

"Yes, every damn cent of it," Bob growled.

Ayres made another trip to the strongbox, to return loaded with gold coins. Then and there, Bob Dalton should have been satisfied with the amount of the loot, gathered up his followers and blown out of Coffeyville. Instead, he demanded again if this was all the plunder in the vault. Ayres, coolly risking his life, swore that it was. Leaving Emmett to handle the captives, Bob strode into the vault himself, rummaged around and came up with two packs of bank-notes totaling $5,000 each.

"What's this?" he shouted. Leaving the vault, he threw the currency into the sack. Then he returned to the depository to find piles of silver coin, which he tossed contemptuously on the bank floor. He picked up a box that was filled with gold watches left by a customer. One of the bankers called to him that there was nothing except papers in the box. Bob replaced it, unopened.

He turned from the vault, then ordered the three bankers and the four other men to march to the front door. Hands aloft, Bob and Emmett walking behind them with cocked guns, the seven Kansans reached the pavement. Two shots rang out from the drugstore as the bandits appeared at the door. George Cubine had let go with his Winchester, C. S. Cox with a revolver, both aiming at the Daltons.

The shots were not on target. The Daltons dashed back into the bank, followed by Shepard and Bert Ayres. Tom Ayres ran to Isham's hardware store, grabbed a rifle, and stood ready for battle at the north door, where he could keep an eye on the bank. Knotts, Hollingsworth and Brewster had scattered. Tom Ayres stood, tensely watching, expecting the Daltons to emerge from the bank again.

Instead, Bob stepped to the side of the First National's front door, raised his rifle, and coolly fired across the square. Guns began booming in answer from every corner of the plaza.

Gruffly Bob ordered Emmett to bundle up the swag for what was going to be a contested departure.

Holding his rifle under his arm, Emmett hurriedly wrapped a string around the top of the sack. Shepard, the teller, was ordered to open the back door for the bandits. They followed him to that exit, ran into the alley—and began tasting the bitter homecoming that Coffeyville had prepared for them.

The roster of citizens who turned out to resist the Daltons on that day is as honorable as that of any roll of professional Western lawmen. These plain everyday people were of the mettle of the Minnesota settlers who had wrecked the attempt of the James-Younger gang to plunder Northfield.

Charles T. Gump, a drayman who had known the Daltons all their lives, was the first casualty of the day. He was struck by the bullet that Bob fired from the bank after the release of Tom Ayres and the four townsmen. Gump was standing behind an iron awning post, facing the bank and waiting for the robbers with a double-barreled shotgun borrowed from Isham's store. He sustained a severe hand wound when the bullet from Bob's high-powered weapon hit the shotgun, which fell shattered at Gump's feet.

Lucius Baldwin, the young store clerk and Methodist Church standby, was the second. Baldwin was waiting for the bandits when they came out the rear door of the bank opened for them by Shepard, the teller. He stepped forward, holding a small revolver, muzzle pointing down. The Daltons pointed their rifles and told him to drop his weapon. Baldwin stood there, paralyzed after his initial courage in confronting the bandits, but his possession of the gun doomed him.

"I'll have to get that man," Bob said to Emmett. He

pulled the trigger. The shell struck Baldwin's left breast
and ripped through his body. The young clerk died three
hours later, after townspeople had carried him to a doctor.

Twenty-one thousand dollars of home-town money in the
sack clutched by Emmett, the two brothers ran north along
the alley, then turned west toward Eighth Street. They must
reach their horses, in that first alley. They hoped grimly
that Grat and Dick and Bill would be through with their
work at the Condon Bank. Then the whole gang could ride
out together.

Still heading west, Bob and Emmett reached Union Street,
where they paused and glanced quickly around. They fired
two shots, hoping to drive away anybody who might be
waiting to snipe at them. They kept moving toward the middle of the street, their eyes searching every doorway. A
grocer, standing in front of his store, shouted to them:

"You're killing innocent people."

Emmett raised his rifle. "Get back in there or I'll give
you some of it."

The merchant scurried back into his store. The Daltons'
foes seemed to be holding their fire, although later on Emmett was to assert that bullets hailed around them. The
brothers maintained their sharp scrutiny of store entrances,
their guns menacing.

They sighted George Cubine, standing armed at his post
in front of Rammel's drugstore. Cubine was watching the
entrance of the First National, not knowing that the brothers had escaped through the rear.

Emmett and Bob both fired at him. Of four shots from
their guns, three found their mark. Cubine sprawled on the
pavement, one shot having penetrated his heart, a second his
left thigh, a third his ankle.

An old man, Charles J. Brown, a shoe cobbler, rushed
from his shop toward his fallen friend. Seeing that Cubine
was dead, he grabbed the gun that his friend had dropped
and began shooting at the Daltons. He kept on firing till the
rifle slid from his hands with his last conscious breath.

Four more shots it took the Daltons to kill a Civil War
veteran who had once been their close friend. As Brown lay
dying two feet from his partner, Emmett raised his gun for
a finishing shot.

"Go slow, Emmett," Bob said. "I can whip the whole
damn town."

Emmett laughed. Coffeyville surely looked whipped. All
that money from the First National in that bulging bag.
More to come from the Condon Bank in the sortie led by

Grat. Four Coffeyvillers plugged for daring to buck Daltons.
One dead on the spot. Two dying.

Only about fifteen minutes had elapsed since Bob and
Emmett had left the First National. Coffeyville had been
treated mightily rough in that quarter of an hour. Four gun
victims and so much cash should have evened all scores
that the Daltons ever had chalked up against it in their
warped minds. But there had to be another trump played,
a final trick taken with a Dalton ace.

Cashier Tom Ayres was standing with his rifle by Isham's
store. The Daltons had reached the west side of Union
Street on their way to the alley where the horses had been
staked. Bob Dalton's roving gaze spotted the banker.

Earlier victims had been potted at ranges of from forty
to fifty yards. Mr. Ayres was a bit farther away—seventy-
five yards. Still pie, for a Dalton. Bob raised his Winchester.
It was a neat shot, and a deadly one, hitting the banker
below his left eye and emerging from the skull.

Rob the bank and shoot the banker. That was really telling off Coffeyville!

Bob and Emmett, after firing a salvo of nine more shots
to discourage any possible avengers of Mr. Ayres, disap-
peared into the alley where they had staked the horses. Grat,
Broadwell and Powers should be waiting there for them.
Hell, the Condon Bank was no more guarded than the First
National, and three men had tackled it.

There were no signs of the second raiding party when the
brothers reached the alley. Bob lost some of his cockiness.
"What's keeping the boys?" he asked anxiously.

Suddenly there was a roar of gunfire, a barrage such as
Daltons had never heard in all their lives. Then came shouts
and the long, piercing cry of someone who had been hit
hard.

Bob Dalton stared at his brother. "Emmett," he said, "the
boys are in trouble; we'll have to go back and help Grat
and them out."

Clutching their rifles, the pair ran back down the alley,
ready to give more battle. The volume and tempo of gunfire
mounted. Emmett and Bob might have guessed what had
happened. Grat's stupidity had wrecked the play.

30

TWO BUSHELS OF MONEY

QUIETLY, almost unnoticed, Grat Dalton had slipped into the Condon Bank with his masked confreres, Bill Powers and Dick Broadwell. The first man to glimpse them was twenty-year-old Thomas Clark Babb, who occasionally worked here, writing out government checks paid to Indians through the bank.

He recognized Grat Dalton, having known the whole family when they had lived briefly on a farm eight miles east of Coffeyville, in adjoining Labette County. Babb had no desire to revive old acquaintance, the less so in that Grat and the others all were carrying Winchesters. Without raising any alarm, Babb slid from his desk on the east side of the bank's front room to the near-by vault. There he hid behind a high rack filled with journals and ledgers.

Grat and the boys didn't notice Babb. Nobody in the bank seemed to notice them, either, till Grat made announcement of their presence:

"We've got you, God damn you! Hold up your hands!"

This was his greeting to the bank's co-owner, C. T. Carpenter, who stood bent over the customer's counter in the right front of the bank. He recognized the intruder. Up went his hands. Carpenter couldn't place the other two gun toters accompanying the home-town boy, but they looked like men it wouldn't pay to meddle with.

Dick Broadwell placed himself on guard near the bank's southeast entrance. Bill Powers took up a post not far from the southwest door. Grat was hurling curses at the helpless Carpenter, his raucous voice echoing back from the bank's walls like a steer's bellow. Charles M. Ball, the cashier, stepped from his office in the northwest section of the big room to see what the commotion was all about.

Charlie Ball got the same threats of harsh treatment as Carpenter, his white-faced employer, as the three guns swung toward him. Ball put up his hands, lowering them only when Grat, striding behind the counter, tossed him a seamless grain sack and ordered him to hold it open while Carpenter filled it with cash.

Ball gingerly followed instructions under the menace of Grat's Winchester. He noticed that it was a two-bushel sack. Grat was going to collect two bushels of money from this county where his old man had scarcely grown two bushels of corn.

Carpenter was nervous and tense. Ball was cool and collected. The proprietor sullenly dumped all the currency from the counter and drawers into the bag. The cashier was as calm as a drummer cashing a check during the few minutes when stacks of bills and coins were being tossed into the bag by his boss. As he held the sack open, he was trying to figure some way to outwit a man he remembered as not having much wit.

For by this time, Ball had placed the burly outlaw. Grat, the oldest son of the bad Daltons, was reckoned the "slowest."

The two went into the opened outer section of the vault. An inner compartment was closed. As Carpenter and Ball entered the huge safe, Grat caught sight of Tom Babb, cowering behind the rack. He burned Babb's ears with oaths, then commanded him to come out with his hands high. Babb obeyed.

Grat then spied in the vault three bulging canvas bags, each of which contained a thousand dollars in silver. These he ordered Carpenter to throw into the sack still being held by Cashier Ball.

"What is this you're putting in there?" Grat asked abruptly.

"Silver dollars," Ball answered truthfully.

Grat looked disappointed. Gold was what his paws itched for. He started cursing again. Then he noticed the locked inner chest. That must be where the most precious possession of any damn bank was kept, he thought.

When he pointed to the chest and said, "Open it up," Ball answered matter-of-factly, "Can't. It's set automatically. Isn't time for it to open."

Grat fell for the dodge. "What time does it open?"

"Half past nine," Ball told him.

Grat asked innocently, "What time is it now?"

Ball pulled out his watch and looked at it. "Twenty minutes after nine."

Grat didn't bother to check the timepiece himself. "We can wait ten minutes," he said.

Actually, the time was nine-forty by Charlie Ball's watch, set precisely, as a banker's should be. Actually, too, the automatic time lock on the chest had opened at eight A.M., so that its contents would be available at nine when the bank began its day's business. Ball would have needed only to swing open the door for Grat's greedy hands to get at the gold inside.

One minute passed. A shadow of suspicion gathered on Grat's face. He remembered Charlie Ball as having been a pretty smart article during boyhood. Banker Carpenter, who had understood the clever play of his employee, proceeded to give it some backing. He made a fake pass at the handle of the door to convince Grat that it was locked.

Another minute passed. Time was important if he were to rejoin Emmett and Bob without mishap, Grat knew. Distrustful again, he said to Ball: "God damn you, I believe you're lying. I've a mind to put a bullet through you. Where's your gold?"

The cashier answered solemnly, "We haven't any."

Grat looked at the bag of loot scooped from the counter. "How much is in this sack?" Ball replied that the amount was $4,000. Grat revealed a glimmer of intelligence. "How much did your books show last night?" he demanded.

"Four thousand dollars," Ball said quickly. "A thousand in bills that you took from the counter; three thousand in silver from those sacks. There's nothing in that chest except some nickels and pennies. We ordered some currency from the mint, but it hasn't been delivered from the express office yet."

Into the bank wandered a couple of customers: John D. Levan, who lent money to citizens not considered good risks by the banks; and D. E. James, a clerk in a local dry-goods store. They were immediately taken into custody by Bill Powers. Levan turned pale around the gills when he looked into the Winchester held by the bandit.

Grat turned impatiently to see what was happening. The time must be almost up.

A volley of bullets from outside shattered the plate-glass windows. Dick Broadwell and Bill Powers fired back six shots apiece. A second crashing wave of lead came from the guns of citizens gathered under crack marksman John Kloehr, at Isham and Mansour's hardware store across the street. The bankers and the two customers prudently dropped to the floor, faces hugging the stone surface. Kloehr's men had mobilized during those few minutes when Charlie Ball had been putting the Indian sign on Grat Dalton.

Trapped, Grat glanced around wildly. Brother Bob wasn't there to do his thinking for him. Dick Broadwell, was swapping lead with some antagonist outside, a sniper named Parker L. Williams, perched on the awning of the Boswell hardware store on the opposite side of the square. Armed

with a Colt .44, Williams was making things hot for Broadwell. The desperado steadied his rifle against the edge of
the southwest door and fired at Williams, whose form he
could barely make out through the curling clouds of gun-
smoke. Broadwell missed a second shot, the bullet plowing
upward to whizz through an upstairs window of the Barndollar Brothers department store and shatter some fancy
china on a shelf.

Williams and Broadwell then raised their weapons and
fired simultaneously.

"I'm shot!" Broadwell howled when Williams's bullet
caught him in the shoulder. "I can't use my arm. It's no use,
I can't shoot any more."

Grat Dalton got the idea it was time to leave. "Is there
a back door we can get out through?" he shouted to Cashier
Ball.

Ball answered no. Grat let himself be fooled again. His
mind had reached the limits of its functioning. Broadwell
was out of commission. Powers's life also hung on the big
fellow's judgment. But all that Grat could think about was
holding onto as much of the loot as he could. He couldn't
leave Coffeyville empty-handed.

Hell was raining through the front door, but Grat ordered
Ball and Carpenter to carry the two bushels of money to it. It
was a literal invitation to death but, menaced by the bandit's
Winchester, the bankers picked up the sack at either end
and marched from the vault toward the entrance. The
hail of bullets was too much for the bankers when they
reached the lobby. They dropped the sack and fled to a
back room. Grat ordered Ball to return to the hall and fetch
the sack.

Ball complied. Grat then commanded him to cut the
string with which the bag had been tied and separate the
currency from the silver. Ball emptied the loot on the floor,
divided the paper money from the metal, and handed the
bills to the desperado. Only a thousand dollars, Grat would
now have for a rough morning's work.

The gunfire had become deafening. There was only one
route of exit: the one past Coffeyville's crack shots—or so
Grat thought. Likewise, there was only one sensible thing
for the three outwitted plunderers to do. Surrender and forget the damned money. Call calf rope, even if it meant risking the lynch rope.

Instead, with a great shout, the outlaws ran through the
door, Grat clutching the slim take. They had gone barely
six steps before the citizens cut down on them.

31

"ALLEY OF DEATH"

NO man could say that Grat Dalton didn't die gamely. He went out as courageously as had his brother Frank, on the side of the law, now bone and dust in a Coffeyville graveyard.

Grat took about twenty steps outside the bank doors before bullets fired by ex-neighbors begin puncturing his big torso. He bled like a pig stuck for slaughter in Coffeyville's hogpens. His feet tangled. His chin sagged. His breath came in sobbing spurts.

"We got Grat!" somebody called jubilantly from the group of marksmen headed by hardware merchant Henry Isham.

Wobbling and weaving, Grat kept a waning hold on life but he lost his grip on the sack of loot. The bag dropped to the ground. His boots dug into the sidewalk for some precarious balance. Blood, oozing from his mouth, spotted the false whiskers. In a staggering half-run, he reached a barn standing on the south side of an alley some 200 feet off Walnut Street. Here, he had a little protection from those determined sharpshooters in front of the Isham and Mansour hardware store. Their bullets were being deflected by an outside stairway leading to the second floor of Slosson's drugstore in front of the alley.

Propping himself against the barn, gasping and groaning, Grat stood waiting for the arrival of Bob and Emmett. They must have heard the shots; they must be on their way to help him. Daltons always helped Daltons. . . .

Kaleidoscopic blurs began skip-hopping before Grat's eyes. The blurs got bigger and darker as the blood saturated his shirt and jacket.

Grat didn't have much breath left in his body but he still had bullets left in his Winchester. His faltering fingers groped for the trigger. He could barely see where he was aiming, but he fired several shots in the direction from which a babble of voices came faintly to him. The slugs passed uncomfortably close to the heads of several men standing near

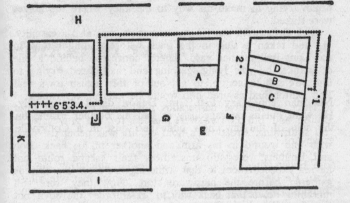

1 Where Lucius Baldwin fell.
2 Where Cubine and Brown fell.
3 Where Marshal Connelly fell.
4 Where Bob and Emmett Dalton fell.
5 Where Grat Dalton fell.
6 Where Tom Evans fell.
A Condon's bank.
B First National bank.
C Isham's store, where Ayres, Gump and Reynolds were wounded.
D Rammel Bros. drug store.
E Plaza.
F Union Street.
G Walnut Street.
H Eighth Street.
I Ninth Street.
J City Jail.
K Maple Street.
† Where the horses were tied. The dotted line marks the course of Bob and Emmett after leaving the bank.

the Masonic Hall at the intersection of Walnut and Ninth Streets.

Grat fumbled once more with the trigger but there was a growing numbness in his fingers. Blood streamed from his nostrils. He was bleeding to death.

Emmett . . . Bob . . . what was keeping them? Powers and Broadwell . . . where were they? They had left the bank with him. . . .

Bill Powers had been hit almost as soon as Grat in that flight from the Condon Bank. Then he had fled to the back door of an adjoining store and beat desperately upon it with his fists, hoping that someone would open it and admit him.

The door was locked. Nobody heard his frantic banging. Still clutching his Winchester, bleeding and cursing, Powers began trying to make his way to the alley where the horses were staked.

Dick Broadwell, the Kansas maverick, was also a casualty. He had taken a slug in the back before finding refuge in the Long-Bell lumber yard. There, concealed behind a pile of planks, he was lying, gasping and half-dazed, trying to find strength to go on, to get out of this hellish town that Bob Dalton had assured him would be such an easy mark.

Three of the five desperados now were casualties. Grat Dalton and Bill Powers were headed for the graveyard, if still squirming. Broadwell's hold on life was nebulous, what with one wound in his arm and another in his back. Bob and Emmett were still unscathed, their escape route not having exposed them to that withering fire from the citizens gathered before the hardware store. Now they were still marching down that back way to "re-enforce" the boys, not knowing what had happened but anxiously quickening their pace to match the tempo of the barking guns.

Three respected townspeople—Cubine, Baldwin, and Brown—had gotten mortal wounds from the weapons of the Daltons. Two others had received severe injuries—Charley Gump, the drayman, and Arthur Reynolds, one of Isham & Mansour's two clerks. Flourishing a rifle borrowed from his employers, Reynolds had rushed to the Condon Bank where he had been one of the eighty citizens standing outside as eyewitnesses to the robbery. A bullet fired by Dick Broadwell, guarding the southeast entrance, had struck the rash young clerk in the foot.

Now there came a lull in the battle. Bob and Emmett were trying to effect junction with their beleaguered comrades. Decimated the gang might be, but Bob was holding on grimly to that fortune seized from the First National. Emmett was ready to help him keep it. Grat, Broadwell, and Powers were still desperately clinging to life in their various hiding places.

With none of the bandits in sight, Henry Isham stepped back into his hardware store to see about the condition of his wounded helper, Arthur Reynolds. Isham's handlebar mustache was bobbing indignantly. He had been quietly accepting payment of a bill from a customer when the Daltons had started their murderous larking.

He found Arthur Reynolds reclining inside the store, blood from his foot puddling onto the floor. Isham's second clerk, Lewis A. Dietz, was still outside, hoping for a second round with the bandits.

Along with Dietz stood M. N. Anderson, a carpenter, Charles K. Smith, a barber's son, and other members of the party that had fired at the three men as they emerged from the Condon Bank. All had rifles. In front of the Boswell hardware store across the street stood a dozen men behind some parked farm wagons that had served as a barricade. These were bearing rifles and shotguns with which they had subjected the fleeing outlaws to a withering crossfire.

Near Read Brothers general store on the south side of the plaza were John Kloehr, the sharpshooting livery-stable keeper, lean and gaunt; Carey Seaman, a slouchy barber with drooping mustaches; and bearded city marshal Charles T. Connelly, looking more like a devil-wrestling Methodist preacher than a bandit-bucking lawman.

The battle resumed in a lower key, with the men at Isham and Mansour's firing scattered shots in the general direction of the half-hidden Grat. Propped against the side of the barn, Grat was still standing, still maintaining a wobbling hold on life, still keeping a grip on his Winchester. At that distance of 300 yards, the Isham squad could make out his form. But the range was too great for a *coup de grace*, the the drugstore stairs too deflecting an obstacle.

John Kloehr, posted at Read's store, feared that this slow-down might tip the scales in favor of the bandits. They must be dealt with before they reached their horses to carry off the money from the First National.

So Kloehr, barber Seaman, and Marshal Connelly started up Ninth Street, to block any attempt to escape by saddle-back. In doing so, they moved toward Grat's refuge. During the short walk, Connelly spoke to his friend, the livery-stable keeper.

"Kloehr, I went off from home this morning without a gun. I need one for this job."

John Kloehr motioned toward Swisher Brothers machine shop. "Borrow one in there, Marshal."

Kloehr entered his livery stable, intending to come at Grat through its rear. Seaman remained outside, hoping to flush Bill Powers from the lumber yard. Connelly, armed with a carbine obtained from the machine shop, hurried across a vacant lot toward the corner of the alley where Grat stood. He should have brought down the dying Dalton as the first order of pending business. But Connelly was

too anxious to prevent the bandits from getting to their
horses to put first things first.

His back was to Grat when he turned toward the place
where the horses were hitched. Grat's blurred vision could
still make out his shape. Too far gone to take aim, the outlaw fired blindly at that moving shadow, only twenty feet
away.

Charlie Connelly fell forward on his face. Snarling like an
animal in its death throes, Grat wheeled around ready to do
more carnage. At this moment, Bob and Emmett joined
him. Townspeople who had heard the shot that killed
Connelly began raking the alley with murderous gunfire.
The boys were hemmed in. The place, ever since, has been
named "Death Alley."

Raising their guns, the brothers, including the dying Grat,
fought desperately. The men in front of Isham and Mansour's
had moved back into the store for better vantage points
from the doors and windows of the establishments. The
milling, cursing Daltons were open targets.

Bill Powers, meantime, had reached that end of the alley
where the horses were hitched. A bullet caught him in the
back as he tried to mount. Dick Broadwell had crawled
from the lumber yard and managed to reach his pony. He
spurred the horse feebly as his blood flowed in rivulets
down the saddle girth.

He had ridden approximately twenty feet when a bullet
from Carey Seaman's rifle ripped into his flesh. Still he
managed to keep boots in stirrups and escape beyond the
city limits. Only the three Daltons, one of them already dying,
were left to fight all of Coffeyville.

They were trapped but, defiantly, they hung onto the
cash stolen from the First National. "We've got the swag, boys,
and we'll keep it," Bob said as a fresh volley from the
hardware store stirred clouds of dust all around them.

Bob looked toward Slosson's drugstore to see Frank Benson, on whom he had paid the midnight call, creeping
through a rear window, holding a gun. At thirty feet, Bob
shattered the glass. Benson renounced his bid for fame and
was seen no more.

Then Bob made a fatal mistake. He stepped into the
middle of the alley to get a good look at the roofs of the
buildings in front, believing that some of the shots being
fired at the beset brothers were coming from them.

In so doing, he placed himself squarely in range of the
snipers at the hardware store. One bullet hit him in that

flurry of instant fire. Bob reeled across the alley, to sit down heavily on a pile of curbstones in the rear of the city jail. He stared unbelievingly at his gun for a second. Then he looked up to see that one of his foes had overtaken him.

John Kloehr was standing inside the drugstore's back fence after having emerged from the rear door of the livery stable. Kloehr's gun was raised for action, his eyes searching the alley.

Bob Dalton tried to raise his gun to shoulder height, but was too weak and confused for the effort. He fired a low shot, which went harmlessly to one side. Then he staggered to his feet and walked slowly toward an old barn that was a part of the jail establishment. He leaned against its southwest corner and fired two more futile shots. John Kloehr looked at him without pity and drew a clear bead.

Kloehr's shot smashed into Bob's chest. He fell on his back against another pile of stones.

Grat was stumbling along, trying to reach his horse. He passed the fallen Marshal Connelly, and advanced a few feet farther. Again Kloehr took steady aim.

His shot struck Grat in the throat, breaking the burly neck. Grat fell back, tumbling across the dying Connelly. Now only one Dalton still battled. After his brothers went down, Emmett ducked along the alley, hugging the building walls, till he reached the horses. Four were still there, Dick Broadwell having ridden away on the fifth. Let Coffeyville have three. Emmett wanted now only his charger, Red Buck. Wanted his horse and the bag of loot he had retrieved when Bob dropped it. Wanted, besides, to get Bob out of Coffeyville alive.

The oil tank in the alley had slowed his progress; half a dozen shots had pursued him as he had made that daring flight. Citizens were pouring out from different places to thwart the escape of this last, lone robber. Emmett reached his horse. A salvo of bullets just missed him, killing the two horses hitched to the tank as well as the two that had belonged to Bob Dalton and Bill Powers.

Emmett mounted, swinging the treasure sack across the pommel of his saddle, but two bullets found their mark as he lifted the reins.

One hit him in the right arm. Another entered his left hip, to lodge in his groin.

The embattled citizens discharged more rattling volleys in Emmett's direction. He sat straight in his saddle, though badly

wounded. Watchers expected him to make a break for liberty.
Townsmen began heading toward mounts, intending to run
him down, as well as the already fleeing Broadwell.

Then Emmett Dalton did an incredibly heroic thing. He
performed the one act that graced the Dalton invasion of
Coffeyville.

Under a raking fire, he turned Red Buck back toward
the spot where Bob lay dying. Bracing himself erect in
the saddle, his teeth clenched, holding his Winchester in
his uninjured arm, Emmett paused not a second in that
tornado of lead. He reached Bob and stretched down a hand
to lift him into the saddle.

"It's no use, Emmett," Bob wheezed, and closed his eyes
as if he just wanted to be left alone.

Then both barrels of a double-barreled shotgun belched
their loads into Emmett's husky frame. He toppled from his
saddle. His Winchester, still trailing little wreaths of smoke,
dropped with him. A moment later, the loot sack fell
from the pommel to lie near the shattered outlaw and the
silenced gun.

Barber Carey Seaman coolly wiped his double-barreled
shotgun. Now all his customers, all Coffeyville, would be
pointing him out as the dead shot who had downed Emmett
Dalton.

Townspeople surged forward, intending to make an all-
out civic project of it by lynching the helpless Emmett.
They were stopped by David Stewart Elliott, publisher of the
Coffeyville *Journal*. Elliott had known Emmett Dalton since
childhood. Attorney as well as editor, he had once rep-
resented Adeline Dalton in a divorce action she had in-
stituted against sorry old Lewis.

"We won't disgrace our community by lynching a dying
man," Elliott said in that emphatic manner of his.

The murmuring crowd scattered. Emmett Dalton, bleeding
from sixteen wounds, was holding up his fluttering right hand
to beg for mercy.

A young Coffeyville boy, John R. Tackett, stood over Emmett, fanning him. Montgomery County Sheriff Tom Callahan
arrived to take charge. Both Emmett Dalton and Marshal
Connelly were carried to Slosson's drugstore to be given
medical attention. Connelly died on the way to the place.

Souvenir hunters were already tearing at the clothes of
the three corpses, Bob and Grat Dalton and Bill Powers,
in that enclave of slaughter. Four dead horses lay near the

three dead men. Hats, rifles, still warm from battle, and other memorabilia of conflict were scattered up and down the passageway.

There were eight dead: four citizens and four bandits, counting Dick Broadwell, who got only half a mile away from Coffeyville before tumbling out of his saddle, to bleed to death from his wounds.

Banker Tom Ayres miraculously recovered, though he was at first believed to have been a fatal casualty from that searing shot so near his skull.

There were four wounded, including Ayres: three citizens and one outlaw—Emmett, the lone survivor of the bunch that struck the Kansas town.[1]

Coffeyville, mourning its dead, seethed with mounting hate for Emmett. Weeping women and cursing men filled the square.

32

BURYING THE DEAD

ALL the loot from the two banks was recovered and re-placed in the righteous tills. All but twenty-two dollars. Twenty-two dollars minus two cents, to be exact.

At the end of that strident day, the banks balanced their books. The Condon bank, where Grat had been undone, showed a deficit of twenty dollars, a trifling loss which Mr. Condon, owner of still another cash depository at Oswego, Kansas, could easily make good from his own ample pocket. The First National, visited by Bob and Emmett, showed a shortage of one dollar and ninety-eight cents—just the price of a pair of flannel pants at Barndollar's department store.

But in less than twenty-four hours, the Dalton raid was proving the biggest windfall that had ever blessed the boom-ing young city of Coffeyville. The morbid and the curious poured in from miles around, jamming the passenger trains of the three railroads serving the community. They sauntered along Death Alley, where the blood had barely dried on the cobblestones, listening to garrulous townfolk bragging about their personal acquaintance with the Daltons. They packed the streets and the hotels and the shops, leaving Coffeyville its first, but not its last, fortune in tourist dollars.

Yes, the boys turned out to be mighty good for their home town. The Daltons had come back seeking money, only to meet what might be called blunt disappointment. Now see how they had brought money *into* Coffeyville!

It was enough to pay off all the deceased Lewis Dalton's debts at the different stores, if the merchants would only look at it in that light. All that money floating around now, with greedy Emmett, a shot-up prisoner, lying flat on his back and unable to collect a nickel of it! Yet there was a way in which of the last of the Dalton band did collect, and handsomely.

He wallowed in fame, which he had been courting ever since he rampaged around Cass County on Jesse James's mare. If there was one unprescribed medicine which pulled Emmett Dalton through, it was the glory he lapped up like water from a springhole, even if some bibulous, unadmiring citizens, none of whom had fired a round in the battle, kept making lynch talk.

Only the quick emergency surgery of Dr. W. H. Wells kept Emmett from dying boots down when he was transported to Slosson's drugstore. Dr. Wells, a polished citizen from Maryland, called in two colleagues, Dr. G. J. Tallman and Dr. W. J. Ryan, to help patch the bandit's shattered guts. Emmett was lying across a table and the physicians were busy with their surgical instruments when a mob charged into the improvised operating theater. The leader was a town character who had been nowhere in view during the fight, but who was now swinging a rope with an ominous noose.

"Hand the son of a bitch over, Doc," he demanded. "We're gonna make Emmett Dalton kiss rope."

"No use, boys," the Marylander answered. "He will die anyway."

The rope swinger looked doubtfully at the groaning outlaw on the table. "Doc, are you certain he'll die?"

Dr. Wells's laugh was a forced one. "Hell, yes! He'll die. Did you ever hear of a patient of mine getting well?" Somebody in the mob haw-hawed. That broke the tension. The doctor turned back to his patient while the mob scattered down the stairs.

Within a very few hours, the substantial residents who had borne the brunt of the battle were insisting that Emmett Dalton must be tried, through regular judicial process, if he lived.

Who would openly dispute John Kloehr, president of the rifle club and slayer of two Daltons, if he delivered such a dictum? Or courageous Henry Isham, whose store had been turned into a citadel from which the citizens had counterattacked the bandits? Or Coffeyville's wealthiest resident, Attorney Luther Perkins, owner of the building in which the Condon Bank was located? Or that enlightened newspaperman, David Stewart Elliott, whose coverage of the robbery was dramatic but not mob-inciting, whose editorials were sober and restrained.

Still, Sheriff Tom Callahan from Independence, the county seat, kept a watchful eye on the drugstore during the tense night that followed the morning of the robbery. Lynch talk was still floating around in the speakeasies or "blind tigers" of the officially dry town. Some bunch of idiots might get tanked up just enough to try it. On the next morning, Emmett was moved to the Farmers' Home Hotel. Officers guarded him against possible violence, but in the easy-

going fashion of those days, anybody could come in to take
a look at a real, live—if barely alive—bandit, a boy just
turned twenty-one but now outdoing in notoriety another
ex-Coffeyville delinquent, Billy the Kid.

Anybody could talk to him, when he wasn't in one of
those semi-conscious spells which made Dr. Wells wonder
if he could pull the patient through to face a Montgomery
County jury. Emmett seemed to enjoy the company, too,
though his replies to questions were often jerky and more or
less incoherent. For the first few days, he seemed a bit
worried by the presence of some hard-faced strangers, but
he perked up when old cowhand partners began drifting
into Coffeyville and ascending stairs to his room. "You got
a lot of grit and vinegar left in you yet," and "You'll pull
through, boy," they would assure him. Some of their voices
were husky, as if they actually didn't believe what they
were saying. Some of them shook their heads sadly, once
they were out of the shot-up boy's sight. Many were carrying
concealed guns, ready for a second battle of Coffeyville if
the big talkers and the big boozers laid a hand on the de-
fenseless Emmett Dalton.

The visitors kept pouring in by every train, kept crowding
the hotel to take a look at an authentic bandit. Wispy ladies
carrying reticules arrived to feel maternally sorry for the
Bad Boy. Preachers swarmed in also, hoping to get some large
measure of credit on the books of paradise for converting
an outlaw. But the youngest Dalton wasn't showing penitence,
however close to eternity he might be. Farmers, with little
excitement in their lives, wandered into the hotel to take long
looks and engage Emmett in brief conversation. To the end
of their days, they would be bragging to their grandchildren
about "knowing Emmett Dalton," of having actually spoken
to him and actually shaken his limp hand.

Emmett kept glorying in all the attention he was getting.
Under modern criminal procedure, he would have been held
virtually incommunicado in the prison ward of some hospital, with reporters having to write conjectured feature stories
about him. Right then, he was hot copy, and any newsman
could see him. He had given his name as "Charley McLaugh-
lin" when he was captured. Citizens had ripped away his
disguise to confirm their belief that he was that pest, Emmett Dalton. Grat and Bob had previously been recognized,
beyond all doubt, when the bogus whiskers had been ripped
from their corpses. Emmett also had said that Dick Broadwell was John Moore, alias Texas Jack, and had identified
Bill Powers as Tom Evans, alias Tom Hedde. Then, under

questioning by Sheriff Callahan, he had admitted that he'd lied.

Coffeyville now had four dead villains and one dying one —dying by inches, according to the prognosis of the town's best doctor. It also had four dead heroes. Two of these four —Marshal Charles Connelly and George Cubine—were buried in Montgomery County. Connelly, the ex-schoolteacher who never should have worn a badge, was buried with the rites of the Methodist Episcopal Church at Independence. Left to mourn him were a wife and three grown children.

George Cubine was laid to rest at Coffeyville, with his lodge brothers of the Modern Woodmen of America conducting ritualistic funeral services. Everybody in town had loved the gossipy old cobbler. The body of the other shoe mender, Charles Brown, was shipped to his old home in Rapid City, South Dakota.

The remains of youthful Lucius Baldwin were transported to his mother in Burlington, Kansas, where he was buried, like his friend, Connelly, in Methodist style. More than one Coffeyville girl shed tears in her handkerchief when the train bore his remains away.

Coffeyville's stores were closed; federal and state flags were hanging at half-mast from many places when the funerals were held for Connelly and Cubine. Less respect was paid to the cadavers of the four dead outlaws—Bill Powers and Dick Broadwell, gents who had picked the wrong men to ride with; Grat and Bob Dalton, who had returned to the town as adult delinquents after having pestered it as juvenile delinquents.

For two hours after the fight, the bodies of Grat, Bob and Broadwell lay like untended dead dogs in the fatal alley. During that time, searchers brought back the corpse of Bill Powers, after having found it on the Maple Street road that had been the entrance route for the gang. All four were then propped up, after all disguises had been removed, for a grisly joint photograph, snapped either by young John Tackett or another local photographer, C. G. Glass. Meanwhile, the curious were having a ghoulish play party with the ghastly corpses. Folks who wouldn't voluntarily have come within a hundred feet of a live outlaw were showing off their bravery in the presence of dead ones.

They hurled jokes and challenges at the mute men, whose faces and arms were covered with swarms of blow-flies from Kloehr's livery stable. But it was Grat—Grat, the shattered bumpkin—who gave them the most fun.

Somebody discovered that raising his right arm would start blood gurgling from that wound in his throat. So

they kept raising that arm—Grat's gun arm, now power-
less to mow down these despised grangers.

Finally the bodies were thrown like cordwood into Marshal Connelly's tight little city jail. The doors were left
open for the carnival to go on unchecked. The gruesome
farce of Grat's uplifted arm and bleeding throat was repeated to the point of nausea, even after the corpses had
been placed in four black-varnished coffins with lids unattached.

Coffeyville had its macabre holiday, and the deaths of
the Daltons and their partners would give the town an heroic
tradition.

Perhaps there was the recognition of an emerging legend on that day following the fight when the dead bandits
were buried by the tense community. The level heads like
John Kloehr had informed the hotheads that there were to
be no demonstrations at the funerals, no assembling of any
lynch mob to finish the battered Emmett. Perhaps that post-
mortem carnival of hate had one positive effect, draining
off energies that might otherwise have been directed into the
murder of Emmett, supposedly dying.

Rumors, however, were sweeping the town that outlaw
friends of the Daltons were planning to invade Coffeyville
and shoot it up, as Quantrill's guerrillas had sacked Lawrence,
twenty-nine years before. The reports were fanned by tele-
graphic offers of help sent to Coffeyville by other communities across the country, including ones where the
Daltons had never set foot but where numerous unsolved
crimes were attributed to them. Again Kloehr and the leading
citizens moved to squelch the obviously false reports.

Grat and Bob Dalton were buried decently and lie today
in Elmwood Cemetery, not far from Frank, whose memory
they had desecrated. A small stone marks each end of the
Dalton family plot. A graphic marker is a rusty iron pipe
reforged into an arch with each end resting in the ground.
That piece of metal was originally a hitching rack in the
alley where the two maverick brothers went down before
the citizens' guns.

Bill Powers, the nondescript, and Dick Broadwell, the
black sheep of the respectable family, were interred in a
common grave in potter's field. No friend or relative showed
up to do any better by the remains of Powers. No kin or
connection of his has ever been traced since. Powers may
have been no more his real name than those bogus ones of
"Evans" and "Hedde" which he sometimes used.

A few days after the funeral, two of Dick Broadwell's

family arrived in Coffeyville from Hutchinson: his brother, George, a salesman for a Chicago tea firm; and his brother-in-law, E. B. Wilcox, a Hutchinson grocer. Impeccable, good-mannered, well-dressed men they were, who would never have been taken for kinsmen of a gunslinger.

These two had Broadwell's corpse exhumed and reburied, in expensive clothes and expensive coffin, at a Hutchinson cemetery. Luckless Bill Powers now had to lie all by himself, until his corpse was also moved to Elmwood Cemetery.

Following Dick Broadwell's second interment, his brother put in a claim for $92.40 that had been found on his corpse that day in the alley. George Broadwell also demanded the horse from which the bandit fell to his death, offering to put up indemnifying bond for both money and mount in case the "inheritance" should be contested.

A now forgotten Coffeyville citizen had seized possession of what might be called the estate of the late Dick Broadwell. Believing that finders were keepers, this gentleman held onto what he had appropriated. George Broadwell and brother-in-law Wilcox correctly decided that it was best to forget the whole thing. But the claim excited the greed of sundry characters, like those still itching to lynch Emmett.

These post-valiant ones began insisting that all the corpses of all the outlaws should be dug up and the linings of their clothes inspected to see if they had cash or other portable assets sewn inside. Colonel Elliott's stomach turned over at the idea. Once again, he and other civilized residents exercised a veto.

George Broadwell and E. B. Wilcox went home. Three women in Hutchinson would mourn one Richard L. Broadwell, who had managed to keep his outlaw doings concealed from his family by using the alias of "Texas Jack." These respectable ladies were his mother, Mrs. Broadwell; his sister-in-law, Mrs. Wilcox; and his unmarried sister, Jennie. Broadwell kin are still found in Kansas, and they are nice people.

No Daltons were present at the hasty funeral of Bob and Grat. Emmett obviously couldn't attend. While his brothers were being buried, with no assurance of a better shake on the other side, he was arguing desperately with two doctors who wanted to amputate his swollen right arm.

Emmett kept the arm. It was the one triumph scored by the Daltons at Coffeyville.

Brother Bill barged in a few days later. The one bad Dalton who had kept his hide whole now was looking for triumphs that would count—and pay off.

NEW GANGS A-COMING

KNOWING the nature of the man, Chris Madsen expected
to hear from William Marion Dalton after Coffeyville. The
sharp lawman foresaw that communication would be prompt,
and for two very good reasons.

One was Bill's need to establish an alibi for himself, however the cards fell for his brothers during that insolent sortie
on boyhood ground. The other was the smart Dalton's concern for his own future. Chris Madsen was one lawman
whose brain matched Brother Bill's subtlety and caution.
What checker games those two might have played had they
been on closer terms! Yet, unlike many Western officers,
Madsen wasn't much for casual camaraderie with criminals.

What turn would Bill Dalton take, once his brothers had
made their strikes at Coffeyville? How would the result of
the raid, one way or the other, affect the future behavior of
that booted wench of the prairies, Florence Quick? Apparently Madsen had no knowledge of the Mexican idyll that
she had planned with Bob. He did expect her, however, to
drop in on him should Bob draw a wrong decision of the
trigger in the forewarned Kansas community.

The United States Marshal's office in Guthrie had been
almost as tense as Coffeyville itself during those few days
before the showdown. Madsen and the marshals stationed
in the Oklahoma capital were keenly expectant on the night
of October 4, when, according to an informant, the Daltons
would plunder the banks.

That evening passed quietly, however, and next morning
the office staff reported for work as usual, ready to handle
any Oklahoma side developments should the Daltons carry
through their raid on Coffeyville. Madsen and Chief Marshal
Grimes expected that the bandits would flee back into Oklahoma if they escaped from the Kansas community. In that
event, the lawmen hoped to run them down, then stage a
mass roundup of their sympathizers in the Territory.

But a deliberate clock ticked off a routine morning that
5th of October. At noon, the office staff went out for din-

ner. Madsen stayed behind to hold down the headquarters, meaning to step out to a restaurant after his colleagues returned.

He was all alone when the big news came from Coffeyville. An excited telegraph messenger rushed into the office and handed him a brown window envelope.[1] Madsen tore it open to read what the town's mayor had wired him:

AN ATTEMPT TO ROB OUR TWO BANKS HERE WAS MADE BY THE DALTONS. THE CITIZENS ARE FIGHTING THEM IN THE STREETS. THREE OF THE ROBBERS HAVE BEEN KILLED AND ONE CAPTURED SO BADLY WOUNDED THAT HE WILL DIE BEFORE NIGHT. ONE ESCAPED AND WENT TOWARDS THE OKLAHOMA LINE RIDING A FAST HORSE. PLEASE TRY TO CAPTURE HIM IF HE REACHES OKLAHOMA.

Which three outlaws had been killed? Madsen wondered. Which one was wounded? Which had escaped? The number of casualties told him one thing, though no names had been given in the mayor's frantic message. If four bandits had tasted lead, two or more had been Daltons, by simple deduction. Five men comprised the gang beaten at Coffeyville. According to Marshal Yoes's informant in the penitentiary, three of the brothers—Bob, Emmett and Grat—were scheduled to be in the raiding party.

Hurriedly Chris Madsen began writing telegrams to be sent to field deputies, instructing them to be on the watch for the escapee. But before the messages reached the telegraph office, a second wire was received from Coffeyville's mayor.

This telegram identified the captured, wounded desperado as Emmett Dalton. The fleeing outlaw, name still ungiven, was reported as having been found dead, full of bullet holes, after having been thrown by his horse. That one would turn out to be Dick Broadwell. A Coffeyville youth named T. N. Russell would later claim, without witnesses to prove it, that he had killed Broadwell in flight.

Madsen called in reporters from Guthrie's two newspapers to give them copies of the two telegrams. Both journals got out extras that sold faster than corn liquor in a prohibition town. The papers were hardly on the streets when a fishy character came into the marshal's office to make inquiries.

The lawman recognized him as a friend of Bill Dalton. So, Madsen guessed, this was Bill's initial move in a situation which might have some very negative repercussions:

send a partner to sniff the lay. If anybody got locked up on suspicion as an accomplice, let it be the sidekick. Or so Madsen thought.

Naturally the visitor wanted to confirm the reports of the Daltons having been shot up at Coffeyville. Madsen kept his suspicions to himself. His answer to the visitor was courteous: "If the papers say that the Daltons were wiped out at Coffeyville, you can be sure that it is correct."

Bill's emissary left. Madsen, so beset that morning, should have had him followed. Possemen might also have killed or captured Bill Doolin, in the camp at Cowboy Flat. But Madsen did not, and who should return in another hour but Bill Dalton's friend—bringing along Bill Dalton in person.

The surviving Dalton brother expressed great shock over what he had learned, and deep disapproval of the fatal caper cut by his kin at Coffeyville. Madsen listened politely, taking it all with copious grains of salt.

"Marshal," Bill Dalton asked, "would it be safe for my mother and myself to go to Coffeyville? My brothers are dead, but we'd like to see Emmett." Chris Madsen's answer was again correct and humane: "I don't know, Bill, but I'll wire the mayor of Coffeyville and find out."

Once more the telegraph buzzed from Guthrie to Coffeyville. Soon came a reply that any members of the Dalton family wishing to visit Emmett would be given protection if they would report to the mayor immediately on arrival.

Bill said a quick good-by. He had announced that he wanted to notify his mother in Kingfisher of the tragedy. After he had left, Chris Madsen expected momentarily a visit from Miss Florence Quick.

The lady didn't appear, and was nowhere to be found in any dive of the Oklahoma capital. Actually, she was still waiting in the Ozarks for Bob and the capital to start the ranch in Mexico. When she did learn of her lover's death, she wasted no time on Coffeyville, but set about memorializing him in the most appropriate way.

She organized her own gang of train robbers.

The Dalton family first heard of the mop-up at Coffeyville through the consideration of Chris Madsen, and not from the lips of Julia Johnson, racing madly to inform Mother Dalton, as Emmett has Julia doing in his ghostwritten account. Madsen was also the first federal marshal at Coffeyville, not Ransom Payne, who made such a claim by inference in his book, *Eyewitness*.

On October 6, the day after the double robbery, Madsen went to Coffeyville for an investigation of the facts. Since the Daltons had been wanted by federal authority, he was required to make some kind of a report in order to close cases pending against them.

This was the day on which the slain outlaws were buried, with sentiment for lynching Emmett still running high. Madsen found the community still too confused for him to get a correct report from anyone. "One fact, however, was not disputed," he wrote; "none of the outlaws had gotten away and the banks had lost no money."

Only on October 8, three days after the robbery, did Ransom Payne arrive to play his bit part in the Dalton drama. He called on Emmett, sick and shot up, in the Farmers' Rest Hotel. According to *Eyewitness*, the maimed bandit grasped Payne's hand and cried:

"So you have got us in, after all."

What Emmett actually said was probably unprintable, particularly when he learned that the sterling wearer of the badge had come to take down his confession. The confession, evasive as its author, was a mishmash of whatever fact and fiction might best serve a Dalton before a bar of justice. That the blistering, epic battle of Coffeyville should lead to two largely faked books, *Eyewitness* and *When the Daltons Rode*, is the sorriest fillip of the whole Dalton story.

One bandit organization, the Dalton gang, had been shattered in Coffeyville when the wounded outlaw talked to the amateurish badge man. Two more bands, both stemming from that combine, were already quietly forming as Marshal Payne posed and strutted on Coffeyville's streets.

The short-lived Florence Quick gang was one. The formidable Doolin-Dalton gang was the other.

The one led by Florence Quick was destined to be of short duration. An angry grief-stricken girl was unable to lead effectively.

The longer-lasting aggregation, led by Bill Dalton and Bill Doolin, was something else again. That outfit would make its parent group look like a flock of desert quail.

THE LAST GASP

ALL of the officially bad Daltons were now ex-bandits. Bob and Grat lay beneath the unfriendly turf of Kansas. Emmett was holding precariously onto life, aided by his own gall and expert medical attention. What had happened should have been enough to make any Dalton with a whole hide blanch at the thought of further outlawry.

Every Dalton met the grim family crisis in some highly personal manner as the clan gathered at the bedside of the wounded Emmett. Adeline Dalton had lived to see four of her nine sons go down before gunfire, three of them fatally. Frank, Bob, and Grat all lay in their graves here in Coffeyville. Now Emmett's fate was in the hands of her vengeful —but sometimes pitying—God. Quietly but fervently, she hoped that the Dalton gang was finished, that what was left of her family henceforth could live in obscurity and peace.

Ben and Littleton Dalton shared that hope, praying that their children might grow up not emulating their three infamous uncles. The brothers talked freely to Marshal Ransom Payne after their arrival in Coffeyville on the 8th of October. Their conduct toward neighbors was circumspect and gentlemanly, as it had been when they were youths in the community long ago. Naturally, they had to do all they could for the shattered Emmett, but that was brotherly loyalty, understood everywhere.

Nannie May Whipple, the Dalton sister, a pert young woman, also was at Emmett's bedside. She recently had fallen out with her husband, who had come to Chris Madsen, offering information, for a price, on his brothers-in-law. Madsen, who didn't relish that kind of pigeon, had shown him the door.[1]

Julia Johnson, prospective member of the family, was hovering over the stricken Emmett too. Loving and solicitous, the spirited girl from Little Caney River was whispering determined promises of loyalty, whatever the future brought, begging him to live so there might be that future. It was evident, though, that wedding bells would not be figuring in Emmett's life for a while.

All these members of the family were playing a rough deal straight. Not so Brother Bill; he was playing it Bill Dalton's way. His first response to Coffeyville had been one of extreme caution: he had asked Madsen to exact some guarantee of safety from the local authorities before he would venture into a place that hated Daltons. Fidelity to his wounded brother required that Bill rush to Emmett without delay and take care of such necessary chores as getting the boy a lawyer.

However, he waited those three days before showing up and bringing the other kinsmen with him. His excuse was that his mother had been in bed with a cold when the bad news came, and finally had risen from her sickbed to make the trip. Emmett also tried to cover up for him later, claiming that Bill had been in California at the time of the slaughter. Madsen knew better; so did Bill Doolin.

Bill Dalton scrupulously followed the protocol set out by the mayor for the journey. He placed himself and the other Daltons under His Honor's protection as soon as they stepped off the train. Coffeyville's decent citizens were prepared to back up the guarantee of safety; they made sure that the wounded outlaw's kin were treated with respect, especially that poor old Mrs. Dalton.

Bill acted friendly not only toward Marshal Payne but even toward the men who had gunned his brothers down. As he walked along the street, shaking hands with old acquaintances, Bill was stewing inside. What was next for him? . . . what caprices of luck? . . . what undertaking that would put some dollars in his poke?

He could not ignore the stark, grim fact: he was ruined by the aftermath of Coffeyville—just as he had been in California when his own good name was linked with the dubious ones of his wayward brothers. No bank in Oklahoma or Kansas ever again would lend him money, not as much as a dime, for his land speculations. And he might as well forget that nebulous hope of a demagogic political career. No party was going to jeopardize its stand with respectable voters by putting a Dalton on its ticket.

Bill Dalton hadn't been in that battle of Death Alley, but he had been sure-enough ruined by it.

He went on pussyfooting, being cordial to everyone while Emmett lay in the hotel bed. No use doing anything that would fan the smoldering spark of lynch-mob fever. It was still alive, he knew, ready to be blown into consuming flame.

On the day after the battle, the Union National Bank of Minneapolis had called upon the American Bankers' Association to raise a fund among its members for the wives and families of the law-abiding Kansans killed or wounded while defending Coffeyville against the raiding Daltons. Already the goal of $20,000 was being approached.

Many citizens, greeted warily by Bill upon his arrival, were still angry and tense after a mass meeting held in the town. Both the local banks had made $500 donations for the survivors during the course of the rally. An appeal for more contributions had been prepared, to be circulated among railways and express companies, as well as banks. It would have been a dangerous time for a Dalton to "get smart" in Coffeyville.

With the visiting brothers—Bill, Littleton, and Ben—on their best behavior, however, the mood of the community relaxed a bit. Besides, the family circle included those three women—Mother Dalton, Nannie May, and Julia Johnson. Coffeyville, insofar as it knew Julia, had no opinion about her one way or the other. Many citizens, however, remembered favorably both Mrs. Dalton and Nannie May, who had been the best regarded of the Dalton girls. They shrank from the idea of making a gruesome tragedy worse on these already hard-hit, innocent women.

Emmett began to mend. It is doubtful that any outlaw in American history ever had been worse shot up and lived to tell about it. Bill Dalton became a little more aggressive in his deportment, but not to the point of inviting a bushwhack shot from some other alley. Jealousy was eating into him, now.

Papers reaching Coffeyville were full of the doings of the bad Daltons. What copy the bloody business made, even for such august journals as the New York *Tribune* and the Kansas City *Star!* Bill, devouring every account, was mighty annoyed by the fact that references to him were only incidental.

Why, it wasn't right for him, the smart member of the connection, to be given this kind of second-rate treatment! The three reckless Daltons—two of them retired by death, mind you—were blazoned in headlines. Every news story he read made Bill recall those man-to-man talks he'd had with Bill Doolin at Cowboy Flat.

A good man, that Doolin—good on the shoot, good in the saddle. Possessed of a following, too. Men Bob either had rejected or had set adrift from the gang . . . Bitter Creek Newcomb . . . Tulsa Jack . . . Ol Yountis . . . Red

Buck Weightman. With them riding behind him, Bob probably *would* have jobbed those two banks at once. And *all* the Daltons would be alive, and flush with money. . . .

With all his old ambitions wrecked, Bill's façade of respectability cracked open. Nothing was left now except to outstrip the boys, to succeed where they had failed, in a trade that had made for them more notoriety than money.

On October 11, 1892, Emmett Dalton was conducted to the Montgomery County jail at Independence by Sheriff Callahan. Bill went along on the short train ride and got his name in the papers, too. Kansans thought that ended, for all practical purposes, the turgid saga of the Daltons. Emmett, they figured, would get the gallows. Bill was behaving queerly, but then, he'd had quite a shock.

Five months after the battle, Emmett stood trial before Judge J. D. McCue, at Independence. To save his neck, he entered a plea of guilty to the slaying of George Cubine, although Brother Bob actually had been Cubine's killer. Murder in the second degree was the charge, and the unhorsed outlaw's attorney was a noted jury coaxer named Joseph Fritsch.

Emmett was hoping to get off with ten or fifteen years. Instead, he drew a life term in the ugly Kansas state penitentiary at Lansing. On the day he entered prison, another band of border buccaneers, tagged with the family name, was rampaging across the counties of Oklahoma and Kansas.

This expanded, cynically audacious combination, called the Doolin-Dalton gang, was composed of three alumni of the original Dalton group—Charlie Pierce, Bitter Creek Newcomb, and the incomparable Bill Doolin himself—re-enforced by nine others. These were Red Buck Weightman, a gent you wouldn't have wanted to encounter after dark; Tulsa Jack Blake, previously an unattached train robber; Little Bill Raidler, said without proof to have been a college graduate from Rhode Island; Little Dick West, a weird bantam Texan who had never slept indoors; Bob Grounds, bearer of an Indian surname common in Oklahoma; Dynamite Dick, a capable craftsman with explosives; Arkansas Tom Jones, a gone-astray Missourian; Ol Yountis, of the old Dalton grapevine; and Alf Sohn, just as mean as the others.

Lastly, there was William Marion Dalton, hitting the long trail when common sense and the fate of his brothers should have kept him walking wide of the whole business. Ironically, Bill was playing second fiddle to a man he rated as his intellectual inferior. The new gang had been organized by summons of Bill Doolin at Ingalls, not many weeks after the rout of the parent band at Coffeyville.

Bill Dalton had hoped to be the chief himself. Wasn't he Bob's heir apparent? Didn't he bear the Dalton name? An election had been held, with the two Bills as opposing candidates for the chieftainship—and Bill Dalton got one vote, his own.

He accepted defeat gracefully, hoping to replace Doolin in some underworld equivalent of machine politics. Nor did he detect any ill omen when Bob's quondam mistress, Florence Quick, shook her skirts of him. Flo felt, scornfully, that while her man had died a hero in Death Alley, Bill Dalton hadn't proved man enough to be there.

Before long, Flo joined Bob in death. This boldest of the West's lady outlaws went out, like Bob, boots down and six-gun smoking.[2] Her own bunch of bad actors wilted away after that.

The year now was 1893, when a great panic shook the country, from the brokerage firms of Wall Street to the farms and general stores of grassroots America. Emmett was being a model prisoner at Lansing, learning the tailor's trade by making pants for other inmates.[3] The other surviving Daltons, except Bill, all were farming, docile residents around Kingfisher and Bartlesville.

Bill was turning into a sorry phantom, robbing openly where he once had done it covertly, looking haggard and ill-kempt, where once he had been so fresh and dandyish. He was becoming more and more envious of canny Bill Doolin.

No one gang would have been big enough for such a pair. Their clashing temperaments produced a centrifugal force that strained the organization at the seams. Yet for that entire year, plus two months, the partnership lasted. The Doolin-Dalton combine robbed a train at Wharton, where the original gang had cut a caper two years before. Two more engines were boarded in two Kansas towns, Spearville and Cimarron, after pursuit by the marshals had temporarily forced the bandits out of Oklahoma. On September 1, 1893, the gang fought lawmen to a fare-you-well at Ingalls, invaded by a posse determined to wipe out that outlaw center and put an end to the careers of the two Bills.

Three marshals of a fourteen-man posse—Dick Speed, Tom Houston, and Lafe Shadley—paid with their lives for the invasion. Bitter Creek Newcomb was badly wounded; Arkansas Tom Jones, firing from the attic floor of Mary

Pierce's hotel, surrendered after Marshal Jim Masterson, brother of the famous Bat, produced two sticks of dynamite and threatened to blow Madam Pierce's disguised brothel "into the middle of next week."

With the outlaws in flight again, Bill Dalton was marked killer as well as robber; it was his bullet that had slain Lafe Shadley, who was trying to stop Bill and the others from escaping across a barbed-wire fence. Now there would be no quarter for the last bad Dalton, particularly since the desperados had slain a youth named Dell Simmons, who innocently had pointed out Newcomb to the possemen. Killing a marshal was a serious offense in Oklahoma; killing a kid compounded the crime.

When the outlaws lost their convenient base in Ingalls, they fled into the hills of the Creek Nation, with jealous rivalry continuing to mount between the two Bills. The one bearing the Dalton surname was becoming almost as much of a drunk as Grat had been. In one transient hideout after another, Bill tapped jugs of scalding Ozark 'shine, brooding over Coffeyville, remembering those years in California, when he had looked forward to conquering Sacramento.

Nobody thought much of Bill Dalton any more. Not the settlers, who once had been so spellbound at his gab. Not the bandits, now doing their jobs in squads of three, what with Oklahoma growing more uncomfortably populated, the recent opening of the Cherokee Outlet having attracted more swarms of hoemen. Not the marshals, now blaming the shooting of every badge wearer on Bill Dalton, with the blood of Lafe Shadler on his hands and a sizeable reward on his head.

On April 1, 1894, Bill and Bitter Creek invaded the general store of part-time marshal T. H. Carr, at an old Catholic mission settlement, Sacred Heart, on the edge of the Seminole Nation. Carr, recognizing Bill when the two asked to buy corn for their ponies, grabbed a gun. Bill's pistol missed fire at first, in a thirty-minute set-to, during which Bitter Creek downed old man Carr and himself was wounded in the left shoulder. Bill did swap some lead with another teenage lad, Lee Hardwick, who came to Carr's aid with his shotgun.[4]

Young Hardwick emerged from the battle unhurt, as did sorry Bill Dalton, but now Bill was an accessory to the wounding of lawman Carr, as he was the principal in the killing of lawman Shadler. Oklahoma's new chief marshal, Everett Dumas Nix, was slated to get an augmented force of 150 deputies to ride down the last remaining outlaw gangs in Oklahoma. The most wanted man on their list was Bill Dalton.

The situation was plainly wearisome for Bill Doolin, who was no friend of law enforcers but who had no yen to spill their blood, either. Nor was shooting youngsters a particular fancy of the lanky Arkansawyer. Relations between him and Bill Dalton became even more strained. Doolin wanted to avoid any actual run-in with the brother of Emmett, whom he had trained in practical gunslinging four years earlier.

So Bill Doolin dumped Bill Dalton—in the friendliest fashion. The gang met in the full force outside Edmond, Oklahoma, for a council and for the division of $6500 in loot, taken at the robbery of the railroad station at Woodward on March 13, 1894. The two Bills had been the operating unit, then, the money seized having been Army pay-roll funds consigned to the paymaster at Fort Supply. Doolin feared that United States troops as well as federal marshals might be assigned to run down the gang.

The Bills shook hands at the parting, the ostensible reason for which was the danger of traveling in large groups, with Oklahoma getting so confoundedly inhabited. It was blackballing Bill Dalton with sweet talk, inasmuch as, technically, every member of the gang was now a freelance whom Doolin would summon when the occasion required.

The Doolin-Dalton enterprise would henceforth be known simply as the Doolin Gang, and no one knew it better than Bill Dalton as he rode away after the adjournment of that session. Not one member of the old firm went with him, though he had paid obeisance to the farce by saying "See you again, boys," after solemnly shaking hands.

It was time for retirement for good and all from that kind of business. Perhaps fate was giving Bill Dalton a last chance to back off from something that had brought the whole family connection so much grief and shame. He should have thought of his six young 'uns; he should have thought of Jennie, a respectable woman. He should have gone off somewhere and lived out a life, admittedly dull but safe and sane.

But a Dalton wasn't going to be dropped, brushed aside and forgotten like a lousy brush popper. Not with Emmett sweating it out in that Kansas pen, not with Bob and Grat fertilizing Kansas sunflowers. Everybody respected his dead, did something for them if he could.

Even before Doolin ousted him, Bill Dalton had been busy with plans of his own. Already he had selected a new area of operation—Texas. He was as determined to be a successful outlaw as he had been bent on being a big politico.

The new "Dalton gang" consisted of Bill and a trio of inept scrubs: George Bennett, a cowboy with the habit of deserting his women; Jim Wallace, a country loafer from around Ardmore, near the Texas-Oklahoma border; and a third fellow, identity not established, who called himself "Bill Jones."

They were sorry material. Bob Dalton would have given such help a meal and sent them along to steal chickens. This final Dalton ensemble lasted for just one job in the rough environs of the Lone Star State.

On May 23, 1894, the shabby bunch rode into Longview, a short way from the Louisiana line. There they held up the First National Bank, for a take of $2000, in ten- and twenty-dollar bills. In a battle that was almost a replica of the Coffeyville slaughter, Bennett was shot and killed by Will Stevens, a deputy city marshal. Chief Marshal Muckelroy took a fatal slug through the bowels. Another man, named George Buckingham, was slain by Bill Jones, doing lookout duty in an alley. Saloonkeeper J. W. McQueen and citizen Charles S. Leonard were hit by wild shots, Leonard dying two days later.

As at Coffeyville, bandits used bankers temporarily as shields while emerging with the loot. Bill Dalton and his two surviving henchmen rode west toward Paris, near the Oklahoma border, hid in a canebrake after outracing a posse, then crossed over into the Territory.[5]

Bill made his way to the Ardmore area, where Jennie and the kids were staying as paid guests on the farm of Houston Wallace, brother of the erring Jim. Oklahoma marshals traced the stolen currency after two characters had paid for a new wagon with identifiable greenbacks at Duncan, in the Chickasaw Nation.[6] Ardmore also was a part of that Indian republic. The federals concluded that the bank robbers were roaming its stretches. Bill Dalton, it was believed, was their leader.

Even so, Bill's luck might have held had he not gotten thirsty in country that was officially dry. Bill was expecting a shipment of whisky, via railway express at Ardmore, twenty-five miles away. He decided to send Houston Wallace for the booze, and to pick up ammunition and groceries. Mrs. Dalton and Mrs. Wallace also elected to make the trip; the girls needed an outing.

Wallace and the two women stocked up on cartridges and victuals at a general store. The tally was more than $200,

and the farmer shelled out spot cash. This aroused the suspicion of Deputy Marshal T. S. Lindsay and other officers
hanging around the store. Houston Wallace was regarded as
a "worthless fellow who never had a cent."

The officers followed the party to the express office and
arrested all three after the farmer picked up nine quarts
of whisky, labeled as something else and addressed to a
consignee named "Hines." The wagon that Wallace was driving
turned out to be the one bought with the bank loot at Duncan.
Jennie Dalton gave a false name, but the deputies had a
pretty good idea who she was.[7]

Next morning, June 8, 1894, at seven o'clock, Lindsay led a
posse of nine to do in the last of the bad Daltons. They
surrounded the house and Bill, trying to make a run for it,
was downed by gunfire after he jumped from a window
and made for a tiny ravine. Marshal Loss Hart got him with
a forty-four slug that tore into him at his waistline.[8]

The Daltons were finished.

DALTON REDIVIVUS!

AFTER he had served fourteen and a half years Emmett Dalton shook the dust of Kansas state prison by grace of a governor's pardon. It was 1907, the year Oklahoma entered the Union as the forty-sixth state—a blessed event that Emmett and his brothers had done their best to delay. In fact, Oklahoma attained statehood only after nervous Congressmen were assured that outlaw aggregations like the Dalton gang had disappeared, having given way before the usual alliance of Bible, badge, and baby buggy.

The Dalton record had cost the Territory a good many votes in Washington during all those years while the bill for its admission was kicking around in Congressional committees. Many, many times Oklahoma's nonvoting delegate, Bird Segle McGuire, had to remind his colleagues that the Daltons were out of business.

"But for that bunch, we would have been in the Union ten years before," N. A. Gordon, reading clerk of Oklahoma's first state legislature, once told this author. "To outsiders, Oklahoma was synonymous with the Daltons, and the Daltons were synonymous with outlawry. Thank God Congress had passed the statehood bill before Governor Hoch of Kansas turned loose Emmett Dalton."

One thing was sure: something of the Dalton mood would forever be superimposed upon Oklahoma. The Daltons would be remembered longer than Delegate Bird McGuire, who got Oklahoma admitted in spite of them.

Being a living legend protected Emmett when he returned to Oklahoma after getting out of prison. Most of the Dalton family had moved to Bartlesville during those years while Emmett was atoning for the sins of all its bad sons. Julia Johnson and her folks were still living in the general area when he joined his people to plant and hoe corn in a more than symbolic surrender to civilization.

Naturally Emmett began wooing Julia, even though during his absence she had been in and out of successive marriages with two lusty gents who had died standing in their

boots. No tame suitors ever got very near Miss Julia, and nobody but her daring Emmett could hold her volcanic af-
fections permanently.

In 1908 the couple got married, the wedding getting no
play from Oklahoma's society pages. Two years later, with
Emmett tired of plow and hoe, they drifted to Tulsa, now
in the throes of a rip-roaring oil boom. Here Emmett, the
retired gunman, felt at home, rubbing shoulders with other
trigger artists, active or reduced to semi-circulation. Then
briefly, in an odd rounding of a circle, the lawman turned
outlaw became a law enforcer again.

Emmett was made a special officer to handle the hardest
of the hard cases who came to the suddenly rich town looking for big pickings. Many of them packed in a hurry and
took the first train out when they heard that a Dalton would
be coming after them with a Winchester and a warrant.

Emmett proved himself a good policeman, as he had been
a middling good marshal in the old days. But now he had a
new interest—in the novel form of entertainment, projected
in moving shadows, for moments of cliff-hanging suspense,
on sheets hung in gaudily decorated buildings.

He became a movie fan. The very first story film produced
by any studio had been a one-reeler called *The Great Train
Robbery*—and train-robbing had been a Dalton art before
it became a showman's artifice. Fortunes were being made in
films, particularly films that dealt with the Old West. Why
couldn't this make-believe, so profitable to others, be made
to yield lucre to one who had himself cut such a figure in
its true-life parallel?

About when World War I was beginning, Emmett wound
up his affairs in Tulsa and with Julia went to California,
where Governor Hiram Johnson had broken the political
power of the Dalton's arch foe, the Southern Pacific. But
of greater importance than that, now, the state was becoming the center of the rising film industry.

Emmett was avid to see his name on movie marquees.
John Tackett, the Coffeyville photographer and showman,
was in California trying his luck with the new medium. He
and Emmett decided to produce a film, *Beyond the Law*,
which would be a "true" representation of the Dalton Gang
—it's star: Emmett Dalton, last of the notorious four brothers, in person!

Some fifteen films, all of them largely fictitious, have
been made about the Daltons since that first one. *Beyond
the Law* was, by all odds, the sorriest. Of all the actors who

have portrayed Emmett Dalton, the worst was Emmett himself.

Cool and capable while facing sixshooters and shotguns, Emmett was not up to coping with klieg lights and movie cameras. His posture on screen was sloppy, his gestures wildly overdone, even for that unsophisticated era. The shoddy production had a brief run across the country. It couldn't hold a candle to the exciting horse operas starring William S. Hart and Tom Mix.

Emmett did better as a building contractor in growing Los Angeles. Better than he ever had done as a bandit back in Oklahoma, for that matter. He liked to observe that he made more money from one good real-estate deal out here in California than he did in all the jobs he'd turned as a freebooter back home.

Emmett was sitting pretty, for an outlaw turned honest taxpayer. Julia made sure that he stayed on the plumb line of respectability. No doubt Bob Dalton would have had to make the same resigned adjustment to society had he and Flo Quick lived to make that altar march.

Years passed. With the First World War over and done with, America hoped there wouldn't be a Second. Girls began to roll their stockings, bob their hair and smoke cigarettes, developments that had Julia and all other good women clucking in disapproval. Emmett's figure was spreading, keeping pace with the growth of his bank account. His weight went up to 200 pounds; he had more money tucked away than that twenty grand he'd grabbed from the First National in Coffeyville.

The routine of honest living had brought Emmett that dull, scrubbed-up look he had resisted so fiercely in the old, wild days. He loved the feel of the good suits that Julia selected for him in the best men's shops. He liked the fine gold watch he carried, paid for with honestly earned cash. Best of all, he liked to walk into a bank and have its officers greet him with deferential bows.

Emmett Dalton had it made. Coffeyville was history. So were Red Rock and Adair and Columbus, and all those other bullet-bitten places of his youth. He could join the Rotary Club; no one would blackball him. He could cut loose from the past while enjoying the present, if he would.

That was asking too much of Emmett Dalton, though. As long as he lived, he insisted on making the Dalton story and tradition his own private preserve, a continuing stage for the spotlight of publicity that he loved even more than he loved money.

No authentic history of the Daltons could be written during his lifetime; invariably he threatened to sue the author. No magazine article could be published unless it featured his distorted interpretations, making the brothers look like lightly transgressing angels.

He was constantly on the lookout for writers who would do the Dalton story according to Emmett. His closest friend in Los Angeles was a leading writer for the pulp magazines, Chuck Martin. A fine man besides being a successful author, Martin became fascinated with the former outlaw and published a number of articles, inevitably reflecting Emmett's viewpoint, on the gang's career.

Once, Martin kept Emmett from staging a personal sequel to Coffeyville on the streets of Los Angeles. By prearrangement, Martin and the now middle-aged Dalton met a threadbare old bucky, now tarrying in California, who it turned out had been a bad friend of Emmett's while both of them were dodging hemp in Oklahoma.

The reunion lasted about ten seconds. Upon seeing his contemporary in crime, Emmett hauled out an ancient forty-five that had been concealed in his pants. The old-timer fanned it out of there, almost as fast as he had ever scooted from posses back home. Martin managed to get Emmett, still sputtering, back to his house. There Chuck and Julia finally talked some sense into the head of the retired outlaw, whom the sudden meeting had catapulted deep into the past.

"Emmett," Martin told him, "the police are mighty tough on an ex-con who totes a gun. Better let me have yours."

Martin had to do a lot of coaxing before Emmett finally gave up his old hog iron. Even then, he yielded only when Julia added wifely authority to Chuck's friendly persuasion. Martin got the gun and kept it as a souvenir. Emmett's cartridge belt later fell into the hands of Tom Murray, another Angeleno.

Then the aging trigger artist struck up an acquaintance with A. B. McDonald, a Kansas City newsman who was itching to write books about the Wild West. Under Emmett's inspiration, McDonald turned out a work on Oklahoma outlawry titled *Hands Up!* McDonald also acted as unofficial press agent for the bona-fide badman whose life had been considerably more authentic than were his stories about it.

McDonald had much to do with the restoration of good relations between Emmett and Coffeyville. He accompanied the prodigal on one of several visits to the home town during Emmett's later years. During those trips, the son of

Lewis Dalton tasted that triumph he had always wanted with the home folks—acceptance mingled with awe.

Men who had flung lead at him now rushed forward to shake the hand of the famous ex-resident whenever he came to town. One of the chummiest of them all was Charlie Gump, the drayman. Duly impressed, crowds followed Emmett to Death Alley and the doors of the two banks, listening while the last living participant in the double haul gave his version of what had happened.

Once, shooting at a Dalton had been a mark of distinction in Coffeyville. Now it was knowing a Dalton, shaking his hand. The old outlaw was being accorded the affection that zookeepers give aging tame lions.

It was in the summer of 1937 that Emmett returned to his home town for the last time—almost half a century after the shambles of Death Alley. More accurately, what was left of Emmett's shot-scarred frame came back to Coffeyville, in an urn. On July 13 he had died peacefully in Hollywood, where he had moved to be near film folk. He was sixty-six.

The year before, he had collaborated with Jack Jungmeyer on a well written, but undocumented opus, *When the Daltons Rode.* For some years, also, he had been an active crusader for prison reform in California. He begged successive state-prison wardens to institute trade-training for convicts, and asked them to take steps to prevent the overcrowding that cause so much trouble behind the bars. Once he had pled before a state legislature committee for the abolition of capital punishment.

"Murders are never committed in cold blood," he remarked to his friend, California governor James Rolph. "They are the result of a moment's passion. All killers are crazy."

Emmett's prudential judgment, so expressed, coincides with the more considered opinions of most experts in psychology and criminology today.

Eminent political figures and film celebrities came and paid their last respects to Emmett Dalton while his remains lay in a Hollywood mortuary. So did people for whom he had built homes, as well as ex-convicts he had helped with a needed dollar or two. One or two cousins showed up, some of the family connection who had migrated to the movie center hoping to crash some studio or other by virtue of their kinship with him.

On July 14, Emmett's corpse was removed to a crematory. Perhaps it was appropriate that he should go out, finally, in a blaze. A handful of the old-time outlaws survived him, although he claimed he was the last of the breed.

The Daltons have kept on riding, though, if not in flesh.
They made some kind of negative contribution to the society that they professed to despise, and with which Emmett eventually came to terms. America's central mythos—
the one of the Old West—would be considerably less than
it is without such raring-tearing, raggletail freebooters as
the Daltons and the Jameses. The outlaws in our history seem
to have been as necessary, natural parts of national development as the law-abiding, orderly souls who always,
somehow, rise up and smite them.

The "bad" and the "good" are the indispensable po-
larities of any culture. Our Rawhide Empire comprehended
the Buckshot Belt. Chris Madsen and his fellow lawmen were
no more integral to the American scene than were the outlaw Daltons.

NOTES

CHAPTER 1

1. By the records of the Kentucky state adjutant general's office, Lewis Dalton served as a fifer in Company I of the Second Regiment of Kentucky Foot Volunteers during the Mexican War. He served for exactly one year—June 9, 1846, to June 9, 1847. Members of Company I were listed as casualties at Buena Vista so Dalton probably took part in that battle, although his name is not included among the others recorded.

2. The term "Scotch-Irish" is used to distinguish Irish Protestant settlers in early America from Irish Catholic émigrés. The Daltons actually were descendants of early French-Norman emigrants to Ireland, the name originally having been spelled D'Alton.

3. Neither Kentucky nor Missouri records indicate any close kinship between Cole Younger's family and Adeline Younger Dalton. Marriages of Youngers are recorded in Logan County, Kentucky, where Lewis Dalton's family originated, but according to the Kentucky Historical Society "no Younger-Dalton connection" appears. Neither were the Daltons related to the Jameses, although Cole Younger seems to have believed they were, the *Kansas City Star*, October 7, 1892, quoting him as follows:

"I think a third cousin of mine married a Dalton in Kansas years ago, but I know absolutely nothing about the Kentucky family. I cannot see where anyone got authority to say that because these men were related to Frank and Jesse James, they were related to me."

Cole, who was seeking a pardon, made this statement two days after the Daltons met disaster in Coffeyville, from his cell in Minnesota State Prison; he also denied having fathered Belle Starr's daughter.

Mrs. Kay Wade of the State Historical Society of Missouri, says in a letter dated February 7, 1962, that she had been unable to find any real bases for the statements made in some books that the Daltons were related to the James family, and, through the Jameses, to the Youngers, but, she adds, "once they appeared in print they have been repeatedly quoted and misquoted."

4. Cousin Kit Dalton was a weird character who went around telling whoppers about having been a Texas Ranger in disguise after having turned outlaw. He gave lectures and sold a lurid pamphlet called "Under the Black Flag." Like Lewis Dalton, he was a native of Logan County, Kentucky. His stories and the facial resemblance shown in pictures suggest he may have been the same man as one "J. Frank Dalton" who would pop up at the age of 101 in 1950, claiming to be Jesse James. He died destitute in Austin, Texas, some years ago, having been abandoned by his promoters.

CHAPTER 2

1. The Kansas-Missouri post-Civil War troubles themselves deserve an authoritative history. My own ancestors, the Shannons, had to leave Newton County, Missouri, in 1866 as Unionists who previously had earned the enmity of the Confederate guerrilla chieftain, Bloody Bill Anderson. Grandmother Catherine Shannon Preece remembered Lewis Dalton as "a trifling horse trader," but said that his wife Adeline was "a right nice woman." The savage little conflict continued almost to the Spanish-American War, when, as Missouri-born author Keene Wallis recalls, his father and others got together "to disarm the old hotheads on both sides." In fairness, it must be said that the pro-Southern Missourians were retaliating for a Union military order that, during the war, almost depopulated entire counties, forcing the inhabitants to find refuge in Kansas, Nebraska and Indian Territory. The Daltons, whatever the "pacifism" of Lewis, were probably a part of this exodus.
2. Information on Lewis Dalton's career as a circus tout was provided the author by the late Reverend James A. Peters, of Sallisaw, Oklahoma. Peters, a former Oklahoma marshal, charitably felt that the wild Daltons might have turned out better, given a more stable father. But then why were a majority of the boys decent and respectable?
3. As another negative fillip to the legend of the James-Dalton relationship, Frank James, when questioned once, replied: "No, I did not know any of them, but have often heard of their raids into the [Indian] Territory."

CHAPTER 3

1. Lewis Dalton may have hit California during his wanderings. Citing Emmett Dalton as authority, the *Fresno Police Annual*, 1956, states that Lewis came there in 1885 to race ponies.
2. Vinita was founded in 1871 by the Cherokee assimilationist and railroad attorney, Colonel Elias C. Boudinot, who worked hand in glove with the railroad lines to abolish tribal govern-

ments that were resisting the advance of the Iron Horse into their lands. Boudinot named the town after the Washington sculptress, Vinnie Ream, reputedly his mistress.

3. Thousands of white squatters gained admission into the Indian republics during the eighties, through the connivance of the near-white mixed-bloods who leased out, for their own benefit, tracts of collectively owned tribal domain.

4. Jordan also held a commission from the federal government. There is no proof of Adeline Dalton's alleged "Indian blood." The Daltons never claimed it, and never applied for citizenship in the Cherokee Nation, as did many whites who claimed Indian forebears. The principal service of Jordan and the Daltons was in a section leased to Texas cattlemen and known as the Cherokee Outlet. Jordan was also a rich rancher in his own right—"a man who'd hire devils or Daltons if he had to," a former Cherokee official, R. H. Brewer, told me in 1930.

CHAPTER 4

1. "Harry Hawkeye" was the house-owned pseudonym of many struggling hacks who turned out flashy stuff for a certain enterprising publisher. They are collectors' items today; of course they are worthless as history.

2. "Frank Dalton was an unsaved man but a brave officer." (Comment made to the author by Jim Peters, ex-marshal and Baptist preacher, in 1949).

CHAPTER 5

1. This pithy description is from Nelson Algren's novel, A Walk on the Wild Side. I do not use it disparagingly, being myself descended from many "gander-necked" clans of Saxons and Scotch-Irish.

2. The fact that Bill Dalton had a wife prior to his marriage to Jennie Blivens was made known to me by Philip Rand, editor of Real West magazine, who is a Kansan and a Dalton authority. Complete information regarding the union has been furnished by Mrs. Thelma Mires, of Modesto, California, Bill's great-grand-daughter, who has never been acquainted with the descendants of Bill and his second wife. According to Mrs. Mires, her grandfather, William Marion Dalton, Jr., never set foot outside of Louisiana and presumably never saw his father.

3. The Johnsons, Julia's people, were Kentuckians; her father, however, was known as "Texas" Johnson, once having been a homesteader in the Lone Star State.

CHAPTER 6

1. The Osage police force was organized under the authority of the U.S. district court in Wichita, Kansas. As both federal marshal and tribal police chief, Bob Dalton was expected to be a link between the U.S. and Osage authority in a joint effort to stamp out crime in the Osage Hills. Possession of two badges doubled Bob's opportunities for graft and robbery.

2. The Starrs were a blazing family of gunslingers. Sworn foes of the Cherokee-independence faction, they were active allies of the assimilationist group and among its trigger men back in the old Cherokee Nation in Georgia. Sam Starr, Winchester virtuoso and no-account, shacked up with Belle Shirley because Lady Belle had a strong predilection for Indian men. Henry Starr, nephew of Sam and Belle, was the last outlaw member of the family; educated, genteel and courteous, Henry was retired from the active practice of banditry February 18, 1921, when gunfire foiled his attempt to rob a bank at Harrison, Arkansas. Dr. Emmett Starr, author of a three-volume history of the Cherokee Nation that faithfully chronicles both fact and tradition, stood in startling contrast to some other members of the family; he died in St. Louis in 1930.

3. It is a romantic notion that most Oklahoma outlaws were cowpunchers thrown out of their livelihoods by the cutting up of ranches into homestead plots. Some were, but most of them were roving hellions moving in to prey on legitimate settlers. Many of them had been driven out of Texas, Colorado and other Western states where posses had their numbers.

4. *Fort Smith Elevator,* May 8, 1891. Files of this newspaper constitute an excellent source on the crimes of the Daltons.

5. Amoral Belle Starr became estranged from her daughter, Pearl, when the girl bore an illegitimate child. Pearl gave the child, Flossie, to an aunt in Wichita for rearing; "She did not willfully abandon the babe as is commonly believed," according to Virginia Marberry, Fort Smith newspaperwoman, "but wanted it brought up respectably."

CHAPTER 7

1. The full story of that fine body of frontier law enforcers, the Cherokee Light Horse, remains to be written. References to it are to be found in the works of Angie Debo, Marion Starkey and other Oklahoma writers. It hunted and caught many bad men and worked closely with the federal marshals, although there were occasional jurisdictional disputes between them.

2. Émigré Missourians of that period were as clannish as itinerant Texans always have been. Lawmen or outlaws, the Daltons were Canty's old neighbors and he remained their friend for life.

CHAPTER 8

This book reveals for the first time the true identity of Bob Dalton's paramour—Florence Quick, alias "Daisy Bryant," alias "Eugenia Moore," even alias "Tom King." For this major revelation in the Dalton story, the author must thank Florence Quick's kinsman, Keene Wallis, a gentle son of the Buckshot Belt and a distinguished American poet. His mother in Cass County was not only Florence's schoolteacher but also her first cousin. In a letter dated July 1, 1962, Mr. Wallis writes: "During her childhood years, Florence was a perfect little lady, thoroughly feminine, pretty, brunette, not at all tomboyish. She could ride a horse and she could shoot—but who except me in the family couldn't? Mother told me of the consternation in Cass and the neighboring counties when 'Tom King' was identified as Florence Quick. Dan Quick, her father, was a real pioneer in both Missouri and Oklahoma, and was *the* bee-tree robber, forever grabbing the honey of wild bees hived in hollow trees. He always claimed that the bees came to him singing, 'Follow us, Dan, we're takin' ye home,' and they wouldn't sting him. Dan was married three times and God knows how many children he batted out. He fattened range cattle for the Kansas City market, was known to carry twenty thousand dollars in a bag. He hid out in the brush not only during the four years of the Civil War, but maybe before and after."

CHAPTER 9

I have not found any written records from New Mexico sources of the fight in the Mexican-American settlement near Santa Rosa. I first heard of it from my uncle, Robert E. Worden, a New Mexico old-timer who was foreman of Albert B. Fall's ranch at Three Rivers just before the Teapot Dome scandal. Marshal Chris Madsen also refers to the battle in his memoir on Oklahoma outlaws; so does Emmett Dalton in *When the Daltons Rode,* and Madsen would have challenged the story if he believed Emmett had concocted it.

CHAPTER 10

The author is indebted to the Fresno County Historical Society and to the local-history section of the New York Public Library for much background information on the early history of Fresno town.

1. Bill Dalton's name does not appear in the complete roster of California legislators from 1849 to 1958, given in the *California*

Blue Book. No other record says that he ever was elected to any office.

2. Personal information on Detective Will Smith is fragmentary. What would have been a main source, the records of the Southern Pacific, was destroyed with the SP's headquarters in the earthquake of 1906.

3. Seven men were killed, four wounded, in the battle of Mussel Slough, May 11, 1886. Two of those slain were U.S. deputy marshals, defending the Central Pacific Railroad, later to be merged with the Southern Pacific. The struggle was precipitated by the railroad's determination to evict settlers who became squatters when the CP refused to issue them land titles which had been promised to them. An excellent short account of the whole violent episode and its causes, "The Mussel Slough Tragedy," was published in the Winter 1960 issue of the lively historical magazine, *Frontier Times.*

4. Adolph Sutro, a great humanitarian, was the one known prominent Jew within the Populist Party. There is no evidence that he and Bill Dalton ever met.

CHAPTER 11

Much background information for this chapter, as well as the preceding one, was furnished by the Fresno County Historical Society; the material included the Fresno County Police Annual for 1956 and photostated pages from a pamphlet, *Garden of the Sun,* by Wallace Smith, a local historian, published in September, 1939. Mr. Smith, an authority on the San Joaquin Valley, records the advent of Bob and Grat Dalton and Bill McElhanie but says nothing of Emmett, who certainly would have made his presence felt at the country dances if he had been around; thus he supports Emmett's claim that he was not in California at the time of the Alila robbery. The preponderance of evidence indicates that Emmett was prowling the Oklahoma brush while his brothers were getting mud on their boots in California.

CHAPTER 13

1. Throughout this work, the author has referred to that first dubious account of the Daltons as "Eyewitness," since it is so called by Dalton-material collectors. The opus's full title was *The Dalton Brothers and Their Astounding Career of Crime by an Eyewitness* —the "witness" being Marshal Ransom Payne, earnestly trying to grab glory he never earned. It was a quickie job, put out in 1892 by a Chicago firm, Laird & Lee, as a paper-covered yellowback. The Daltons had scarcely been finished at Coffeyville when the first copies were being hawked by train butchers and circus vendors. Much of its content is in the present tense, declaring, for

example, that "bad" Daltons still were being seen around Coffey-ville, although three of these Daltons were harmless: Ben, Little-ton and Charles. Obviously the firm rushed some hack to Coffey-ville to get the Dalton story first. He may have been one Will Ward: an expanded version of the booklet, with many identical passages, appeared under that byline in 1908. Ward, looking for a gloss of authority for his production, must have run into Marshal Payne, always ready to talk about Marshal Payne. In 1954, Frederick Fell, Inc., issued a cloth-bound reprint of *Eyewitness*, with an introduction by Burton Rascoe, a native of Oklahoma. Rascoe pointed out, correctly, that "the author had little interest in and knew almost nothing about the Daltons until after the Coffeyville raid and that what little he did, finally, learn about them he gathered in his talks with Ransom Payne, the U. S. Dep-uty Marshal, whom the author celebrates very fulsomely in his book, without supplying any evidence to show that Payne merited any of the honor that 'Eyewitness' bestowed upon him." Rascoe surmises that Payne was either an "incompetent fool" or else a "tip-off man for the Daltons and possibly for other bandit out-fits." Payne *was* incompetent and no doubt a fool, but Rascoe had no warrant of history or tradition to suggest he was an ac-complice of outlaws; he was much more like the bumbling police-men portrayed on today's TV screens. Unfortunately, *Eyewitness* furnished the model for much purplish trivia later written about the Daltons, and was its chief source.

CHAPTER 14

1. The existence of this hideout in the Ouchitas, described by Em-mett Dalton, was verified in correspondence between the author and Jim Peters during 1949.

CHAPTER 16

1. Figures on the amounts of loot in the Dalton train robberies have had to be estimated from all sorts of conflicting accounts; in each case, I have given the sum that seems to be most plausi-ble. Rule-of-thumb has led me to strike a midway balance be-tween the extravagant claims of Emmett Dalton and the figures announced by the railroads. The big lines were so cagy about things that not even the Pinkerton archives give precise figures on any Dalton train job. All told, the boys didn't make too much from their trade.

CHAPTER 17

1. Much the same thing is said in the previously cited *Garden in*

the Sun, Wallace Smith there pointing out that "trains had been held up before the Daltons arrived in California, and they continued to be held up after they left." Smith declares further: "The ineffectual attempts of the officers to locate the bandits resulted in a great deal of criticism and they writhed under the jibes directed their way. That explains their anxiety to pin the guilt on someone and their apparently unjust treatment of the Daltons."

2. John Sontag and Chris Evans were close friends who allegedly combined to rob Southern Pacific trains after the SP failed to pay Sontag compensation for injuries received as an employee. A man referred to as "A. Dalton" was connected with this gang but no evidence has been found to establish any kinship with *the* Daltons.

3. The account of this meeting of Chris Madsen with Bill Dalton is from Madsen's memoir, "Oklahoma Outlaws." So is the account of the trick that Bill pulled at the expense of the California detectives, mentioned later in this chapter.

4. Information on Coffeyville's probationary attitude toward the returning Bill was given me by the son of the Kansas attorney mentioned in this chapter; for personal reasons, he asked that his and his father's names be withheld.

CHAPTER 18

The background of this chapter was supplied by the Madsen memoir and by personal conversations of the author with Keene Wallis and with old outlaw Riley Martin, who knew the Daltons.

CHAPTER 20

1. The best account of Grat's jailbreak and subsequent sojourn in the snow is to be found in Kathleen Small's *History of Tulare County.* That hair-raiser, *Eyewitness,* has Grat melodramatically leaping from a train as Detective Will Smith was taking him to the California state prison. Other authors have copied the myth— there was no such train ride or daring jump to freedom.

2. This is Grat's route of flight, as given by Emmett in *When the Daltons Rode.* Emmett can probably be trusted here: it would have been the best possible back way for an Oklahoma-bound fugitive to take.

3. Mrs. Small tells of the incident involving the money order in her account of the Daltons. The "sympathizer" was probably a scrub outlaw eager to grab some of the reward money.

4. The Madsen memoir identifies Dover, Oklahoma, as a place where Ma Dalton secretly met her erring sons.

5. A full account of the Red Rock robbery appeared in the *Fort Smith Elevator,* June 10, 1892. The author has accepted Emmett's account of Grat's behavior on the job: it squares with what we know of the older brother's general character.

6. The story of Bill's "triumph" over the federal officers in Kingfisher is related in the Madsen memoir, and has been adapted
from that document by Homer Croy in his biography of Madsen,
Trigger Marshal.

CHAPTER 21

1. John Hixon was another competent Western lawman who has
been forgotten in favor of the Earps and the Hickoks. Like them,
Hixon loved publicity, but he had less luck getting it.
2. *Stillwater Gazette*, June 10, 1892.

CHAPTER 22

Flo Quick's gulling of the youth is related in Madsen's memoir.
Madsen, who wrote this document in his old age, gives the impression that Mundy and Flo's transient victim were one and the
same, but her family tradition says otherwise.

CHAPTER 23

1. Charles Le Flore (sometimes spelled La Flore) was an Indian
aristocrat who ranked with John Jordan and Sam Sixkiller among
the outstanding lawmen of the Cherokee Republic.
2. The author, as a fledgling newsman in Austin, knew J. K.
Lane, whose politicking and evangelizing extended over two states.
"Bill Dalton always exaggerated his political prospects," Mr. Lane
said once. "He hung around Guthrie a lot, trying to make friends
with different party leaders. But we knew he'd been in trouble in
California and that the bandit Daltons were his brothers. So we
never encouraged him to be a candidate for any office." Lane always denied the story that he had ridden out with a Bible after
the Dalton boys, hoping to convert them. It's a little hard to im-
agine Grat "getting religion."
3. Emmett Dalton gives the impression that Woodward was a
good-sized town when Bob and Flo were there, and that they
openly walked the streets together. Actually, it was then no more
than a railway depot and a general store or two, with no streets
except some crisscross country lanes.
4. Information on Jim Riley's troubles with nester neighbors was
graciously provided by the Santa Fe Railroad.
5. Adair today is becoming a peaceful writer's colony where rents
are low and the atmosphere is free.
6. A long account of the Adair holdup appeared in the *Stillwater
Gazette*, July 16, 1892.

CHAPTER 24

1. Madsen tells something about his strategy in his memoir but
leaves much to inference. Probably he wanted to protect men then
still living from possible retaliation at the hands of elderly surviving friends of the Daltons.

2. Bill Dalton's use of hired gunslingers to get hold of land was
revealed to me by the son of his attorney. Bill was not the only
"realtor" to use such tactics in early-day Oklahoma.

3. This is the first book to tell of the advance tip that the officers
had on the Pryor Creek-Adair holdup.

CHAPTER 25

1. Riley Martin was the most colorful of the "retired" outlaws
that this author has known. The name is one of the man's aliases,
which I have used out of consideration for relatives trying to live
down the reputation of being a two-gun Texas family. As a child
in the Texas hills, I first heard from him of the Daltons, whom
he had known so well that my mother didn't want me to have
much to do with him. He always said that his Indian wife, Tanasi,
kept him from being at Coffeyville. He claimed that the Daltons
wanted to hire him; perhaps they did.

2. Only one other known Western outlaw ever tried to rob two
banks at once. This was Henry Starr, already mentioned, who led
a band of five men into Stroud, Oklahoma, for a double holdup
on March 27, 1915. A posse caught him while he was trying to
make his getaway and an unsympathetic judge handed him
twenty-five years in the pen. He was pardoned within a few years
—unreformed, as it turned out. Henry Starr once declared,
"There's a sort of hypnotism about a man or a bunch of men
who come coolly into a town in the middle of the day, walk up
the main street, rob a bank and walk out again, doing just enough
shooting to show they can hit anything. The very daring of it
puts a spell on people, paralyzes them with surprise and awe.
Before they recover, the bandits are gone." Maybe so; but Henry
didn't hypnotize the people of Stroud, any more than the Daltons
did Coffeyville.

CHAPTER 26

1. Coffeyville's best local historian, David Stewart Elliott, and his
paper, the *Coffeyville Journal,* always insisted that the citizens
had no advance warning of the Dalton raid. Too much evidence
has turned up to accept this claim—including Madsen's memoir,
giving the story behind the story.

2. A common legend has Bill Doolin riding out with the Daltons toward Coffeyville, then turning back because his horse cast a shoe. After his capture in 1895, Doolin told Chris Madsen that he had refused to lend a hand because of Bob Dalton's short-potting. After a spectacular career as an outlaw leader on his own, Doolin was slain in an ambush by possemen led by Marshal Heck Thomas, August 25, 1896.

CHAPTER 27

1. The information on the stores at Gray Horse came from Riley Martin, who claimed to have the same kind of informal business arrangements with the town's merchants. A reference to the Daltons' last visit to the hamlet also appears in an unidentified newspaper clipping furnished the author by Homer Croy.
2. The leading authority on Dalton armament is George E. Virgines, a writer for *Guns* magazine. In his March 1962 *Guns* article, "Guns That Rode with the Daltons," Virgines said: "As time goes by, more 'Dalton guns' will appear. How well they will be able to tell their own history will depend on the records that come with them." Peddling old weapons alleged to have been used by famous outlaws is a busy little industry. Various guns said to have been used by the Daltons can be seen at the following places: Los Angeles County Museum; the Davis Collection, Mason Hotel, Claremore, Oklahoma; Donnin's Arms Museum, North Miami, Florida; and the Dalton Defenders Museum, Coffeyville, Kansas (the weapons shown here are the best authenticated ones).

CHAPTER 28

This chapter is based principally on David Stewart Elliott's excellent pamphlet on the showdown at Coffeyville.

CHAPTER 29

1. Jack Long's recollections of the robbery were published in the October 5, 1949, issue of the *Coffeyville Journal,* fifty-seven years to the day after the memorable raid.

CHAPTER 31

1. Long after the collapse of the Daltons, the legend of a sixth man among the raiders at Coffeyville would circulate. The brunt

of the story was that this man was left to stay with the horses during the holdup but left in a hurry when the shooting started. This sixth man, according to the particular storyteller, was:

(1) A small-fry badman named Alley Ogee, who had moved his residence from Coffeyville to Wichita at the urgent suggestion of the local badge-wearers. Ogee, who would have been recognized, just as the Daltons were, had he returned with them, was so upset after learning of the battle that he wrote to the Coffeyville paper denying that he had done any cutting-up with old acquaintances.

(2) The younger brother of Jesse Evans, of the Sontag-Evans gang in California.

(3) A precious old relic known as Buckskin Ike, a Saroyan-type Westerner who claimed to have been everywhere with every long rider.

(4) An obscure bushwhacker named George Padgett, mentioned previously in the text. Years after the raid, Padgett wrote a letter to a friend, Clint Riggs, of Sullivan, Indiana, which is here quoted in part (spelling and grammer are his own):

"I left Indiana in 1886 with a sawmill [meaning a sawmill crew] going to Fort Scott, Arkansas; did not do any good with the mill, so I moved to the Cherokee Nation near Live Oak, got to peddling whiskey over there in 1891. I got to going with the Dalton Gang. On October the first we planned the Coffeyville bank robbery which we tempted to do. The following day we rode in town from the west about nine o'clock in the morning. They left me tending the horses but when the battle began, I soon saw the battle was going against us and everyone was going to get killed so I rode out south into the Nation which I think was about three miles south. I did not fire a shot."

T. C. Babb, who hid in the bank vault during the robbery, claimed that he saw a sixth man after he had left the bank but could not identify him.

Emmett Dalton always asserted that the horses were hitched in the spot that proved so fatal because Negro workmen were tearing up the pavement at the site originally chosen.

In the absence of convincing proof, the author leaves the question of the sixth man open. If such proof is presented, it will be included in a later edition of this work.

CHAPTER 33

1. The wording of the telegram is copied from that given in the Madsen memoir. All the other vital facts of this chapter have been taken from that important and long unpublished document.

CHAPTER 34

The Daltons' disaster at Coffeyville disposed of one bothersome question for Alan Pinkerton and his famous detective agency, who had been trying to persuade the nation's railroads to subscribe to a common war chest for the crushing of the gang. The agency's archives in New York show that the jealous, competing lines refused to do so.

A total of $40,000 was outstanding in rewards offered for the bandits who bit the dust at Coffeyville. Careful tracing of the claims and their settlements has indicated that less than $3000 of the total ever was paid.

1. Madsen memoir.

2. Information on Florence Quick's death came from her cousin, Keene Wallis.

3. Emmett won favor in prison by refusing to participate in a riot staged by other inmates. After his release, a shabbily written novel about the attempted break was published under his byline.

4. Bitter Creek Newcomb was going under an alias, "George Thorne," in the Seminole Nation, according to a statement made to me by Riley Martin. An Indian woman dressed his wound when he came riding with Bill Dalton to her cabin after the Sacred Heart gun scrape.

5. I am indebted to the Pinkerton Archives for a full account of the Longview robbery.

6. *Oklahoma State Capital*, July 11, 1894. The Wallaces were a hard lot, said to have come originally from Texas and to have kept a convenient distance from its border.

7. According to a history of Carter County, Oklahoma, Jennie Dalton called herself "Mrs. Jones" on that ill-fated trip to Ardmore. Her companion, obviously Houston Wallace's woman, told officers her name was "Miss Pruitt."

8. The identification of Bill Dalton's corpse by his brother Charles was confirmed by Sheriff Howard of Longview, Texas, and two employees of the bank that was robbed there. Burial was delayed to accommodate the crowds of the curious who flocked in to Ardmore to see the body of a Dalton. It was badly decomposed when Jennie Dalton loaded it on a train for California, six days after the slaying. Bill first was buried under a palm tree on the property of his father-in-law at Livingston, later reinterred in a cemetery at Atwater, both in California. Descendants of Jesse James also live in California. Present-day Daltons, Jameses and Youngers are eminently respectable people.

CHAPTER 35

Newspaper files in the Los Angeles Public Library indicate that Emmett Dalton resided at 1224 Meyer Avenue, Hollywood. His funeral services were conducted by the Loyal Order of Moose, which Emmett evidently joined after settling down to respectability and Julia. Emmett's last testament of the gang, *When the Daltons Rode*, appeared during the year of his death, 1937. Harry Sinclair Drago, well-known author, has furnished this thumbnail sketch of him as he was during his later years: "I last met Emmett Dalton in Hollywood, in 1928. He was a tall, lean, handsome man, a well preserved man somewhere in his early fifties, with a springy step and straight as an arrow, truculent and highly opinionated. He was looking for a writer to assist him in putting on paper the 'true' story of the Daltons. His need was the need without exception of all the leftovers from the bygone days of the horseback outlaws who had achieved some claim on fame. Each was convinced that he had a 'great' story to tell; all he needed was a writer to write it. Eventually, most of them got into print; unfortunately, the books they produced, including Emmett Dalton's *When the Daltons Rode,* had little to say that had not been said before."

BIBLIOGRAPHY

Adams, Ramon F. *Six-Guns and Saddle Leather,* 1954.
    Adams is our foremost Western bibliographer.
Barnard, Evan G. *A Rider of the Cherokee Strip,* 1936.
    A good, colorful book about an area where the Daltons
    often rode.
Block, Eugene B. *Great Train Robberies of the West,* 1959.
    Excellent general background material on engine-boarding
    but sparse on Dalton exploits.
Botkin, B. A., ed. *A Treasury of Western Folklore,* 1951.
    See the section, "Law and Order, Ltd."
Canton, Frank M. *Frontier Trails,* 1930.
    This autobiography of a noted Oklahoma lawman contains
    much material on the state's more prominent agents.
Coffeyville Journal—various issues for 1892, 1937, 1939.
Croy, Homer. *He Hanged Them High,* 1952.
    Judge Parker and his court.
————. *Trigger Marshal,* 1958.
    Authorized biography of Marshal Chris Madsen.
Dale, Edward Everett. *Cow Country,* 1942.
    Makes only minor mention of Oklahoma outlaws but does
    describe graphically the breaking up of the ranges for
    homesteads, a process that contributed to the development
    of outlawry there.
Dalton, Emmett. *Beyond the Law,* 1918.
    First printed serially in *Wide World* magazine, London,
    this came out at the same time as a movie of the same
    title—starring Emmett Dalton.
———— (with Jack Jungmeyer). *When the Daltons Rode,* 1937.
    Jungmeyer was a newspaperman whom Emmett roped in
    to do this dubious first-person account of the Dalton saga.
    The present work has quoted excerpts that can be verified
    from other sources.
Dalton, Kit. *Under the Black Flag,* 1931.
    This second cousin of *the* Daltons claimed to have ridden

with Quantrill's guerrillas during the Civil War and to have raised hell all over the Southwest afterward.

Elliott, David Stewart. *Last Raid of the Daltons*, 1892.

This is the only completely trustworthy account of the gang's disastrous attempt at double bank robbery. Elliott was the publisher and editor of the *Coffeyville Journal*. A reprint of the pamphlet can be secured from the Dalton Defenders Museum at Coffeyville.

Federal Writers Project. *Oklahoma: A Guide to the Sooner State*, 1941.

Sparse information on the Daltons but a great deal of material on the towns they honored with their presence.

Fort Smith (Ark.) *Elevator*—various issues.

Fresno, California, *Police Annual*, 1956.

Contains valuable material on Grat Dalton's connections with the gaming fraternity in Fresno.

Glasscock, Carl Burgess. *Bandits and the Southern Pacific*, 1939.

Casts doubt on the Daltons' alleged participation in the Alila robbery, and impugns SP detective Smith.

Graves, Richard S. *Oklahoma Outlaws*, 1915.

A valuable book written by a local historian.

Harlow, Alvin F. *Old Waybills*, 1934.

Written from the express-company records, but not unfavorable to the Daltons.

Harman, S. W. *Hell on the Border*, 1898.

The first account of Hanging Judge Isaac Parker's court in Fort Smith. Read judiciously, it is an invaluable source of information on the lawlessness in Oklahoma and Indian Territories.

Harrington, Fred Harvey. *Hanging Judge*, 1951.

A fine book on Judge Parker, this also gives the most accurate picture of the law-abiding Dalton brother, Frank.

Hendricks, George David. *The Bad Men of the West*, 1941.

The author tries to analyze the Daltons and other Western outlaws by outmoded theories of criminology, but he does show some understanding of the social reasons for outlawry.

Holloway, Carroll C. *Texas Gun Lore*, 1951.

Good supplemental reading for banditry buffs. Contains an index of 800 different outlaws.

Horan, James D. *Desperate Women*, 1952.

Especially valuable for its information on Bill Doolin, Bitter Creek Newcomb and other Dalton retainers.

Hunter, J. Marvin and Rose, Noah H. *The Album of Gunfighters*, 1951.

A notable pictorial collection, including photographs of the Daltons.

Hough, Emerson. *The Story of the Outlaw*, 1907.

Written on a basis of the most complete sources then available to Western historians. Some of Hough's findings have been superseded by the results of more adequate information.

James, Marquis. *They Had Their Hour,* 1934.
> This roundup of outlaws by a native Oklahoman is generally trustworthy, except that Dalton henchman Charley Pierce is wrongly identified as Tulsa Jack Blake.

Jones, W. F. *The Experiences of a Deputy U. S. Marshal of the Indian Territory,* 1937.
> Jones was one of many old-time lawmen whose recollections, while colorful and interesting, are seldom completely accurate.

King, Ernest L. *Main Line: Fifty Years of Railroading with the Southern Pacific,* 1948.
> A loyal company man, King expressed perfectly the railroad's point of view on outlaws, homesteaders, politics, and such subjects.

Lamb, Arthur H. *Tragedies of the Osage Hills,* 1951.
> Living in the heart of the old Osage Nation, Lamb still gives very little detail about Bob Dalton's tenure as its chief of police.

McNeal, Thomas Allen. *When Kansas Was Young,* 1922.
> McNeal ranks with Paul Wellman, Harry Sinclair Drago and Edwin V. Burkholder among authorities on Kansas outlawry.

McReynolds, Robert. *Thirty Years on the Frontier,* 1906.
> Contains an interesting portrayal of Bill Doolin.

Masterson, Vincent. *The Katy Railroad and the Last Frontier,* 1952.
> Highly informative on the spread of the rails across Indian Territory; sparse in detail on the Daltons' depredations against the Katy line itself.

Madsen, Chris. "Oklahoma Outlaws" (typed memoir, c. 1942).
> Cited extensively in the text of the present book. Madsen was an exceptionally reliable figure among the old-time marshals.

Morris, Lerona Rosamond, ed. *Oklahoma: Yesterday, Today, Tomorrow,* 1930.
> Devotes a long chapter to Oklahoma's long riders.

Nix, Everitt Dumas. *Oklahombres,* 1929.
> Nix succeeded Bill Grimes as chief deputy marshal of Oklahoma Territory and helped plan the campaign that shattered the Dalton-Doolin gang.

Oklahoma City *Daily Oklahoman; Oklahoma Farmer-Stockman; Oklahoma State Capital*—various issues.

Preece, Harold. *Living Pioneers,* 1952.
> Some material on Western outlaws; see especially "Ring and a Hat," dealing with Riley Martin and the Daltons.

Raine, William MacLeod. *Famous Sheriffs and Western Outlaws,* 1931.
> The old master among Western writers devotes a fine chapter to the Daltons.

Rascoe, Burton. *Belle Starr, the Bandit Queen,* 1941.
> Rascoe made such frolicsome mistakes as presenting Belle, the Daltons, the Jameses and the Youngers all as kinfolks.

Rister, Carl Coke. *No Man's Land*, 1948.
    Fine material on Marshal Ed Short.
Shirley, Glenn. *Law West of Fort Smith*, 1957.
    A long-needed restatement of Harman's *Hell on the Border*, with much important factual material added.
——. *Six-Gun and Silver Star*, 1955.
    A carefully documented work on the outlaw crisis in Oklahoma Territory, with particular reference to such gangs as the Daltons'.
Small, Kathleen Edwards. *History of Tulare County, California*, 1926.
    Extensively cited in text.
Stillwater Gazette and Stillwater Populist—various issues.
Tilghman, Zoe A. *Outlaw Days*, 1926.
    This work, by the widow of that stellar lawman, Bill Tilghman, contains much background material on the members of the Dalton band.
Tulsa World—various issues.
Ward, William. *The Dalton Gang, the Bandits of the Far West*, 1908. *Eyewitness*, 1892; reprint, 1954.
    Cited together because both were evidently written by the imaginative Mr. Ward from the verbal outpourings of Ransom Payne.
Wellman, Paul I. *A Dynasty of Western Outlaws*, 1961.
    Traces the sequence of outlaw bands in Oklahoma, Kansas and Missouri from Quantrill through the Daltons and the Jameses down to Henry Starr and Pretty Boy Floyd in our own century.

INDEX

◯

More SIGNET Books You'll Enjoy

☐ **THE BORDER TRUMPET by Ernest Haycox.** The powerful story of the soldiers who were sent to win the West and were caught in bitter battles with huge forces of Apache Indians, the most deadly fighters in the world.
(#Q6035—95¢)

☐ **CANYON PASSAGE by Ernest Haycox.** One of the most famous novels of the West and an enormously successful movie, **Canyon Passage** is the story of men drunk with gold fever, men who fought the land and one another to gouge riches from the mountain wilderness, and it is the story, too, of the women they loved along the way.
(#Q5986—95¢)

☐ **CONQUERING HORSE by Frederick Manfred.** A superb novel about a young Sioux chieftain in the days when great legends were a way of life, and the Indian ruled the land.
(#Y5492—$1.25)

☐ **AN OWL ON EVERY POST by Sanora Babb.** An enchanting true story of a childhood on the plains. "This book should not be missed. The days of the sodbusters, the sod houses and the tough, independent, dry land farmers have rarely been so well chronicled."—Newsday
(#Q5246—95¢)

THE NEW AMERICAN LIBRARY, INC.,
P.O. Box 999, Bergenfield, New Jersey 07621

Please send me the SIGNET BOOKS I have checked above. I am enclosing $_____(check or money order—no currency or C.O.D.'s). Please include the list price plus 25¢ a copy to cover handling and mailing costs. (Prices and numbers are subject to change without notice.)

Name_____

Address_____

City_____State_____Zip Code_____
Allow at least 3 weeks for delivery